The Hockey News

TOTAL GRETZKY

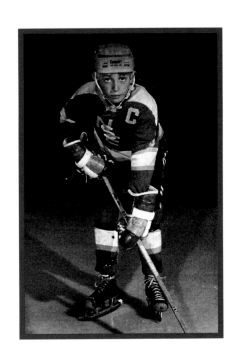

The Hockey News

THE MAGIC, THE LEGEND, THE NUMBERS

TOTAL GRETZKY

Foreword by **PETER GZOWSKI** • Tribute by **ROY MACGREGOR**
Edited by **STEVE DRYDEN**

CONTENTS

Copyright © 1999 by Transcontinental
   Sports Publications

All rights reserved. The use of any part of this publication
reproduced, transmitted in any form or by any means,
electronic, mechanical, photocopying, recording, or otherwise, or stored in a retrieval system, without the
prior written consent of the publisher – or, in case of
photocopying or other reprographic copying, a licence
from the Canadian Copyright Licensing Agency – is an
infringement of the copyright law.

Canadian Cataloguing in Publication Data

Main entry under title:

Total Gretzky : the magic, the legend, the numbers

Based on articles by Hockey News magazine.
ISBN 0-7710-4177-2

1. Gretzky, Wayne, 1961-   . 2.Hockey players – Canada
– Biography.
I. Dryden, Steve, 1957-   .

GV848.5.G78T67 1999   769.962'092   C99-931851-9

We acknowledge the financial support of the Govern-
ment of Canada through the Book Publishing Industry
Development Program for our publishing activities.
We further acknowledge the support of the Canada
Council for the Arts and the Ontario Arts Council for
our publishing program.

Canadä

Research by Shi Davidi
Design by Sheldon Coles and Gary Westgate,
   The Hockey News
Typeset by *The Hockey News* and M&S, Toronto
Printed and bound in Canada

McClelland & Stewart Inc.
The Canadian Publishers
481 University Avenue
Toronto, Ontario
M5G 2E9

1   2   3   4   5   03   02   01   00   99

FOREWORD

By PETER GZOWSKI

He looked like a squirrel, as I remember – a slim, solemn blond, not unattractive kid in a hockey jacket but, nevertheless, a squirrel. He was 13, though not by much. His coach had driven him from Brantford into Toronto so he could tape an interview with *This Country in the Morning*, the CBC Radio program I was hosting at the time. *This Country* didn't talk to many hockey players; hockey just wasn't our beat, though only a couple of seasons earlier, in September of 1972, I'd opened one program by asking the listeners to put their hands on their radios and join with me in willing Team Cana-

WAYNE GRETZKY: THE SQUIRREL.

da to beat the Soviets in their final game – a reminder, if we needed one, of how much hockey meant to all Canadians. Now, the kid from Brantford had caught my eye, if not those of my producers. I'd read some newspaper clippings about his phenomenal statistics – he was nearing his 1,000th minor hockey goal when we met – and we'd decided to make an exception, not only to our lack of interest in jocks but to our reluctance to try radio interviews with pre-adolescents in any field, for we had learned that no matter how pleasant they were or how impressive their achievements, they tended to be monosyllabic in public conversation.

And here he was.

"Hi," I said. "Have a good trip in?"

"How do you do, sir," said the solemn young squirrel. I liked him from the start.

In the quarter century or so that followed, I've thought a lot about that interview. Although not particularly memorable in itself – except, perhaps, for one passage in which I suggest to him with Austin Powers–like awe that, if he continued to progress as he had started, he might make as much as *a million dollars* out of hockey – it became a factor in my life, much more so even than other early meetings I had with such Canadian figures as the law professor Pierre Elliott Trudeau in his mother's house in Outremont before much of

the rest of the world had heard of him or a nine-year-old Ashley MacIsaac as he step-danced and played the fiddle one night at a ceilidh in Sydney.

Not that I knew Wayne was destined for anything like the greatness or the stature he'd achieve. Far from it, in fact. I was coaching a bit of boys' hockey myself in those days, nearly always with teams my own sons were playing on, and I knew the incredible odds against even the most promising of youngsters making it to the pros. ("Do you think he has a chance?" the fathers of our most gifted players would ask the coaches, and, as gently as we could, we'd remind them that there were then about 200,000 kids playing in the Metropolitan Toronto system alone, and that the average number of graduates to the NHL from their numbers each year was one.) Further, for all Wayne's astronomical statistics, most people who followed minor hockey had far too many memories of other prodigies who had flamed out all too soon and had ended up pumping gas or selling beer or, if they were lucky, getting out of hockey altogether. But, as I say, I liked him, and as he continued to draw superlative reviews and to leave his mark at every level he moved through, I kept an eye on him and cheered him on. I was doing nightly television when he had his year of major junior in Sault Ste. Marie and was packing arenas wherever he played. I took a film crew up and renewed our acquaintance – I still sometimes wonder what happened to the two young wingers who were lucky enough to play with him that season and reach scoring figures they'd never imagined possible – and, a few years later, I looked him up again.

This was 1980. My television career had collapsed. I'd written one mildly successful book and found myself with both the time and resources to tackle something I'd always wanted to do: a book on hockey and the part it played in our lives. I made a couple of false starts, looking for a framework. As much on a whim as anything, I called the

young man I had first met as a boy and who, contrary to skepticism – including mine – had continued his rocket-like ascent to the top. A couple of seasons earlier, the high-rolling Vancouver millionaire Nelson Skalbania had flown Wayne, his father, and his agent, Gus Badali, out to British Columbia and convinced them that Wayne should sign with his Indianapolis franchise in the upstart World Hockey Association, which was hungry enough for headlines that it was taking players still too young – or in some cases, already too old – for the NHL. Then, Skalbania's friendly but fierce rival and former partner Peter Pocklington, through a combination of old debts and skillful bargaining, had wrangled Gretzky's contract for his Edmonton Oilers, who would be one of the few teams to survive the early demise of the World Hockey Association and join the ranks of the NHL. In his first year in the true big time, Wayne had proved conclusively that he belonged, tying Marcel Dionne for the most points and losing the scoring title only because Dionne had more goals – just as he was denied the rookie of the year award because of his season in the WHA. He was, you will remember, 18. He'd long outgrown his pubescent resemblance to a squirrel and was already an attractive and remarkably poised young man. The solemnity was often broken by a self-effacing grin. He agreed to meet me for a round of golf, at the Cutten Club in Guelph, Ont., near where I was living at the time, and not far from Brantford. Typically, I was to learn (for he has always been as good about remembering his childhood friends as he is about being generous to reporters who covered him on the way up), he showed up with a friend of his youth. On the golf course, he showed a graceful natural swing, a reminder that he probably could have been a professional baseball player if he'd been bent in that direction. As we played, I told him about my plans for a book. I was considering following one team for one season, I said, and wondered if he had any thoughts about which one. "Why not us?" he said. "The Oilers." I said I hadn't even thought about them – other than his own scoring exploits they'd had a pretty mediocre debut season – and, with genuine enthusiasm, he began to talk about some of his teammates, the general manager Glen Sather and even the larger-than-life character of the owner.

THE KING OF HOCKEY.

The next day, at his urging, I wrote to Pocklington, and after a visit to Edmonton, was delighted when he and Sather agreed to my looking over all their shoulders for a year.

It was quite a season. It began at training camp in Jasper in August and stretched through till May when, at last, and after having risen up and smitten the mighty and historic Montreal Canadiens, three games to none, the Oilers, laughing and singing on the bench, confident already that they were the team of the future, fell to the aging New York Islanders. The Oilers were a wonderful team to watch, and for those of us who had learned their hockey on the sloughs and lakes of Canada, an inspiration. They took us back to the hockey we loved: swooping, darting, ad libbing, reminding us there were other ways to win at the world's most beautiful game than to play the grinding, shoot-it-and-chase-it style that had dominated for so long.

I wish I could say that during that year I became close to the Kid, as I came to call him. He was unfailingly gracious to me always, and would sometimes steal a glance at me when the working press was, as they increasingly were, besieging him with questions, and wink as if there was something only he and I knew. He would, in fact, often grant me private time away from his teammates or the constant brigade of hangers-on. If any scholars of the future are diligent enough they can find our names on consecutive lines of the guest book of a certain fern-bedecked restaurant in Edmonton where Wayne drove me in his 4x4 for lunch one day and, ever loyal to his sponsors, sent back the ginger ale I'd ordered for him in favor of a 7-Up, and settled in to talk about such matters as his growing fame. I remember warning him that the press might turn on him one day, and that he might suffer the fate of, say, Pierre Berton, who after a round of admiring stories was now subject to occasional and undeserved attacks. "Is Pierre Berton Canadian?" Wayne asked.

At one point in the year he had agreed to sit with me and watch a slow motion video of one of his goals, so we could go through it together and he could try to explain to me, second by second, what was going through his incomparable hockey mind – how much was reflex and how much conscious thought. The evening after our session turned out to be one of his greatest exhibitions of the year. Against the St. Louis Blues, whose goaltender Mike Liut had been a nemesis through much of the season, he ran up three assists and five goals, including what most of us were pretty sure (we couldn't find the record) were the four fastest ever scored by one player. After his extraordinary display, clattering his way toward the TV studio under the stands of the Northlands Coliseum, he noticed me among the throng of celebrants and called me aside. "Did you get what you wanted from the tape?" he asked.

Sometimes he would ask me for the kind of favors only a friend might presume to. Once, in Boston, he was invited to appear at the local NBC television outlet for an early morning spot on *The Today Show*. He was trepidatious about making his debut on American network TV – how long ago this seems now in light of the places he has been since and the poise he shows in front of the camera – and asked me to rise early and accompany him to the studio. I was happy to oblige and, in the taxi to the studio,

THE SLICKEST OILER OF THEM ALL.

him reading a particularly flattering newspaper profile, and nodding in agreement at its wisdom. Walter had shown a rare outburst of temper. "You're a very special person," he'd told his oldest son. "Wherever you go, people are going to make a fuss over you. You've got to behave right. They're going to be watching for every mistake."

He made some anyway, of course: an occasional burst of petulance (including three laughable encounters on the ice when he tried to do his own fighting), times when he'd keep the lesser mortals on the team bus waiting while he signed just one more program or flirted (always innocently, as far as I know) with one more adoring fan. But for me at least the wonder always was not how often the halo slipped but how few and minor his transgressions were. Aside from my never-ending amazement at his hockey artistry, and despite or maybe because of the fact that "sir" had long given way to "Peter" or even "Gzowsk" – or usually in public "Mr. Gzowski" – I liked him then as much as I had at the outset. And, over the year I spent shadowing him and his teammates, I came to think of

was charmed once again by his shyness.

All that year, and later as I traveled around to promote *The Game of Our Lives*, the book that came of my experiences, people would ask me, "But what's he really like?" Invariably, I'd say, "Exactly as he appears to be – polite, decent, gentlemanly." Sometimes, as his fame and the constant attention and adulation grew, I'd add that he maintained those characteristics in the face of more reasons to be arrogant that anyone I'd ever met. We'd talked about that, I remember, at our fern-surrounded lunch, and, as he did with so many things, he credited his father. Once, he said, when they'd been away at a minor tournament, Walter had caught

him as a friend. But close? Not quite, I'm afraid. Not really.

It was Ken Dryden who first explained to me why writers could never really understand hockey players – though he of course was both. "Writers," he said one day in his measured, thoughtful way, "particularly the good ones, tend to assume hockey players, particularly the great ones, see the world and reflect on it the way they would, if they were in the athlete's place; they want the athlete to explain what he does as they would explain it if they could do it. They don't understand that it's a different world. That's why, for instance, so many people were surprised when Guy Lafleur said hockey and his team were more important to him than his family. They thought it was outrageous; even in his place, if they'd thought that, which they probably didn't understand anyway, they'd never have said it. But for Guy, it was just the way it was. Hockey players simply think about different things."

That conversation with Dryden took place long after I'd finished my work on hockey. I'd returned to radio by then, in fact, and we were talking about Ken's own studious and compelling book, *The Game*. But his observation gave me, in retrospect, some insights into my own shortcomings as a reporter; I had, as he suggested, expected the young men I'd been traipsing around after to explain their world as I'd have tried to explain it if I'd been the insider and they the observers. It also cast more light on a phenomenon I had noticed: that the team formed a kind of group identity (even though its members – always aware that anyone could be traded at any time – were wary of forming too close friendships) that no outsider could ever penetrate, not the management, not the coaches or even the trainers, and certainly not the ever-present press. However much we tried, and whatever the similarity of our experience – for nearly everyone in the entourage was a failed hockey star himself – the rest of us would never quite get it.

Even in this respect, Wayne tried to be an exception. After he and I had looked microscopically at the goal he had tried to explain to me, and still determined to figure out what he had that his peers didn't – for he was neither the fastest skater nor the hardest shooter among the Oilers – I turned to the academic literature of both sports and psychology. I found some fascinating things. At the core of my discoveries – or discoveries for me, since some researchers may already have known them – was the realization that what set Wayne apart from his peers, and, indeed, perhaps even from the dominant players who had preceded him, was not his physical gifts (although, particularly in the shadow-like shiftiness of his skating and his remarkable sense of balance, they were greater than he was sometimes given credit for) and not even his visual talents – or not as we usually understand that phrase.

Instead, his mastery was a matter of perception, not so much what he saw around him on the ice but how he processed that information. Where most players saw an assortment of individuals, both teammates and opponents, Wayne saw *situations*. The clearest parallel I found came from chess, where a series of experiments showed that a grand master looking at a board sees and remembers no more than the average club player – if the pieces are placed at random. But if it's a game in progress, the grand master recalls everything much more clearly; he absorbs not only where the various chessmen are on the board, but all the lines of force that are in play and all the diverse possibilities

that present themselves. In these terms, Wayne was a grand master of hockey: one glance around and his mind told him not only where people were but what they were likely to do next. That's why, I figured from my studies, he always made so many passes to apparently open spaces only to have a teammate suddenly appear in position to gather them in. "Don't go after the puck where it is," Walter used to tell him. "Chase it where it's going to be."

This theory, and Gretzky's implementation of its principles, takes most of a chapter in *The Game of Our Lives*, and I have scarcely done it justice here. But what has always interested me about it was not the cleverness of my academic research, but the fact that when I finally had a chance to explain it to Wayne he both grasped it fully and he agreed with it entirely. "That's it," he said. "That's what I see."

A gift? Well, sure. The patterns Wayne has always seen in a game, and to which he would react so quickly, are stored in what psychologists call "long-term memory," as are, for instance, the telephone numbers everyone carries around in their heads. All of us know people who seem to have a better gift for recalling phone numbers than we do. But hockey patterns, with their constant kaleidoscopic rearrangements, are not phone numbers, and learning them and what they mean – seeing them in the first place – takes concentration and work. And no one who has followed Wayne around for a while could fail to be impressed by how hard he practiced and how resolutely he studied the game he played so brilliantly.

❑ ❑ ❑ ❑ ❑ ❑ ❑ ❑

Not long after *The Game of Our Lives* was published, I changed careers again, going back to radio, where I spent the next 15 years, and writing about other things. Without me, the Oilers – and Wayne – more than fulfilled the promise I had seen beginning to blossom, winning four Stanley Cups in five years and, in Wayne's case, setting enough scoring records to clearly establish himself as the pre-eminent player of his time. Then the team began to disintegrate, as a financially challenged Peter Pocklington first traded Paul Coffey to Pittsburgh, and then, one by one, heaved overboard all the young stars who had made the Oilers what they were. The most dramatic moment of this dispersal, of course, occurred on August 9, 1988, just 24 days after Wayne's wedding to the Hollywood actress Janet Jones, when Pocklington shocked the hockey world by trading Gretzky to Los Angeles (if trading is the word for a transaction that brought him $15 million [U.S.] in cash) and ending forever any hopes that the dynasty he had been such a part of could continue to carry on. At the press conference to announce the trade, Wayne wept, and across the country, I'm sure, so did a lot of other Canadians. To people who felt the game and its most illustrious star belonged in the nation that had made it and him, the Gretzky trade was almost as sad an event as the death in Montreal of Howie Morenz – from heartbreak, some said – must have been half a century earlier.

From my base in Toronto, I shared in the national sense of loss. My radio job had kept me pretty well out of touch with my young friend – I was unable even to attend his wedding, though he was kind enough to invite me (along with a few hundred of his other closest friends). But I still felt a bit proprietary about him, dropping his name on every possible occasion (my producers once pleaded with me to stop using it as a synonym for greatness), watching his every televised game and catching every Oilers visit to Maple Leaf Gardens I could manage. (Once, I almost lost the woman I was courting when Sather arranged for me to sit in the gold seats adjoining the Oiler bench and she was treated to an intimate exhibition of the profanity, bodily odors and machine gun expectoration I had forgotten existed in the professional game.)

We talked on the radio once or twice, and, though I missed the informality of our private chats, his open, relaxed manner with me remained steadfast (that old loyalty to people who knew him on the way up). By now, I suppose, with his television appearances on everything from soap operas to variety shows – "Don't quit your day job, Gretz," I would sometimes chuckle at the screen – *he* could have helped *me* overcome my nerves for network TV. And there were those who'd known him before who said that after his marriage to Janet and his move to Los Angeles he had "gone downtown"; he had always been a bit starstruck. But the Kid I talked to on the radio or watched on the screen never struck me as very far removed from the young squirrel I had interviewed in the early 1970s: polite, gentlemanly, self-effacing and, at whatever age, full of a kind of natural grace.

On the ice, he continued to astound us all, winning three more scoring championships, to go with the seven he'd picked up in Edmonton, being chosen the league's most valuable player one more time, and leading the unlikely Los Angeles Kings to a Stanley Cup final. His scoring figures continued to mount until there were virtually no mountains left to climb; somewhere along the line – I'm not sure where – he'd set the record for setting records.

Whatever blow his departure had struck to the future of professional hockey in Canada – and he continued to be a pillar of our international teams – his skills and his attractive persona spread the popularity of our game throughout the U.S., until there were more cities in the NHL where you could wear shorts to the rink than ones where you needed a parka. Old-time fans continued to sing the praises of such historic figures as Richard, Howe, Orr, Hull, Béliveau and even Morenz, and, for a while at least, the immensely gifted Mario Lemieux emerged from Wayne's shadow to challenge his dominance of the game, but no one who had ever seen him play could ever deny that he was the greatest player of his age, or the most prolific scorer in history, or that by reminding us that hockey was a game of artistry and quickness, as well as strength and physical aggression, he had left his mark upon the sport – and our lives – for ever.

❑ ❑ ❑ ❑ ❑ ❑ ❑ ❑

In the winter of 1998-99, I had left daily radio again, and was dabbling in television. I wanted one last interview with the Kid, and the CBC, sensing his impending retirement, was enthusiastic. My producers called his agents in New York. A couple of days later, the phone rang in their office. "Hello," said a pleasant voice, "this is Wayne Gretzky."

"Sure," said the person who took the call, used to dealing with various celebrities through the filter of their "people." "And I'm Céline Dion."

I know how she felt, and eventually they did work out a date, but I'd still have preferred it if all she'd said had been a simple, "How do you do, sir."

THE MAGIC OF NO. 99

WAYNE GRETZKY POSSESSED AN INTUITIVE GRASP OF THE GAME'S RHYTHMS

CANADIEN

CANADIEN

Fortune SMILED Upon Us

By ROY MacGREGOR

He had built an entire career out of surprise and deception, and yet, in the end, he willingly telegraphed his final play to a crowd that had no wish to see it. It would be one more day and another city before Wayne Gretzky, 38 years old and still the best player on the ice this night, would officially announce, "I'm done," but there was no one in Ottawa's Corel Centre the balmy evening of April 15, 1999 who could not see it coming as surely as if they had been asked to sign the retirement card and chip in for a suitable gift. His good friend John Davidson had dropped the loudest hint on a previous *Hockey Night In Canada* broadcast, but Gretzky himself had been sending out quiet signals for weeks: talking about the

possibility with close friends, signing more sticks and autographs than usual, even weeping at one point in Calgary when a crowd that had had its collective heart broken so many times by a younger Gretzky and his Edmonton Oilers rose in salute, somehow sensing that his kind would never pass this way again.

This night, however, the final road game of a bad season for the New York Rangers, Wayne Gretzky found himself in Ottawa, the capital of a sprawling, harsh country where the national game, like the country's literature, was originally based on survival, a game where keeping in constant motion once had as much to do with defying winter as it did the opposition. Such a country by nature – and perhaps because of nature – has always been known

TO ALL HOCKEY FANS, GRETZKY WAS MUCH MORE THAN JUST THE GREATEST PLAYER EVER. HE WAS A LIVING LEGEND, A CULTURAL ICON THAT TRANSCENDED THE GAME.

more for reserve than spontaneity, a place made up of stoic and stubborn people who have so often appeared reluctant to celebrate the success of their own. It once caused author Morley Callaghan to lament that Canada "has some kind of an ingrown hatred of excellence," but

there, fortunately, the comparisons between hockey and literature stop, for it has never been so in the national game where teamwork and triumph have always been the image others saw when they looked Canada's way. In hockey, perhaps alone, excellence is cherished by

Canadians – which may explain the mass reluctance this night to be witness to Canadian history.

There had never been any official announcement that this would be his final game, ever, on Canadian ice. The occasion, as originally scheduled, was merely to be a final regular season National Hockey League game between the surprising Ottawa Senators and the sinking New York Rangers. At best, a six-point-type summary the following morning instead of 36-point headlines around North America – which is what it became, spontaneously, gloriously and, of course, tearfully. On the surface, the story was a closing chapter on the story of a working-class kid from Brantford, Ont., who had become a multi-millionaire from New York, a Canadian who had left the country more than a decade earlier, married a Hollywood actress, appeared on Letterman and, singlehandedly, paved the roads south for treasured Canadian hockey franchises to follow. Had he been a performer in any other field but hockey, he might well have been resented, but just below that surface – and really, not all that far below the supposedly tough Canadian exterior – Wayne Gretzky's departure was not unlike the passing of a beloved monarch. For more than a quarter of a century his remarkable hands had been touching a nerve that runs straight into the heart of the Canadian identity.

It came as no real surprise, then, that with 4:45 left in an otherwise unremarkable game that would end 2-2, the 18,500 fans representing their country rose to give thanks to a man who had over the years made Canadians feel more Canadian about themselves. An insecure country nose-to-nose with the United States, a small country of smalltown sensibilities if not realities, Canada had found in Wayne Gretzky the face they wished to put forward to the rest of the world: shy and polite, deferential to elders, not braggardly but capable, sly and resourceful and gifted with heart, a good-humored, good-looking, smalltown kid who always remembered where he came from, and who took his country to where the people wished to be. Stanley Cup championships. Canada Cups. Canadians victorious – not always, but enough – in the game that matters most to them.

It had been telegraphed, yes, but it was still a night of incredible emotion, all the more moving because it was in no way contrived. The crowd reaction as the game wound down was, like the best of Wayne Gretzky's play, entirely spontaneous, invented on the spot, magical in its results. The *formal* announcement would be the next day in New York, but here, informally, and in a manner so very Canadian, the 18,500 would chip in for the most suitable imaginable retirement gift: "One more year!" they began to chant. "One more year! One more year!" And it was all hap-

pening, so very appropriately, in the capital of the country that had produced a Gretzky, and before him a Lafleur, an Orr, a Béliveau, a Howe, a Richard. Happening here, in the city where the Stanley Cup had originated and where the game's first dynasty, the Silver Seven, had ruled. In the city where such Hall of Famers as One-Eyed Frank McGee and Cyclone Taylor had first invented and reinvented the way in which a puck is moved up an ice surface and ends up, somehow, in the opposition net. Perhaps, as hockey lore has it, Taylor once did score a goal by skating the length of the ice backwards, but even Cyclone Taylor would have been amazed by the later inventions Wayne Gretzky gave their beloved game.

Surely in spirit, both Cyclone Taylor and One-Eyed Frank McGee would have happily joined the people of Ottawa who stood that night at the end of a fruitless over-time and cheered and wept for a member of the *opposing* team. The people of Ottawa cheered when their own team, at first tentatively, then in a rush, swarmed over to touch and wish well a player they had minutes before been trying, rather unsuccessfully, to check. They cheered through a hastily assembled video and musical tribute – a whiff of Gretzky's magnificent career flashing on the scoreboard while Carly Simon's "Nobody Does It Better" filled the arena – and they cheered so long after Gretzky had waved back and left the ice that he came back out for two long curtain calls, the second in his soaked underwear with his team jersey draped childlike over a thin frame that could not possibly just have played the violent, crushing game of giants the fans had watched.

And yet, in this, his final Canadian game, he was passing from the national scene as he had first come onto it – the best player on the ice – his teammates missing passes that should have been goals, his reflexes so acutely tuned that no one else could track his frequency, his imagination so far ahead of all others that it seemed, at times, as if two games were being played at once: one in his head, another around their feet. He could, if he so wished, play on for years and, certainly, some of the cheering was vainly trying to argue that very point. The stinging hands of a sold-out house clapped on, growing louder rather than diminishing, almost as if an entire country believed if the cheering never stopped, Wayne Gretzky could never quit.

And yet he was quitting. In less than 24 hours, the telegraphed play would be completed. He was, as he said, done. After three decades of domination at every level he had played, Wayne Gretzky was finally saying himself what had been said so many times before by others that it had become part of the Gretzky myth. Too small for junior, too slow for professional, too skinny, too weak to survive. He had been written off after a back injury and charged back to one last Stanley Cup final, with the Los Angeles Kings. He had been added to Canada's Olympic Team in 1998 largely because the organizers could not bear the public relations disaster that would follow his being left off, and he had been penciled in as a third line center and possible power play specialist, only to emerge as the team's best player and top center. He had been brought to the Rangers as a draw and a second line center, only to carry the burden of a bad team to the end as the best player and the one who cared the most all the way to that final whistle that Sunday after-

decide on their own to quit, decide at the right time and decide forever, are the only ones among us who get to attend their own funerals and enjoy their eulogies. Play with the notion of quitting for good, fall for what they always tell you – you can still do it, you can still play – and the second, sometimes third, send off will never be so sweet. Those who have quit at the very top are rare indeed. Rocky Marciano, undefeated champion of the world, is the most famous, but football's Jim Brown did it, baseball's Sandy Koufax did it, golfer Byron Nelson did it, hockey's

IN A STORYBOOK ENDING TO A STORIED ALL-STAR CAREER, GRETZKY EARNED MOST VALUABLE PLAYER STATUS AT THE 1999 NHL ALL-STAR GAME IN TAMPA BAY.

noon in New York. His brilliant, baffling passes were still the on-ice signature that will forever defy forgery, and if only his teammates had been able to read as well as he wrote, the Rangers might have been headed into the post-season instead of the off-season. He had played, only months earlier, in his final NHL All-Star Game and had so dominated play that he had, once again, been voted the Most Valuable Player among the very best players in the world. Far from done, he was, instead, doing – doing the right thing even if, at the time, it seemed so wrong.

Shakespeare may have claimed the valiant taste of death but once, but the Bard knew nothing of the elite athlete, who dies twice if he's smart, three or four times if hopelessly vainglorious. The few truly great athletes who

Ken Dryden and Mario Lemieux did it, J.D. Salinger did it, the Beatles did it. Perhaps they all did leave early, but the secret of a perfect career is to know when to go, and when is by definition as close to the top as possible. Sports, with its seductive money and easy fame, is riddled with the rarely successful, usually regrettable comebacks of those who changed their minds – Gordie Howe, Guy Lafleur, Bobby Hull, Muhammad Ali, Archie Moore, George Foreman.

"I don't want anybody telling me when to retire," he had said a decade earlier, not long after the Edmonton Oilers sent him to the Los Angeles Kings in a trade that is now part of Canadian history. "I know it's going to be tough. I just don't want to hang on past my welcome."

By leaving with the brilliance untarnished, he would shine forever. He knew it, and the Ottawa fans – even if they temporarily regretted it – knew as well that this, in fact, was what they wanted for him and for themselves. Canada may not be the world's most important country, but when it comes to hockey, Canada not only gave the world a marvelous game, it gave the world the greatest player of all time, no matter what may become of the game in the years to come. Wayne Gretzky might take himself out of the game, but the game could never lose track of Wayne Gretzky, and what he has meant to hockey.

Even after the lights had dimmed at the Corel Centre and the sweepers were in the stands, the fans lingered in the parking lots and in the hallways. If all 18,500 could have squeezed into the press conference that followed they would have done so gladly, and they would have seen the Wayne Gretzky that they always believed was at the core of their hero, no matter where he went or what he did. He was polite, considerate of his parents, humble, a team player, kind and patient. When they tried to cut off questions, Gretzky cut off the organizers, saying he would sit and answer until there were no more questions. It was a strange press conference, only peripherally concerned with news and more like a heart-to-heart between two parties – a country and its national icon. Nothing really needed to be said, but since they hadn't spoken in a while, the two just needed to hear each other's voices.

He spoke with the expected and usual humility: "I've always said that no player is bigger than the game," and no one stood to point out the 61 NHL records, the nine Hart Trophies, the 10 scoring championships, the 3 MVPs in All-Star games and Stanley Cup playoffs, the perfect pass for the winning goal in the 1987 Canada Cup, the four Stanley Cups, the 92 goals in a single season, the four years of 200-plus points, the 894 goals and 1,962 assists for 2,856 points (up to that game) – more assists, in fact, than any other player had ever reached in total points. No one pointed out the absurdity of such a statement any more than anyone demanded he say, officially, that he was quitting. It was all too obvious for such a question. Without ever actually using the word "retirement," Gretzky had talked about his career in the past tense, about the satisfactions he had had and the lessons learned and, hopefully, passed on. "I've never considered myself bigger than any person I ever played with," he said as the clock ticked toward midnight. "I was lucky enough to be gifted." Perhaps, he wondered aloud, it came from God.

He paused then, smiling sheepishly at what he had said, the Canadian in him rising quickly to deflect such vanity.

"Maybe it wasn't a talent He gave me," he said on reflection. "Maybe it was a passion."

A passion. The greatest gift a country can give its people, its people can give a country, a parent can give a child.

❑ ❑ ❑ ❑ ❑ ❑ ❑ ❑

It has long been noted in sports that the greats rarely, if ever, are able to pass on their knowledge. Whatever it is that they know that others do not, it appears to be kept in some part of the brain that cannot be accessed by words or diagrams or even demonstration. Most successful sports coaches were, at best, journeymen players in whatever game they chose. Rocket Richard lasted one game as a coach and gave up. Bobby Orr grew frustrated trying to teach, and quit. Most others have never tried. Each of the truly gifted, however, would understand innately what Pablo Picasso meant when, after he was asked by a fan how long it took him to complete a painting, he answered, "All my life."

In hockey, no one is closer than a parent to the beginning years, and yet even at such close quarters the spark of genius is difficult to see, and virtually impossible to explain. In December 1994, during the National Hockey League owners' lockout, Wayne Gretzky and several of his closest hockey friends – Mark Messier, Paul Coffey, Brett Hull, Steve Yzerman, Marty McSorley, Sergei Fedorov, Russ Courtnall, Steve Larmer, Al MacInnis, Rob Blake, goaltenders Grant Fuhr and Kelly Hrudey – headed off for a series of exhibition matches in Europe. They called themselves "The Ninety-Nine All-Stars" and four of the players – Gretzky, Messier, McSorley and Coffey – took along their fathers to pay them back for all those early-morning practices and bad arena coffee. It was a charming, relaxed trip, the hockey superb and the interplay between hockey fathers and sons fascinating. At one point, at the Finnish Hockey Hall of Fame in Tampere, Wayne had his father sit beside him during a press conference, and Walter sat there patiently, like everyone else, while the predictable questions were asked and answered. Just when he thought it was over, however, a young television journalist raised her hand, was recognized, and stood to face a surprised Walter Gretzky.

"Mr. Gretzky, Sr.," she asked in halting English. "What kind of son do you have and how did he become the ultimate hockey player?"

Wayne grinned and pushed the microphone over in front of Walter. Walter cleared his throat and shook his head as if to fight off the jet lag. He wasn't sure what to say.

"Wayne always did like hockey," Walter Gretzky said, clearing his throat again, reaching. "Even when he was three years old – and it just kind of happened."

It didn't, of course, just kind of happen. But easier, perhaps, to say just that than keep the press conference rolling right through the upcoming game and well into the new

EVEN AT 38, THE GREAT ONE STILL HAD DEFENSEMEN AT HIS MERCY. NEVER TIPPING HIS HAND, GRETZKY WAITED UNTIL THE LAST POSSIBLE MOMENT TO ACT.

year. A year and a half later, with the NHL labor battles behind them and the first World Cup of Hockey under way, Wayne broke away for a few quiet minutes of idle chatter with a couple of longtime hockey writers, and spoke about how it had happened for him. The talk of the summer had been all about a rising national concern over developing hockey skills. The Canadian team, led by Gretzky and Messier, were the oldest team in the World Cup. Concerns had been raised by coaches about the skill level of young Canadian defensemen. And apart from young Canadians Eric Lindros and Paul Kariya, the stars of tomorrow all appeared to be coming out of hockey rinks in Russia and Sweden and the Czech Republic. Three games had so far been played by the Canadian side in the tournament they would eventually lose to the United States, and it had not passed notice that Gretzky, then 35, was the best Canadian on the ice.

He talked about the fan mail he'd been getting all summer long from concerned parents. They wanted their child to excel in hockey, of course, and they wanted, from him, advice on how to raise that child in the game. What hockey school, many of them asked, did he go to as a youngster?

The answer made him laugh. "None." His father wouldn't hear of it. Summer, in Walter Gretzky's world, was for baseball and lacrosse and any one of a dozen other sports that will improve hand-eye co-ordination and keep the appetite fresh for hockey. Walter's son held the same belief. "The only complaint I have about hockey," he said as the arena crew moved the three of us over to begin a fresh flood of the ice, "is that kids play too much." Parents, he said, "should just back off a little bit."

He hated to hold himself up as an example, but knew that everyone would anyway. If he had to tell people how he became the player he had become, he said, he would have to tell them it had not been through organized hockey or any particular coach or school or, for that matter, in any game or practice that needed to be booked into a 50-minute slot at the local rink.

Where it happened for Wayne Gretzky was, he said, "right in my own back yard."

He was thinking of "Wally Coliseum," the Gretzky kids' name for the extraordinary rink built each winter by Walter Gretzky in the backyard of 42 Varadi Avenue, Brantford, Ont. Perhaps Walter might have tried to explain the significance of this annual ritual to the reporter back in

Tampere, but some of it would make little sense to any but those who grew up at Wally Coliseum. How, for example, could Walter explain to anyone but close family the embarrassment he once felt standing at a Canadian Tire counter on a freezing February day and asking if they had any lawn sprinklers stored in the back, and if he might buy one for his rink? And how would anyone but those who were actually there relate to the crazy notions this hyper-kinetic man with the the long nose and crinkly smile brought to that frozen backyard classroom: skating around Javex bottles and tin cans, shooting against an overturned picnic table so a young Wayne would learn to pick the corners, sticks scattered flat about the ice surface so he could learn to gently flip a puck over obstacles and still pick it up again in full flight, himself hopping madly over the sticks? And how could Walter ever explain to anyone how it occurred to him that he should tell his young charge to "Skate to where the puck's going, not where it's been" – a single sentence of instruction that has come to explain so much, even to those of us who have had to accept it intellectually, because we could never accomplish it physically?

Where did Walter Gretzky get his ideas? He had himself played Junior B hockey. He had once had a tryout with the Junior A Marlies in nearby Toronto, but he'd been slowed by a bout of chicken pox and been cut for the very reasons he had feared: too small, too light. He'd been a nifty, gifted player, a fine playmaker, but he had never played professionally and had not traveled widely. He knew nothing of European hockey, and knew nothing, absolutely nothing, about the Soviet secrets – soccer formations, lateral skating, drop passes, five-man units and the time-gathering trick of pausing – that were first unveiled to shocked North American hockey fans in the 1972 Summit Series. Wayne Gretzky was all of 11 years old when the Soviet Union came to play Team Canada. He was himself already a bit of a national figure, having scored 378 goals the previous season for the Brantford Nadrofsky Steelers and having been featured in cross-Canada articles as a coming phenomenon. "When the Russians came over here in '72 and '73," Wayne later told CBC Radio's Peter Gzowski, "people said, 'Wow, this is something incredible.' Not to me it wasn't. I'd been doing those drills since I was three years old. My dad was very smart."

Walter Gretzky *was* smart, in an uncanny way. Even his son's famous signature sweater tuck – seen as vanity by many – came not from the father wanting his child to stand out, but from Walter noticing his child was too short to shoot unless that side of his over-sized sweater was somehow tucked out of the way. Walter's greatest gift, however, was to nurture a craving, an itch for the game, and to provide the space to play and the time to experiment, and then

to pass on the small things that he himself had learned while playing so that his son's own creativity could one day take them for his own.

"People say you can't teach anticipation," Walter told Gzowski in 1981 when Gzowski was writing *The Game of Our Lives* about the early years of the Edmonton Oilers. "I'm not so sure. I used to get them out on the ice and I'd shoot the puck down the boards toward a corner and I'd say, 'Chase that.' Well, they'd all go right into the end after it. Then I'd say, 'Wait, watch me.' I'd shoot it in again, and let it roll around the net. Instead of following it around the boards I'd cut across to where it was rolling. 'There,' I'd say. 'You've got to know where it's going to go.' "

Other parents have understood the importance of providing their promising offspring with such opportunity, and it was not always the father playing the critical role. Katherine Howe took $1.50 out of her milk money during the Depression and gave it to a struggling neighbor in exchange for a gunny sack that contained, among other things, an old pair of skates. Her son, Gordie, grabbed one, daughter Edna the other, and both headed for the frozen slough back of the Howe home where, as Gordie Howe later related, "She got cold and went in and took the skate off, and that was the last she ever saw of it. I fell in love with hockey that day. I couldn't get enough of it. On the weekends, I never took the skates off." Laurette Béliveau allowed her two boys, Jean and Guy, to keep their skates on when they came in off the backyard rink for lunch, the quicker to then return to their friends and the "marathon shinny" games that broke for nothing but, eventually, darkness. Pierrette Lemieux, Mario's mother, used to cart snow into her house when it got too deep outside for her boys to play shinny. She would throw it onto the carpet and pound it down to a smooth surface and then throw open the doors and turn off the heat, so the Lemieux boys could enjoy their own indoor rink when they were barely toddlers. Left to their own devices, they created their own devices, as any who saw Mario Lemieux at his best will verify.

Nor is such devotion peculiarly Canadian, which may explain Gretzky's quick and deep friendship with gifted young Russian Alexei Kovalev when they were teammates on the Rangers. Both shared heart-stopping abilities, if not similar results, and both recognized the importance of an indulgent, loving father in their early development. "All my spare time I spent with my son," Viacheslav Kovalev wrote in a slim memoir he published about his son's hockey career, "taking him to the hockey grounds. He could think of nothing else but hockey, and on weekends he would spend five to eight hours playing it. During practices he worked so hard that his clothes were soaked wet with sweat: you could wring them.

"We hung a cardboard on the goal and Alex practiced his shots from different points aiming at various pictures drawn on the cardboard...On a plastic floor I would draw three small circles, and Alex had to steer the puck around the floor trying to avoid hitting the circles. Such a game improved Alex's techniques of handling the puck and helped him to be able to play without looking at the puck. When Alex was nearly 12, I began training him with special heavy pucks which I made myself. For that I would drill a hole in the middle of a puck and pour some hot lead into it. Such a puck would usually weigh about a pound. Practicing with a heavy puck exercised his arm muscles. When he would start playing with a regular puck afterwards it would appear to him to be made out of cotton." Viacheslav Kovalev, meet Walter Gretzky.

But, as Wayne Gretzky later pointed out, what mattered most was the backyard rink, and the opportunities afforded by having endless time to experiment. "All I wanted to do in the winters was be on the ice," Gretzky wrote in his 1990 autobiography. "I'd get up in the morning, skate from 7:00 to 8:30, go to school, come home at 3:30, stay on the ice until my mom insisted I come in

GRETZKY WITH JANET, TY (LEFT) AND TREVOR AT HIS RETIREMENT ANNOUNCEMENT.

for dinner, eat in my skates, then go back out until 9:00. On Saturdays and Sundays we'd have huge games, but nighttime became my time. It was sort of an unwritten rule around the neighborhood that I was to be out there myself or with my dad. I would just handle the puck in and out of these empty detergent bottles my dad set up as pylons. Then I'd set up targets in the net and try to hit them with forehands, backhands, whatever. Then I'd do it all again, except this time with a tennis ball, which is much harder to handle."

❏ ❏ ❏ ❏ ❏ ❏ ❏ ❏

In the days of Gordie Howe and Jean Béliveau, the notion of a rink was entirely out of doors, with covered arenas the rarity. It was the outdoor game that the poet Al Purdy was praising when he wrote about how, "sometimes on hard-crusted winter snow I've seen the game escape its limits." Today, the outdoor rink is a rarity, an endangered species threatened by everything from too much organized ice time at the hundreds of indoor rinks built since the 1960s to the increasingly common decision of towns and cities to close up the outdoor rinks to save costs. No one, however, has ever calculated the loss of skills.

And yet even some of today's finest young stars hail the outdoor rink as an essential ingredient in their hockey development. Eric Lindros learned to skate and play on a rink his father, Carl, built for him and younger brother, Brett, behind their London, Ont. home. "The rink," Lindros said in *Fire on Ice*, "was my getaway, my little bit of heaven...It was all so condensed; everything was so simple on the ice. It was just you, your stick and a couple of pucks. The ice was crisp. My blades were sharp. The air was cool and bracing, but I felt warm. That was life.

"Game days held no special attraction back then; I much preferred to stay practicing on the backyard rink where I could run the show. The house league games were like brief interruptions to the more serious business at hand... When the game was over, I couldn't wait to get back to my private haven in the backyard...

"To me, the rink meant free time."

❏ ❏ ❏ ❏ ❏ ❏ ❏ ❏

When Wayne Gretzky stood in that Zamboni chute a few years ago and begged parents to "back off a little bit," he was in fact saying something that experts on child-rearing have been trying, with limited success, to get across now for decades. Back off, and let them play on their own. It is hardly a new notion. "The work of children is play," the great French philosopher Jean-Jacques Rousseau said two centuries ago. "Every time we teach a child something," the renowned Swiss psychologist Jean Piaget said this century, "we keep him from inventing it himself."

"How much can you teach a 10-year-old?" the degree-less sports psychologist Wayne Gretzky asked earlier this decade. "There's only so much he's going to take in. Do the basics – that's all they do (in Russia). You see a 10-year-old team in Canada and all you hear is, 'Shoot! Stay on your wing! Forecheck! Dump it in! Up and out!' (The Russians) get all their 10-year-olds on the ice and say, 'Play shinny!' "

Instinctively, Gretzky understands the significance of play and the dangers of denying the opportunity. Since the 1960s, when Gretzky himself was a child, parents have increasingly devalued play until today it has largely become a penciled-in time slot on the family day calendar, with many deeply involved parents hoping to see a return on their time and financial commitment, just as they would on any other enterprise they take up. "Play to order," the renowned Dutch scholar John Huizinga wrote many years ago, "is no longer play." For those who refuse to believe that the very young learn best on their own, and through play, Huizinga invited them merely to watch puppies: how they "invite" each other to play, how they have rules such as "no biting," how they pretend to get very angry, and how much obvious enjoyment they show as they learn. Play is how they are taught, and much of it by themselves. Too many of today's parents cannot bear the thought of their child playing on his or her own, any more than they can resist interfering with puppies at play. "The way children are interrupted in their play by adults is brutal," Margaret Flinsch, the great American pioneer in early childhood studies, said in a 1996 interview in *Parabola* magazine. "Play is a trying out – experimenting. It's not a joke. Children don't play for fun. They play for real, and adults don't understand that; they laugh at what children do. To children, play is very serious."

It was serious at the Wally Coliseum, as well. Winter was total hockey immersion, with Walter Gretzky the mentor-teacher as well as, at times, the playmate. Walter deeply wanted his son to succeed – driving the precocious five-year-old around the area seeking out a team that would take someone so young – but if he pushed somewhat it must be said that he was not alone in pushing: the child was equally demanding, as were the Gretzky children who followed. "It was definitely pressed on us," minor pro Brent Gretzky told the *National Post*, "but we loved the game. Without the direction of a father, I don't know where I'd be."

Walter Gretzky, who still coaches 10-year-olds, understood the value of teaching, but also of making idle time available in which no adult would be present to point out mistakes. He knew a child is often his or her own best school. "Play," after all, is still the word they use in the game, from the first time a stick is held until the final shift of a long career.

Unfortunately, that notion that supposedly meaningless play leads to meaningful discovery has been under some siege in the Canadian hockey world since Wayne Gretzky first learned the game in his backyard more than three decades ago. Play has become, at least in the minds of so many adults charged with organizing the act, competition, and it begins, at a merciless level, as early as ages seven and eight. Practice time is too often swapped for "exhibition" games against other area teams, so that not one, but two practices are lost in the interest of entertaining the parents and easing the burden of planned practices for the coaches. And even those coaches who hold on to their practice time, and often arrange extra time, will become too oppressive in controlling practices, with children subject to the same discouraging criticism during practices as they are in the highly competitive games. If, as now happens in the NHL, after each shift a player is subjected to instant review, and usually correction, the inclination to try something new, which may or may not work, is soon replaced with a determination to avoid everything but the old and sure, and approved.

In Sweden, where more and more highly skilled players are being produced, skills and fun are the essence of hockey "play" until the youngsters are 12 years old, and even then practice-to-game ratio remains two to three times what it is in Canada. Viacheslav Kovalev counted himself lucky when he sent young Alexei off to the coaching care of a Mr. Guzhenkov, who was, according to the elder Kovalev, "a very kind man (who) always treated the children nicely. He was also not dogmatic and provided them with an opportunity to be creative on a hockey field. Unlike many contemporary coaches in our country, and especially in the United States, who make their players act only according to definite patterns, he never made his trainees act in a straightforward way."

The more Wayne Gretzky played, the better he became. Walter and Phyllis Gretzky, a Bell Canada worker and a homemaker with a growing family and a backyard rink, had a prodigy on their hands and seemed, somehow, to sense everything that would be involved with such a child: responsibility, sacrifice, even the resentment of others. Walter can remember hearing men in the crowd loudly saying things like, "That damned puck hog – why don't they take the little bastard off the ice?" Parents of Wayne's teammates would sit in the stands with stop watches and time how long he was on the ice compared to their children. He was once booed to the point of tears prior to a peewee tournament in his home town. The women, Walter says, were often worse than the men.

It didn't matter that the youngster would set up, or at least attempt to set up, as many goals as he was scoring. The year he had 378 goals for the Nadrofsky Steelers, he also had 139 assists. It didn't matter that Walter Gretzky, rather than pushing, was suggesting to the coach that Wayne not be given so much ice time. It didn't matter that the coach, Bob Hockin, went out of his way to say that the 10-year-old wunderkind was "more of a team player than most people realize." To parents denied the accrued glory, Wayne Gretzky was a detriment to their own child's success, their own reflected glory.

These early brushes with criticism, in fact, cannot be underestimated in their effect on the player Wayne Gretzky later became. It is possible to understand his sensitivity to criticism, his very deliberate humility and his dedication to teamwork in connection with something his father said to him when he was only 10 years of age. "You're a very special person," Walter Gretzky told his son when the national media attention was only just beginning. "Wherever you go, probably all your life, people are going to make a fuss over you. You've got to remember that, and you've got to behave right. They're going to be watching for every mistake. Remember that. You're very special and you're on display."

That was said in 1971. Twenty-six years later, with five dozen National Hockey League records under his belt and a Hall of Fame induction long a certainty, the sen-

EVEN YOUNG HOCKEY FANS KNEW WHAT GRETZKY MEANT TO THE GAME OF HOCKEY.

sitivity to the spotlight was still very much in play. "When you're a celebrity," Wayne said in an unguarded moment in 1997, "you're guilty until proven innocent." He was then 36 years old, still driven daily to prove himself. He was determined not to "hang on past my welcome," but he also believed he still had something to offer. It was both a matter of pride and a reaction to the sting of real or perceived criticism and doubt. From age 10 on he had shown what The Hockey News' Bob McKenzie calls a tendency toward "rabbit ears and thin skin" – an elite athlete highly attuned to all that is written, said and even whispered about him. Such sensitivity drove him on toward ever greater success, and it would be folly to ignore this personality trait in trying to understand what it was that made The Great One great. As Gretzky himself conceded to McKenzie, "It made me a better player."

It had not worked out for him in St. Louis, where he spent the heel of the 1995-96 season, and over the summer he had signed as a free agent with the New York Rangers, a

multi-million-dollar deal that some had suggested was simply a Big Apple ticket draw; Gretzky, however, still burned for another Stanley Cup. He had risen, slowly throughout the 1996-97 season, to assume the real leadership of the Rangers even though he wore neither the "C" for captain nor an "A" for assistant. He had emerged as the team's finest player and had taken them all the way to the Eastern Conference final against the powerful, Eric Lindros–led Philadelphia Flyers. Months after being dismissed as a novelty, he was being hailed as the leading candidate, at that moment, for the Conn Smythe Trophy that goes to the Most Valuable Player in the Stanley Cup playoffs. He was, by that conference final, carrying the Rangers while Messier and Brian Leetch struggled, and he knew it, but would neither criticize his great friend Messier for his play nor pretend that he himself was anything but a part of the overall team. Superstars, he suggested in a quiet moment in the Rangers' dressing room, are hopeless if they think they alone are the answer. "It's a Catch-22," he said. "You can't do so much you end up running around and wind up chasing your tail."

Two years later, having decided, despite the chanting of that April crowd in the Corel Centre, that he would leave now rather than risk his welcome, he was still conducting himself as the consummate teammate. His Rangers had just missed the playoffs for the second straight season, yet he was still saying, "I've never considered myself bigger than any person I ever played with." In assessing his final career totals, it seemed odd to acknowledge that the greatest scorer in NHL history had been thought of, and thought of himself, as fundamentally not a scorer. He may have scored 894 goals in regular-season play – 93 more than Gordie Howe scored in six more seasons – and scored more in a single season, 92, than anyone ever before imagined (or will ever again threaten, the way the game is now played), but he had two assists for every goal. It was said that, during the 1987 Canada Cup, he had changed the life of a young Mario Lemieux by taking the youngster aside and ordering Lemieux to quit trying so much to set him up. "I'll make the passes," Gretzky apparently told him, "you take the shots." At the same time, the older player took the opportunity to lecture the younger one on the importance of hard work and good habits. A few days later, of course, Gretzky made the remarkable pass for the goal that not only won the Cup for Canada, but gave Lemieux the confidence he required to win his first scoring championship that season and, subsequently, take his Pittsburgh Penguins to two Stanley Cups. Gretzky's handoff, in other words, had involved far more than a mere puck.

So much of this behavior had its roots in Brantford. Always defer to the team. Always credit, never blame, your teammates. Always appear humble. It used to grate some sports journalists that Gretzky would avoid talking about upcoming milestones, even though they knew he was more acutely aware of where he stood in the grand measure of hockey than anyone, but they had not been there at the start to see what so much early success and so much sensitivity in both parent and child could do to a youngster. He was, as Walter Gretzky had said, forever "on display," and perhaps the most remarkable record of all is that, after more than two decades in the North American celebrity spotlight, there was hardly a false step, and never once a scandal.

To the end of his career, the son credited his father with teaching him how to behave in the spotlight. Walter Gretzky, to his great credit, kept a grace about him during those early years. No fist fights in the stands. No abusive shouting matches. He devised ingenious schemes to protect his son, such as having Wayne and a teammate trade jackets before they left the dressing rooms in the hopes of confusing the local critics. He carried on nonplussed by the criticism and anger, convinced that, in the end, it was the children's game that mattered far more than the parents' game. Wayne once said he considered his father to be "probably the smartest guy I know." He admired the work ethic of a Bell employee who kept on working even when he no longer needed to. He worried about Walter's nerves, the headaches and the ulcers and the late nights staying up with an endless string of coffee, but he knew, too, that Walter never worried about himself, always about the family, always about the kids' sports whether it was Wayne's hockey or sister Kim's cross-country running. It has been written a thousand times or more that Wayne Gretzky's great hero growing up was Gordie Howe, but Howe, in fact, was always No. 2.

❑ ❑ ❑ ❑ ❑ ❑ ❑ ❑

It is no small task raising a prodigy. Great accomplishment does not demand precociousness – Einstein was no Einstein as a child, Churchill didn't even *play* war particularly well – but Mozart was a brilliant child composer and Picasso painted well almost as soon as he could walk. Wayne Gretzky, as a child hockey player, had such astounding

talents that he could not help but be tagged special. He had uncommon ability, great curiosity and a natural penchant for inventiveness.

The more he tried untried things, the more he came up with new ideas for the game. Slim and small, Wayne Gretzky found a place behind the net that was, for hockey, unexplored territory. He saw the net as an impediment to others, and protection for himself, something that could offer him both space and time, even if it amounted to little more than a few square feet of ice and a fraction of a second. He had discovered what others would one day come to call his "office."

Only Wayne Gretzky knows what view he saw from behind the net. "Gretzky sees a picture out there no one else sees," Boston Bruins' general manager Harry Sinden once said. "It's difficult to describe because I've never seen the game he's looking at." Perhaps Gordie Howe said it best when he once joked, "I sometimes think that if you part Wayne's hair, you'll find another eye."

The connection between superior eyesight and superior play is as old as professional sport. It is commonly held that the truly gifted athlete – whether Michael Jordan in basketball, Martina Hingis in tennis, Sammy Sosa in baseball or Wayne Gretzky in hockey – have special visual gifts. Rogers Hornsby, the baseball Hall of Famer from the 1920s and winner of six batting titles in a row, refused to read books or go to movies with his teammates for fear it would harm his most effective weapon. Ted Williams, the last person to hit .400 in major league baseball, used to claim he could pick out the seams on a spinning ball, and therefore know what pitch was coming in. Stan Musial, another great hitter, used to claim, "If I want to hit a grounder, I hit the top third of the ball. If I want to hit a line drive, I hit the middle third. If I want to hit a fly ball, I hit the bottom third." In George Will's ground-breaking book on baseball talents, *Men At Work*, gifted hitter Tony Gwynn reduced the mysteries of hitting to only five words: "See the ball and react."

Perhaps the great athletes cannot always explain what they see and how it might be different from what the rest of us see, but there is, assuredly, a difference. There is a famous story told of when American writer John McPhee was researching *A Sense of Where You Are* about 1960s basketball great Bill Bradley (now the U.S. senator) and how Bradley one day complained in a high school gymnasium where he was shooting hoops that the net felt about 3/8ths of an inch too low. It seemed a preposterous conceit to McPhee until he returned that evening with a tape measure and checked. The net was precisely 3/8ths of an inch too low. Vision, McPhee therefore concluded, had to be Bradley's great natural gift, and subsequent tests at

GRETZKY SETS UP IN HIS OFFICE ONE LAST TIME DURING HIS FINAL GAME. THE GREAT ONE EARNED MORE CAREER ASSISTS THAN ANY OTHER PLAYER HAD POINTS.

Princeton University confirmed that the basketball star's peripheral vision was considerably more developed than average. "During a game," McPhee wrote, "Bradley's eyes are always a glaze of panoptic attention, for a basketball player needs to look at everything, focusing on nothing, until the last moment of commitment." For those close enough to watch Gretzky at work in his "office," the sense is the same: he focuses on nothing, he sees everything.

They say of gifted playmakers that they see the ice particularly well, and the scoring statistics would seem to argue that no one has ever seen it as clearly, or in such detail, as Wayne Gretzky. But there is more to it than scoring. He saw danger as acutely as opportunity, and was able to avoid checks to the point that a common belief took hold among many fans that there was an unwritten rule in the NHL that players were not to hit the game's No. 1 star. There was not. As Denis Potvin says, "There was nothing I wanted to do more than hit the guy," but the big New York Islander defenseman could never find him. "He had," says Potvin, "the strongest danger radar of anyone on the ice." Always

cool and methodical, he never rushed his play, never made the critical pass until the last possible moment, usually the perfect moment. In the opinion of goaltender Mike Liut, "He had the highest panic threshold of any player I ever faced."

Studies done on Gretzky and teammates during the early days of the Edmonton Oilers suggest nothing particularly special about the young NHL sensation. Tests done by Dr. Cam O'Donnell, now of the visual attention laboratory at the University of Western Ontario, found that Gretzky's reaction time was no faster than any other player's. Nor was his short-term memory the secret, as those tests found only that the team's highest-educated player, Randy Gregg, now a medical doctor himself, scored highest, yet was never considered anything but a reliable defenseman on the ice. Dr. Art Quinney, dean of the faculty of physical education at the University of Alberta, did early physiological tests on Gretzky and his teammates, yet found nothing scientific to explain the gifts. "It's fair to say," Quinney told the *National Post*, "that Wayne is not gifted physically in any particular way. He had during the years that he was here a very acceptable level of fitness, and some years worked harder at it than others…but I think what sets Wayne Gretzky apart is his intelligence and his ability to see the game and his dogged determination to develop skills."

Nearly 20 years ago, when Gzowski was writing his book on the Oilers and Gretzky, he became fascinated by the notion that Gretzky was neurologically different from mere mortals. Gzowski had noted that there seemed to be "an unhurried grace to everything Gretzky does on the ice." The pause, in fact, can be as effective a move in hockey as the quick break, but much more difficult to do as one is based on pure adrenalin and the other on pure nerve. It is, Gzowski said, "as if, as time freezes, he is enjoying an extra handful of milliseconds. Time seems to slow down for him, and indeed, it may actually do so." Gzowski then turned to scientists who agreed that, for some elite athletes, their neurological motors may run with such efficiency that, for them, the pace is slower. As one of them put it, there is "a great deal more room, in effect, in the flow of time than there is for the rest of us."

Mario Lemieux has said in the past that when things were going well for him on the ice it was almost as if everything moved in slightly slow motion. Raymond Bourque, the Boston Bruins' future Hall of Famer, says he knows the feeling, but would never dare compare what he feels out there to what it must have been like for Gretzky. "When I'm playing well," Bourque says. "I can feel what's coming behind me. You feel the game differently. It's slower for you. But that just comes from confidence, I think. Most guys hurry because they're just not sure what to do." While others panic, the elite players grow oddly calm under stress. "For you," says Bourque, "sometimes it seems so simple and easy you wonder why more guys can't see it that way. You try sometimes to tell them."

Unfortunately for hockey coaches, the power of suggestion alone cannot create in an average player the gifts of the vastly superior one. When journeyman forward Shaun Van Allen was playing for the Edmonton Oilers during the 1992-93 season, he was hit so hard that he barely staggered back to the bench and sat trying to recover as the trainer held smelling salts under his nose.

"Is he all right?" coach Ted Green shouted down the bench.

"He doesn't even know who he is!" the trainer shouted back.

"Tell him he's Wayne Gretzky," Green yelled. "And get him back out there!"

It didn't, unfortunately, work. Once Shaun Van Allen's head cleared, he was still Shaun Van Allen.

None of this, however, sufficiently explains the phenomenon that is Wayne Gretzky. Barely an adequate skater when he broke in, small physically and weak of shot – "You could wear driving gloves and catch one of his shots," Chico Resch once said, "and it wouldn't hurt" – and yet he somehow managed to dominate. "What separates him from his peers," suggested Gzowski back in 1981, "in the end, the quality that has led him to the very point of the pyramid, may well have nothing to do with physical characteristics at all, but instead be a matter of perception, not so much of what he sees – he does not have exceptional vision – but of how he sees it and how he absorbs it." Rather than compare Gretzky to other athletes, Gzowski suggested, better perhaps to compare him to chess masters who, under examination, have demonstrated that they remember "not so much the positions of the chess pieces but the overall situation." The more highly gifted the player, "the more likely he was to see on a board not the individual pieces, but the combinations they formed, the forces at play."

Gzowski was probably onto something. Recent tests on young hockey players at the University of British Columbia to judge "visual attention" – the ability to make sense of what is happening in one's peripheral vision territory – has found that the stars far outsee the grinders. Dr. James Enns, who undertook the study, told the *National Post* that the average person can keep track of only four or five objects on the periphery of vision, but he was certain that a Gretzky could keep track of many more. "I'd love to test him," says Enns.

There is one famous anecdote – apocryphal perhaps – dating back to Gretzky's years with the Oilers in which he stickhandles down the length of the rink and somehow finds time to shout at a linesman that the opposition has too many men on the ice. Whatever it was that separated him from the others on the ice – peripheral vision, vision attention, intelligence – it was a gift others either could not develop or were not given in the first place. "What he does on the ice isn't taught," says Glen Sather, Gretzky's coach from those days. "It comes down straight from the Lord."

Walter and Phyllis and genetics, of course, have a say, as well. It is intriguing that Walter, since he took up golf in recent years, has been steadily accumulating a vast treasure of "found" golf balls, now numbering several thousand, that he finds easily by merely walking along the edge of a fairway, balls that others cannot find in all their hours of searching and rooting about the rough and woods with club heads. No one, and certainly not Walter, understands why it is he finds so easily what others lose so easily, but he does appreciate the cost factor: he will not need to buy a new golf ball for the rest of his life. Walter simply says he's "lucky."

The son thinks the same of himself. At the 1998 All-Star Game in Vancouver, just prior to the Nagano Winter Olympics, Gretzky talked about the joys that had come to him through playing hockey. Everything he had he felt he owed to the game: money, success, joy of work, even family. "When I was growing up," he laughed, "if you told someone you wanted to be a professional athlete, you weren't considered very smart." Back then, he said, the dream of a parent was for their child to grow up to be a lawyer or a doctor, and while he was careful not to say anything negative about such professions, he himself felt that, as a parent, "I want my child to be an athlete." He knew, when it all worked out, how good it could be, how privileged the lifestyle. "I wouldn't trade my life for anything," he said.

He knew he'd been one of the lucky ones, and that unmeasurable, unknowable force – luck – cannot be ignored in any evaluation of what became of Wayne Gretzky and the game he both dominated and transformed. University of Chicago psychologist Mihaly Csikszentmihalyi has spent a lifetime studying and writing about creativity, and while he has concentrated mostly on scientific discovery and literature, he has no problem conceding that the very special athlete, basketball's Michael Jordan and hockey's Wayne Gretzky, also qualify as "creative performers." For his bestselling book, *Creativity: Flow and the Psychology of Discovery and Invention*, Csikszentmihalyi spent years studying 93 major international achievers, including 11 Nobel laureates, and covered a variety of achievers from world-renowned scientists to the Canadian novelist Robertson Davies and the great Canadian jazz musician Oscar Peterson. "Would I put Gretzky in the same league as (polio vaccine discoverer) Jonas Salk or Robertson Davies?" Csikszentmihalyi asks. "Personally, I would not – but I realize this is not based on logic." For those who believe that the value of sport in culture is equal to that of literature in culture, a Gretzky is as creative and valuable as the world's great novelists.

The great joy that Gretzky found in his life, the University of Chicago professor would argue, came out of his own creativity. "When we are involved in it," the professor says, "we feel that we are living more fully than during the rest of our lives." In studying creativity, Csikszentmihalyi found, as expected, that a great commitment and ample time to experiment were crucial, whether it be a brilliant young scientist or a promising young athlete. Wealth is not important so long as there is "strong parental influence" – and he cited here the father of Oscar Peterson, a struggling railway porter who would hand his child a new piece of music before heading out on a cross-country trip and fully expect to hear it played perfectly on his return. Csikszentmihalyi also found that all his interviewees were highly complex, often displaying such contradictory extremes as enormous physical energy combined with an equal ability to enjoy rest and quiet, a playful yet disciplined nature, a sense of humility as well as great pride, and strength in character as well as sensitivity, much as Wayne Gretzky has displayed. And, most intriguingly, a generous portion of pure "luck." The other factors have to be in place, the psychologist found, but then there has to be a certain amount of "luck" to pull it all together.

He would find quick agreement in Jack Coffey. Jack's son, Paul, is the highest-scoring defenseman in NHL history, and has displayed almost as much offensive creativity from the blueline as Gretzky has from the sides and behind the net. It would never have happened, however, says Jack Coffey, if his son – and, for that matter, Walter Gretzky's son – had not the great good fortune of having Glen Sather as coach of the early Oilers teams. "They were kids," Jack Coffey said one day in Oslo as the Ninety-Nine All-Stars were preparing to meet a Norwegian all-star team. "Kids. They grew up together in Edmonton. They learned to play hockey together there. They could make mistakes and they were allowed to learn from their mistakes. That's what made them such a great team."

Sather was young and easygoing, secure in his own abilities and in those of his young, talented team. He was not a "systems" coach, as is so popular today. He did not have an array of assistant coaches waiting for players to come off the ice so they could bend down and tell them what they had done wrong. He did not believe greatly in video breakdown, slicing up each player's shifts until instinct had been replaced with instruction. He let them "play." He let them experiment. And he let them learn from their experimenting rather than from his own lecturing. When he offered advice, it was to encourage. "Carry the puck," he told the young Coffey. "Carry it up the ice and try to do something with it." In later years, the all-star defenseman would say it was that one simple nod of approval – "Carry the puck" – that turned him into the top-scoring defenseman of all time. Jack Coffey would even go so far as to say another coach and another team might well have broken his sensitive son before he had a chance to show what creative gifts he had.

Sather was confident enough in himself and in his own abilities to let his players seek out their own solutions. As Gretzky later revealed in his autobiography, Sather stood by, without questioning, during the 1981-82 season while a young Gretzky completely overhauled his own game. Dispirited by his play during a stunning 8-1 loss to the Russians in the Canada Cup, Gretzky reacted strongly to mutterings he heard about his play, that he was able to score at will against weak teams like the Winnipeg Jets, but unable to come through in the really big games. He had not, of course, yet won a Stanley Cup. He set out to answer his critics.

"I decided the best way to do that was to change my style," he wrote. "I'd been passing 90 per cent of the time. I was too predictable. Every time I'd come down the line, they'd play me to pass, not shoot. The pass was getting too tough and the shot too easy to pass up. Now I decided to try shooting more." He scored 92 goals that

TOUGH GUY DAVE SEMENKO, RIGHT, COULD BE COUNTED ON TO BE BY GRETZKY'S SIDE WHEN NEEDED.

forever as the one who discovered uses for the area back of the net, but it was in his brilliant location passes, his sense of players yet to arrive – perhaps anticipating their role in the larger play long before they themselves did – that he changed, forever, the manner in which this evolving game is played. In other times, the idea was to get the puck to the star, for the star to get the puck to the net, but, as Dryden notes, "He wasn't big enough or strong enough, or even fast enough to do what he wanted to do if others focused on him." And so, "like a magician, he had to

season, still the NHL single-season record.

It is not possible to underestimate the importance of this time in the development of Wayne Gretzky, player. In permitting spontaneity, in encouraging improvisation and in refusing to be overly critical toward effort, Sather let the youngsters have their heads so long as they stayed within the broad outline of what he hoped to accomplish. "Those Oiler teams played ball hockey on ice," Mike Liut says. "They batted the puck out of mid-air, used caroms and bank shots, showed the kind of ingenuity that can't be diagrammed (or defended against) in a book or a between-period chalk talk."

The Oilers, led by the young Wayne Gretzky, were changing the game as it had been known to that time. And Gretzky himself was making himself up as he went along, not reinventing so much as inventing a whole new, unknown way of playing center. As Hall of Fame goaltender Ken Dryden writes, he "made his opponents stop five players not one, and he made his partners full partners to the game." Yes, he did inventive things along the right boards during power plays, and certainly, he will be remembered

direct attention elsewhere, to his four teammates on the ice with him, to create the momentary distraction in order to move unnoticed into open ice where size and strength didn't matter."

"Gretzky is like an invisible man," Igor Dmitriev, the assistant coach of the Soviet National Team, said during Gretzky's brilliant 1987 Canada Cup performance. "He appears out of nowhere, passes to nowhere, and a goal is scored."

It is amusing to note how often, in reaching for description, they have come to speak of Wayne Gretzky as if he somehow lacks substance. Gzowski suggested the youngster moved about the Edmonton ice like a "whisper." George Plimpton, the editor of *The Paris Review*, thought that Gretzky had an ability to "materialize abruptly here and there on the ice." He passed through checkers, someone once said, "like an X-ray." Former NHL coach Jacques Demers has wondered aloud how Gretzky just "seems to disappear out there. I can't believe a man can hide on a sheet of ice that's 80 feet wide and 200 feet long, but he can do it. And when he does appear again, it's nothing but trouble." All were speaking, of course, of an older, mature Wayne Gretzky, but it must never be forgotten that it was Walter Gretzky who told the child to "skate to where the puck is going to be, not where it has been."

He made, perhaps, more sense to the Russian players, so adept with the pause, so willing to try lateral passes and back passes and willing to use the flow of the game against itself. But even as astute an observer as the Detroit Red Wings' Igor Larionov – himself often compared to Gretzky for his inventiveness – found Gretzky's play perplexing when he first encountered it face to face in the 1987 Canada Cup. "We didn't know what to do about Wayne," Larionov says. "Every time he took to the ice, there was some spontaneous decision he would make. That's what made him such a phenomenal player. You never knew what he was going to do. Other players would need maybe two seconds to make a decision. He would make it in half a second and it would always be the right decision." It was Gretzky, of course, who dropped that surprising back pass directly onto the tape to Lemieux for the goal that would not only win Canada the series but would, as Lemieux himself is quick to credit, elevate Lemieux into the superstar status that he would enjoy until his early retirement.

"In '87 I watched Gretzky and Lemieux," says Raymond Bourque, "and I learned so much. I had the best seat in the house. They took the game to another level together, and they took it higher and higher as the games went on. I'd turn to the guy next to me and say, 'Did you see that?' "

Over on the other bench, the Russian players were doing the same. "He was a master," remembers Larionov. "He was improvising all the time."

People remember the winning goal and Gretzky's great pass to Lemieux, but Gretzky once told his friend sportswriter Al Strachan that he has another memory of the 1987 Canada Cup that he holds just as dearly. The Canadians had lost the first game to the Soviets 6-5, and following the game the 26-year-old superstar had received one of the

great dressings-down of his life. He had stayed on the ice too long. He had been tired at the worst possible moment, sagging on the ice when the Soviets scored the winner. "Don't you ever do that again!" he was told.

The lecturer was Walter Gretzky. "That's really something when you've just lost a game and your dad is blaming you for it," Gretzky recalled years later. Next game, Game Two, he set up five goals in Canada's 6-5 victory to tie the series at one game apiece.

He never scored a goal in what he considers the greatest game he ever played.

❑ ❑ ❑ ❑ ❑ ❑ ❑ ❑

Sports is about shared memory, and Wayne Gretzky left us much to remember. The goal that won the 1987 Canada Cup, of course. The behind-the-net passes to Jari Kurri. The overtime goal he scored against the Calgary Flames in 1988, the year everyone but Gretzky seemed to concede that the Flames were bound for the Cup. The trophies, the cars, even the three silly fights he had in his career. The wedding to Janet Jones. The August 9, 1988 trade to Los Angeles that so traumatized

GRETZKY TALKS STRATEGY WITH HIS RIGHT-HAND MAN, JARI KURRI, DURING THE EDMONTON DAYS.

the nation that many hockey fans can still remember exactly where they were and what they were doing when they heard the news.

Only one of the memories was a deliberate creation, however, and that was the December 1994 trip to Europe with Walter. He had talked Messier and Coffey and McSorley into bringing along their dads "to pay them back," but there was another, little known and deeply personal reason for wanting Walter Gretzky along. Three years earlier, the elder Gretzky had suffered a near-fatal aneurysm. For weeks his life had been in some doubt, and though he had recovered miraculously by the time of the owners' lockout, it was by then clear that not every door in his brain would be re-opening. Among the memories sealed off forever to him were the years 1979 to 1991, the very years in which his son had won the four Stanley Cups and established the scoring records that may stand forever. Walter had tried watching video accounts of the series, but

MARTY MCSORLEY, GRETZKY, PAUL COFFEY AND MARK MESSIER WERE BACKED UP BY THEIR DADS, BILL, WALTER, JACK AND DOUG, DURING A EUROPEAN TOUR IN 1994.

it wasn't the same. "I remember the tapes now," he said. "Not the games. It's like I was asleep for 10 years. It's all kind of like a dream."

The European trip, too, had been like a dream – so many of the original Oilers back together; Kurri lining up with Messier and Gretzky for the opening faceoff in Helsinki; Gretzky, Coffey and Messier using the big ice to play the puck control games of old – and, for Walter, standing on the Ninety-Nine All-Star bench as an "assistant coach," it had grown over the weeks to be a brand-new, fully formed and deeply treasured memory. No wonder that, at one point in Sweden, Gretzky had walked by the few journalists traveling with the group and said, "It's kind of like being a kid again – only this time we're in Europe."

He had one more great hockey trip left in him – to Nagano, Japan, for the Olympic Winter Games. It had been said that his day in the sun was over, that at 37 he would be simply too old to be of great use to his country. Canada

had lost the 1996 World Cup, and there were many who believed the time had come to turn a new page, to turn away from the Old Guard represented by Gretzky and Messier, and turn instead to the New represented by Eric Lindros and Paul Kariya. It was time, a thousand stories had said, "to pass on the torch." Messier and Gretzky, with their mammoth reputations, were thought to be now more a problem than a solution, with their intimidating reputations far outweighing their remaining skills.

Gretzky had no problem with passing on the torch, he just refused to consider himself a spent force as he did so. Obviously he was no longer the scoring threat he once had been, but that hardly meant he did not score at all. "The hardest thing for me," he said somewhat bitterly at the time, "has always been that I've been compared to myself. For years, people have been trying to figure a way to knock me off the horse. Now it's like: 'Finally, we can get him. He's not going to get 200 points.' Well, they're right. I'm not

THOUGH HE DIDN'T POSSESS ONE OF THE NHL'S HARDEST SLAPSHOTS, GRETZKY WAS DEADLY ACCURATE, FINDING HOLES WHERE THERE APPEARED TO BE NONE.

going to get 200 points, and I don't think that's a crime when the best players in the game – Lemieux and Jagr and the rest – aren't going to get 200 either. I think I can still play."

He had proved his mettle immediately in New York, where he led the league in assists in 1996-97, with 72, and added 25 goals for 97 points.

By the spring of 1997 he was the best Ranger in the playoffs, proving night after night that "I can still play." With similar point totals the following year in New York – he would again lead the league in assists – his play and, perhaps more importantly, the certain public backlash that would follow his not being named to the Olympic squad, garnered him a spot on the team, though most of the

He came, smiling, to the Vancouver hotel where a mock-up of the Olympic Village facilities was on display, and he was one of the few who refused to ridicule the rooms.

Sure the beds were small, the room tight and roommates necessary, but he himself had been offended by the arrogance of the American basketball "Dream Team" that refused to stay in the Village at the Atlanta Summer Games in 1996 and chose, instead, to take over an entire upper floor of the most exclusive hotel in Atlanta.

"We can stay in any hotel in the world," he said after he'd checked over the accommodations and pronounced them satisfactory, "but how many times do you get a chance to stay in an Olympic Village?"

His arrival in Nagano was an international sensation, completely catching the Canadian organizers by surprise. He came, with the rest of the team, on the bullet train from Tokyo, and more than two thousand Japanese fans were waiting on the platform above Track 11 when he arrived at precisely 11:13 a.m.

The crush of fans and media was so ferocious that, at one point, sportswriter Cam Cole, a large, strong man, was literally picked up by the flowing crowd and carried along behind Gretzky for several meters.

"I almost got killed," said Canadian goaltender Curtis Joseph. But the Japanese fans were thrilled. "This is better than Elton John," squealed office worker Toyoko Sugimoto. "Wayne Gretzky is most famous." Even Gretzky seemed taken aback by the reception. "It was a little unnerving," he said after he reached the safety of the media center. "We didn't expect it. It was one of the first times I got a little nervous."

"It's just stupid," said teammate Theoren Fleury, who was himself somewhat crushed in the onslaught. "Everybody wants a piece of him."

But everyone, of course, has always wanted a piece of him, and the memories of Nagano from off the ice are an indication of how much of himself Gretzky is willing to give. He talked openly of how this would probably be the last time in his hockey career that he would have the privilege of playing for his country. It was the first, and certainly last, time he would ever be an Olympian, and he was determined to enjoy it as much as possible. He was never seen out of his Olympic clothes. Rather than pull rank and command one of the smaller rooms, he moved happily in with three roommates: Martin Brodeur, Rod Brind'Amour and Steve Yzerman. He became a key figure in the late-night ice cream sessions that seemed to bring a cocky new spirit to the Canadian contingent. There was even the bright cold day down by the Big Hat Arena when two Canadian journalists rolled off a media bus and saw, far down the

experts considered him a frill, a power play specialist who might end up centering a third or fourth line.

He showed up for the first gathering of the team, at the all-star break in Vancouver, and he brought with him an attitude that would, before the Games were over, be embraced by the entire Canadian team. He said he felt "like a rookie," and that this, for him, was a dream come true. He was an Olympian. He was a Canadian. And he had been asked to represent his country.

street, the unmistakable rolling walk of Wayne Gretzky, fists pushed deep in his Roots jacket pocket, walking along and stopping to talk to everyone who had a moment to spare. He had walked all the way in from the Olympic Village itself, a walk of several miles, and he had done so alone so he could better take in the sights and remember this golden time toward the end of his career.

He was gracious about his role on the team. He said Eric Lindros was the perfect choice for captain and gladly offered his support. "I've had my time and certainly a long time," he said. "Now is the time to step back and just really enjoy it." There was, in retrospect, a growing sense here that he knew it was all coming to an end, that he had no intention of hanging on "past my welcome" no matter how tough the actual decision was going to be.

The Canadians had trouble with the big ice. They had trouble with the European patterns and the lateral play and the endless, inventive cycling. Some of the Canadian players who had been most expected to shine, such as Brendan Shanahan, played terribly and admitted it. Lindros played as hard as he could every shift, but with precious little result. Slowly, as game after game went by and the concern continued to rise, Wayne Gretzky began climbing through the lineup. He, almost alone among the Canadians, seemed to take to the larger ice surface as if it offered more opportunity instead of obligation – as if, indeed, there was, as Gordie Howe had so long ago suggested, a third eye in there somewhere. In a match against the bumbling American team, it was Gretzky who set up perhaps the prettiest Canadian goal of the tournament when, killing a penalty with Joe Sakic, he and Sakic caused a turnover just as Canadian forward Rob Zamuner got out of the penalty box. Sakic dropped a pass to Gretzky just inside the U.S. blueline, Gretzky drifted toward the net with his stick rising for a direct slapshot, faked magnificently, and then slid the puck across to the oncoming Zamuner, who had but an easy tap-in for the goal. It started the Canadians off to an easy 4-1 win over the Americans, a little retribution, two years later, for the World Cup loss that was supposed to be Gretzky's last international hurrah.

By the final round, and with the elegant Sakic injured, it was Wayne Gretzky who assumed the leadership both on and off the ice. His playing time soared, as he was being sent on not just for power plays but double shifts and even penalty kills. But he could not, of course, do everything. When the Canadians came up against the Czech Republic and Dominik Hasek – who Gretzky now calls "the greatest player in the world" – it was beyond any of them to solve the brilliant, eccentric goaltender. Gretzky played his 37-year-old heart out in that critical game. Between whistles he struck a familiar image from those long-ago, glorious Oilers'

days – bent over, stick across the knees, head down, sweat dropping, mouth gasping – but the moment play began again it seemed he was charged with new energy, stealing pucks, setting up point shots, slipping those exquisite little floater passes out from behind the net, only to see shots missed by his teammates or, just as likely, blocked by the acrobatic Hasek. Those sitting in the stands, including Walter Gretzky, gathering new memories, were smitten with how desperately he was trying to win the game. Smitten, but hardly surprised.

When overtime solved nothing, they went to shootout. The team that scored the most goals on alternating, unimpeded breakaways would go on to the gold medal round in the Olympics; the team that lost would have to hope for a bronze medal. There seemed some confusion as the teams organized their shooters. Pieces of paper were consulted, discussions were held, finally a list was handed to the referee. Shooting for Canada would be Fleury, Bourque, Joe Nieuwendyk, Lindros and Shanahan. Bourque was a defenseman who had rarely played in international competition and never before on a large ice surface. Shanahan had openly said he had lost all confidence and was "lost" out there, unable to find the net.

"No Gretzky?" someone in the press box asked out loud. Others looked across the ice in confusion. The greatest goal-scorer in the history of hockey was not on the Canadian list. The best player on the Canadian Olympic team was not on the list.

Czech shooter Robert Reichel scored on the first shot. Fleury was stopped by Hasek. Bourque was easily stopped. Nieuwendyk was stopped. Lindros hit the post. Shanahan shot wide.

The game was over, the Czechs had won and they poured off the bench to swamp Hasek, skating toward them with both arms raised in victory. At the other end, the Canadians slipped over the boards sadly and skated slowly toward goaltender Patrick Roy.

One player, however, stayed on the Canadian bench.

"Look at Gretzky," a voice said in the press box.

All eyes shifted from the Czech celebration to the Canadian bench, one solitary red jersey still sitting there, bent far over and staring straight down. He looked up, peeking over the boards at the nightmare unfolding, then for a long time into the distance, seeing nothing, then down again, alone with his thoughts.

The Czech stick-throwing and helmet-tossing and hugging and shouting and jumping and slapping went on and on. The Canadians slowly made their way toward the exit, leaving the ice. And still he sat there, with no teammate daring to go to him, no Canadian eye in the building off him.

GRETZKY HAD NO PROBLEM STEPPING ASIDE FOR LINDROS, TOUTED AS "THE NEXT ONE": THE MOST DOMINANT CANADIAN HEADING INTO THE NEW MILLENNIUM.

High in the stands Walter Gretzky had taken up the same position, only instead of staring down at the floor, he was staring straight down at his son, their expressions identical.

The Canadian explanation was preposterous. The ice, they said, was heavy with snow after so much play, and they wanted to go with players with "the strength to get through the shot." No one bothered to point out that Wayne Gretzky was 37, not 87.

But if he was hurt by the slight, he refused to show it. While other players swept through the fenced "mixed zone" at Big Hat as if they were cattle resigned to slaughter, Gretzky, one of the last to come, lingered, turning out to be the last to leave. He stood – eyes red-rimmed, yet clear – and offered no excuses. "Normally," he said, "when you lose in hockey, you can stand there and say, 'We didn't do this well' or 'we did that poorly,' but we can't say that tonight."

He said he was "devastated" by the loss. He said it was pointless wondering if another list of shooters would have been better, as no one was going to beat Hasek. "I really don't believe I would have made any difference," he said. He also said it would definitely be the last time he would ever represent his country in international play, but he wanted it understood that while he was disappointed in the result, he was far from disappointed in the experience.

"We came here," he said, "with a sense of mission and focus and responsibility. And I hope a lot of kids in Canada watched us here, and saw how hard we worked, how much pride we played with, how responsible we were, and how we conducted ourselves as Canadians."

It was a point that would be underlined in the days to come. While the American team bailed out of the Olympics early, leaving behind a legacy of boorish behavior and trashed rooms, the Canadians stayed right through to the end. They cheered their fellow Canadians on, they toured Nagano, they played, but lost, the bronze medal game to a spunky Finnish squad. They shook hands and congratulated the Finns. And they marched in the closing ceremonies, all in Canadian Olympic Team uniform, all led by a waving, happy Wayne Gretzky.

Looking back, there was a sense as he sat there, all alone, on that bench in Big Hat, that he was in fact seeing something as he seemed to stare vacantly into the distance. He was, surely, looking back – he talked later about how "privileged" he had felt to first represent his country as a 16-year-old and how he "felt the same way playing on this team as I did on that team" – but likely looking ahead, as well.

He would play one more season. The 21-year-old who had scored 92 goals in 1981-82 was now a 38-year-old who would score only nine times in 1998-99. He was still the best player, but on a very bad team. He had, in January, one final glorious moment on the ice when, playing with Fleury and Mark Recchi on his wings, he had taken the North American side to victory over the World in what would be his final All-Star Game, his final Most Valuable Player award.

He knew, long before he arrived in Ottawa that April evening, that this would be his final game in his homeland. Friends and family had tried to talk him out of it, but his mind was made up. As he'd said a decade earlier, "I don't want anybody telling me when to retire." The decision was his, and his alone, first tentatively reached, one now suspects, as he sat alone on that empty bench in Nagano. The magnificent career would soon come to an end. As Walter Gretzky had said of its beginning, "It just kind of happened."

He was not interested in one of professional sports' tedious "farewell tours." If there were going to be tears, they would be genuine ones, not manipulated ones, and they would be brief.

GRETZKY IN HIS FINAL INTERNATIONAL APPEARANCE, THE 1998 WINTER OLYMPICS IN NAGANO, JAPAN.

After 21 seasons of professional hockey and nearly 3,000 points, he had already stopped the clock more times than any player the game has ever known.

The only thing he could not do was turn back the clock.

That particular trick he would leave to his fans, and the gift of precious memory. **99**

A PHENOM Is Discovered

By JOHN IABONI *Oct. 28, 1971*

There's a Little No. 9 in Brantford, Ont., who has ambitions of replacing the recently retired Big No. 9 of the Detroit Red Wings, Gordie Howe.

And, as with his hero's prowess in finding the net and beating rival goaltenders, 10-year-old Wayne Gretzky has proven he can score goals, too. Now in his fifth novice season with Brantford's Nadrofsky Steelers, the 4-foot-10, 70-pound defenseman-winger-center has notched 369 career goals.

That's including a five-goal and two-assist performance last Saturday at North Park Arena, which paced Nadrofsky to its seventh consecutive pre-season win, 7-4 over the Metropolitan Toronto Hockey League's unbeaten Toronto Kings West Hill Highland Farms.

The goal production currently stands at 41 for the 1971-72 campaign with league action in the Brantford-participating Hub League scheduled to commence in two weeks.

Wayne impressed his coaches in his initial tryout when he was five years old. He earned a center berth in the 10-and-under novice league then and scored one goal while his team captured the group title.

The following season, Gretzky upped his goal total to 27 as Brantford once again won the group championship.

Prior to the 1969-70 season, Nadrofsky coach Bob Hockin presented Wayne with the No. 9 sweater and Gretzky responded with a 105-goal performance as a defenseman to lead Brantford to the group crown.

Last year as a penalty-killer, power play specialist, center and defenseman, Wayne collected a phenomenal 196 goals as Nadrofsky won the Ontario championship. Along with his list of team and individual firsts, Wayne was selected as an all-star each season. Achievements of this sort certainly deserve a few hearty boasts, but the Grade 5 student at Greenbrier Public School remains a very modest young man.

He really enjoys hockey and doesn't mind playing every shift if coach Hockin asks him to. Yes Bobby Orr, Phil Esposito and Bobby Hull are good hockey players, but as for the first two he doesn't like Boston and with the latter he is enamored only of his slapshot.

"Now Gordie Howe is my kind of player. He had so many tricks around the net no wonder he scored so many goals," Gretzky said. "I'd like to be just like him. And if I couldn't play hockey I'd like to play baseball with the Oakland Athletics and Vida Blue."

"Wayne is a wonderful little hockey player," Hockin said. "He ends up being more of a team player than most people realize.

"I know that some say he has played too often, but every time he's out there he's a threat because he controls the game.

"With Wayne being so dangerous and in possession of the puck quite often, he is in a position to shoot himself or set up his teammates. This is good for team morale–the others know he's giving 150 per cent so they try to give 115 per cent."

Brantford's seven pre-season games have been typical of Wayne's consistent 150 per cent efforts. While most victories have been relatively easy (11-2 over Waterford, 23-0 over Grimsby, 17-0 over Galt, 16-1 over Guelph and 13-2 over Hamilton) Nadrofsky's encounters with Toronto teams have provided spectators with close, exciting games.

And each time, Gretzky has come through to give Brantford the final edge with three goals in a 5-3 victory over powerful Don Valley Jack's Pack and again versus the Kings.

background

THE STORY BEHIND THE STORY ABOUT A 10-YEAR-OLD PHENOM

The first major newspaper article about The Great One almost never made it to print. Reporter John Iaboni's story on the 10-year-old Brantford phenom ran Oct. 28, 1971, in the *Toronto Telegram*. The paper folded two days later. Iaboni knew he was witnessing something special when he watched the 4-foot-10, 70-pound Gretzky. "He was absolutely unbelievable," Iaboni said. *Hockey Night in Canada* produced an intermission feature on Gretzky in the wake of Iaboni's story.

Wayne was on the ice for 40 of the 45-minute Kings' game and tested Toronto goalies Glen Wagg in the first period and Steve Bochum in the final two periods with 18 of his team's 31 shots on goal to account for his high points total.

When Gretzky wasn't shooting at the goalies he was close to the goal area anticipating a possible rebound or congratulating wingers Brian Croley and Len Hachborn when each finished Wayne's rushes with goals.

"To be very honest, I don't like to see him out on the ice all the time," said Wayne's father Walter, who is coach of the Niagara District League Junior B entry.

"I'll leave the coaching up to Bob Hockin. Wayne has always been a good skater, although he has never had the size. As long as he likes the sport, I won't complain."

In the Kings' dressing room, coach Pat Volpe expressed contentment in his team's play and praised Gretzky.

"There's no doubt about it, he's a good hockey player," Volpe said. "They've got a fine team and we're hoping to get them back into Toronto if we can get some ice time."

Judging by the solid body-checking and splendid goaltending evidenced in the first encounter, a rematch in Toronto could fill the arena.

A PROLIFIC-SCORING WAYNE GRETZKY EARNED THE CAPTAINCY ON HIS NOVICE TEAM, THE NADROFSKY STEELERS.

A breakaway goal by Gretzky at 2:35 and a beautiful 2-on-1 passing play from Wayne to Croley at 13:30 gave Brantford a 2-1 first period lead. Art Robbins beat goalie George Hotston at 3:39 for a Kings' goal.

The Steelers were in front after the second period, but center John Goodwin, by far the Kings' best player, tied the score after 32 seconds of the final period. But Gretzky won the game with goals at 9:08, 12:28 and 14:59.

As the players congratulated each other before heading for the dressing room, Darren Thompson, an eight-year-old spectator, asked if your correspondent was a newspaper reporter.

"Yes," came the reply.

"Oh, are you going to write a book on Wayne Gretzky, he's good you know." No Darren, not yet, but maybe someday, soon. 99

Canapress

WALTER'S World

By BOB McKENZIE

Never mind what Wayne Gretzky is going to do now that he has retired, what about Walter, Eddie and Butch? For years now, on the nights Gretzky played, Eddie Raemer and Ron "Butch" Steele would arrive at 42 Varadi Ave., in Brantford, Ont., to watch the game with their longtime friend, Walter.

"We've got our routine," Walter said. "Eddie always brings a dozen donuts. Butch, he always brings a bag of chips. I take care of the pop. We've got our special places where we always sit and watch Wayne's games on the TV."

Just one problem now, though. Wayne isn't playing any more games. What's to become of the three amigos' ritual?

"That's a good question," the patriarch of the Gretzky family said. "I'm sure we'll figure out something."

When Gretzky was finalizing his retirement plans in Ottawa on April 15, 1999, he told his dad to make sure Eddie and Butch were going to accompany Walter to New York for the last game on April 18. "Eddie and Butch showed up at the house before we went to the airport to go to New York," Walter said. "Eddie had his dozen donuts, Butch had his bag of chips. Those guys..."

A party for the last time, perhaps?

"It better not be," Walter said.

As good a story as Wayne Gretzky is, Walter may be a better one. As good a person as Wayne is, and he's a better person than he is a player (which is saying something), he has nothing on his 60-year-old father.

Wayne's unbridled passion for playing the game was incredible, but it no doubt stemmed from Walter Gretzky's love and appreciation of life in general. This is especially true of Walter since he suffered a brain aneurysm that nearly took his life in 1991.

"I wasn't supposed to live," he said. "(The doctor) told Phyllis to call Wayne and the boys because I probably wouldn't last the night."

A Toronto radio station actually reported Walter was dead.

"When you get a second chance, just being here, well, this is all a precious thing to me," he said. "Very precious."

Walter speaks the words, but his actions tell the tale. The retired Bell Canada worker has always seemed to have a firm grasp of the meaning of life, of how it's not

BACK TO THE FUTURE: GORDIE HOWE PLAYFULLY HIGH-STICKS YOUNG WAYNE IN 1972.

Nith, just behind Wayne's grandparents' farm in Canning, Ont., and captured it on the family's movie camera.

It was Walter who flooded the famous backyard rink, dubbed the "Wally Coliseum," but not because he figured he had a future NHLer on his hands.

"It was," Walter said, "for self-preservation. I got sick of taking him to the park and sitting there for hours freezing to death. I told Phyllis, 'I'm making a rink in the backyard and we can watch him from here (in the kitchen).' "

Today, the backyard rink is no more. Now, there's an in-ground swimming pool, a gift from Wayne and wife Janet. The day the diggers broke ground was the same day, Aug. 9, 1988, Gretzky was traded to Los Angeles.

It was Walter who took a little six-year-old

what you take, but what you leave that's important.

Maybe it has something to do with his sister, Ellen. Born with Down Syndrome, she taught them early in life about advantage and disadvantage and how one can become the other. Maybe it's about his mother, who suffered from leukemia. Maybe it's related to having had a child prodigy who garnered national attention as a 10-year-old, a kid who brought out the best and worst in so many people.

"My dad has always been my biggest fan and my biggest critic," Wayne said. "I don't mean he was hard on me. He would talk to me about what would make me a better player. He has always been such a big part of it. There has never been a day he wasn't a big part of my success."

It was as if Walter was chosen to shepherd a special talent into the world and he didn't disappoint.

It was Walter who put Wayne on the ice for the first time, just shy of his third birthday, on the frozen river, the

Wayne to tryouts for a team of 10-year-olds, the beginning of a minor hockey career that is now legendary.

He scored just one goal that season with trainer Bob Phillips giving him the puck and prophetically saying, "You'll score a lot more than this, but here's the first one."

He scored 27 in his second season, 104 in his third, 196 in his fourth and, finally, as a 10-year-old playing against 10-year-olds he had 378 goals in 82 games. As the competition got stiffer the next three years, his totals decreased to 105, 196 and 90, but he was still without peer.

Just as legendary as the stories of his prowess were the stories of resentment and jealousy in Brantford, which Walter rationalized as follows: "Wayne was four feet, four inches. They were trying to cut him down to their size."

Through it all Walter taught his son humility and grace. No story has received more play, or perhaps been a bigger factor in the career of No. 99, than Walter's stinging admonishment after 10-year-old Wayne went through the motions before a packed house at a late-season exhibition game.

"My father said, 'I don't ever want to see you do that again. All these people came to see you play. You have to be at your top level every night, whether it's an exhibition or Game 7'" Wayne said. "That always stuck with me. I knew then I was on display."

That Gretzky has so seldom disappointed, on or off the ice, is a tribute to himself–and his father. Not that his mother Phyllis should ever be forgotten. She often is, though.

"That's the way she likes it," Wayne said. "She doesn't like to be in the foreground. The ironic thing is that as much as I talk to my dad, I probably talk to my mom more. I call her to find out what's new and what's up with my dad. My relationship with her is more about what's going on in life than hockey."

If Gretzky is the ultimate hockey player, Walter is the ultimate hockey dad. He is likely to miss Wayne playing as much as Wayne will miss it–maybe more–though his youngest son, Brent, still plays with the Chicago Wolves of the International League.

YOUNG WAYNE SCORED MORE THAN 1,000 GOALS.

The Gretzky basement on Varadi is a shrine not just to the greatest career in hockey, but all the Gretzky kids and their sporting exploits–Wayne's sister Kim and her track and field trophies as well as the pictures and mementos of brothers Glen, Keith and Brent.

Walter is very much in his element there, proudly displaying Montreal Forum seats autographed by Jean Béliveau, Wayne's Order of Canada medal, even a Ranger sweater Wayne wore for one game with his name misspelled (Gretkzy) on the back. There are hundreds of everything else you can imagine, from trophies to plaques to medals to photos to sticks to sweaters to crests.

Any one is the departure point for a free-flowing conversation with Walter, who is a terrific storyteller.

"What's wrong with that sweater?" Walter asks.

When the visitor notices Gretzky spelled G-R-E-T-K-Z-Y, Walter is clearly tickled and quick with a retort. "That's not just a hat rack you've got there after all," he said, laughing with delight.

It's ironic, too, that of all Wayne's awards in his basement, the one Walter most cherishes wasn't won while playing hockey. It's the Order of Canada.

"My parents, who were from Russia and Poland, always used to tell me how lucky we are to be Canadians," Walter said. "This is a great country and it's something very special to be a Canadian."

And of all the photos that adorn the walls and shelves, the framed snapshot Walter pulled off an end table was of him and the man he credits with saving his life.

In the picture is Walter, arm-in-arm with Dr. Rocco de Villiers, the Hamilton neurosurgeon who operated after the aneurysm.

"That man saved my life," Walter said solemnly. "He said he didn't do anything special, that it was my own will to live, but I don't know about that. If he hadn't operated, I wouldn't be here today."

In the aftermath of Walter's surgery, once it became apparent he would live, there were concerns about his quality of life and whether his faculties would return to normal. For the most part, they have. Walter is as sharp as a tack, picking up on details that would elude many. And yet while his memory has improved considerably, vast chunks of it are gone and will never come back.

"A lot of what happened between the 1970s and 1991, I don't remember it at all," Walter said.

Now, when Walter pushes a button on a talking picture of Wayne scoring goal No. 802 to beat Gordie Howe's NHL record–there's an audio recording of the play-by-play of the historic goal of March 23, 1994–and a visitor talks about being there that night, Walter said: "Was I there?"

When the visitor replied, "I believe so," Walter responded, "If I was, I don't remember."

"That must be hard," he's told.

"It's not so bad," he said. "What you don't think about, you don't miss."

Besides, for Walter Gretzky, there are more important things in life. Like life itself.

He talked about the passing of Arnold Anderson, the well-known local radio sportscaster who was one of the very first to chronicle the exploits of the young Wayne. Three days after Gretzky's final NHL game, Anderson died in Brantford, losing a battle with cancer.

"Wayne phoned Arnold just before he died, but he got the answering machine and left a nice message that Arnold's family will be able to keep because it speaks so well of Arnold," Walter said.

WALTER GRETKZY, ER, GRETZKY SHOWS
THE MISSPELLED RANGERS' SWEATER
WAYNE WORE FOR ONE GAME.

Walter retired from Bell Canada in 1991, but it's a full-time job just being Walter Gretzky. He's still involved in coaching minor hockey and he likes to get out golfing, each weekday if he can, as part of his post-aneurysm therapy.

Still, he has plenty of time for others. The pile of broken hockey sticks on the strip of grass beside the garage has nothing to do with hockey and everything to do with Walter's work on behalf of the W. Ross Macdonald School for the visually impaired in Brantford. The local arena drops the broken sticks off at Walter's house and he takes them to the school, where they're made into hockey-style park benches.

As much as Walter likes to talk hockey, he likes to talk about helping people. He takes great pleasure in phoning recipients of scholarships in Wayne's name for the visually impaired.

"We've always given out five, but now we're going to 10," Walter said, excitedly. "These are special children."

At Christmas, Walter tours hospitals throughout Ontario, distributing teddy bears as part of a drive by the Ontario Provincial Police. On Halloween, a young, visually impaired boy named David, who lives on Varadi, came trick-or-treating at the Gretzky household.

"David talks like a little adult," Walter said. "He said to me, 'Well, Mr. Gretzky, how long after your medical mishap was it before you could talk to your family?' He said it just like that. Now, why would a little boy want to know that? Well, his dad had a stroke and hasn't been able to talk to David and since David is visually impaired, it's hard for them to communicate. His dad is making progress, but isn't that something?"

Walter finds a lot of wonderment in every day, though if every day is like the one a visitor witnessed in the week after Wayne's retirement, the only wonder is how Walter survives. Two elderly widows who live a mile or two away from the Gretzky household knocked on the door, wondering if they could get some autographed pictures of Wayne to take to relatives in Australia.

The next thing you know the women were sitting on the couch in the Gretzky living room, Walter had autographed photos of Wayne spread all over the floor and was down on his hands and knees personalizing the photos and adding his signature while kibitzing with them.

Through it all, the phone never stopped ringing and Walter never stopped running, literally, through his house.

YOUNG BRANTFORD SUPERSTAR MILLENNIUM MAN IN GOALS
The Prodigy, born Jan. 26, 1961, scored a prodigious 1,097 goals during eight seasons in Brantford. Gretzky added another 63 goals during two sesons in Toronto with the Jr. B Seneca Nats.

Year	Division	Goals
'67-68	Novice	1
'68-69	Novice	27
'69-70	Novice	104
'70-71	Novice	196
'71-72	Novice	378
'72-73	Peewee	105
'73-74	Peewee	196
'74-75	Bantam	90
'75-76	Jr. B	27
'76-77	Jr. B	36
10 Seasons		**1,160**

Not long after the women departed, former Brantford mayor Karen George, a friend of the family, dropped by with two Toronto businessmen who wanted to meet Walter and get autographed pictures. More photos were hauled out and Walter was alternately signing photos and posing.

While this was going on, the mailman arrived. He wanted a signature, too, but for a registered letter. On this day, there were more than 20 pieces of mail, some for Wayne, most for Walter and Phyllis.

"Now you know why I golf every day," Walter said. And yet he reveled in it. His eyes were twinkling, his arms were in full motion as he trotted out old stories of what it's like to be the father of you know who.

Like the time many years ago when a car stopped outside 42 Varadi. Two teenage girls got out, pulled up handfuls of grass and hopped back into the car with their souvenirs. The kicker to the story is last fall, at a local appearance, a woman confessed to Walter to being the driver of the getaway car. Walter asked for the names and addresses of the two girls who pulled up the grass–they now live in Nova Scotia–and sent them each a letter suggesting their grass must be dried out by now, so he included a fresh supply.

Or there was the time he was on a plane going to Edmonton to see Wayne. He pulled out a copy of *Sports Illustrated* with Wayne on the cover and the woman beside him proceeded to tell Walter that Gretzky wouldn't be nearly the player he was if he weren't surrounded by so many other Oiler stars.

"Not long after that the stewardess came up and called me Mr. Gretzky," Walter said. "That poor woman couldn't eat her dinner and never said a word the rest of the way."

Spending an afternoon with Walter Gretzky is an exercise in the reaffirmation of life. Maybe that's because few people value it as much as Walter, who has been a much different person since his brush with death.

"Yeah, he changed," Wayne said. "He became more relaxed, more at ease with his family. He spent a lot of time working with his kids, but now he'll just walk to the arena to help kids and coaches. There's less pressure on him, he's having more fun, which I tried to get him to do for 20 years."

Not that Walter's life is stress-free. He still has to figure out which nights Eddie and Butch will show up with donuts and chips and which game they'll watch. **99**

The Best YOUNG Player Gretzky Faced

By MIKE BROPHY

For all intents and purposes, Bob Goodish was finished with hockey years ago–turned off and tuned out. He was a successful businessman who had little time for the sport he dominated as a youth.

Then all of a sudden, the greatest player to ever lace on a pair of skates brings up Goodish's name in conversation. And in glowing terms, no less.

"I can always remember my dad saying, 'Play like (Goodish) and you'll play in the NHL,'" Wayne Gretzky told The Hockey News in 1994. "He had everything; he had speed, he had hockey sense, he had size. In peewee, he was probably a better player than me."

A week after he retired, The Great One again heaped praise on his former foe. "Goodish was the best minor hockey player I ever saw," Gretzky said. "(Future NHLer) Paul Reinhart was a close second.

"(Reinhart) was a rushing defenseman who was hard to play against. He wasn't overly physical, but he hit me one time when we were 10 and in those days there was no glass around the rink. My grandmother hit him over the head with her purse."

While Goodish often stopped Gretzky in his tracks, he escaped grandma's wrath. A native of Burlington, Ont., Goodish was a physically imposing defenseman who at 14 was 6 feet and 195 pounds

Goodish and Gretzky competed against each other from age eight through 16, when Gretzky was a member of the Ontario League's Sault Ste. Marie Greyhounds and Goodish, the London Knights. Although Goodish was not

BOB GOODISH: GRETZKY'S MOST RESPECTED OPPONENT DURING MINOR HOCKEY.

the scoring machine Gretzky was, his size and speed intimidated opponents.

"Wayne was a good player, but we were never awestruck by him," said Terry Bovair, a teammate of Goodish in youth hockey. "Bob was a big kid who was always able to contain Gretzky."

While Goodish allows he had some success against the budding Great One, he doesn't take credit for keeping him completely under wraps. "You would think you had him tied up all game and you'd beat them 6-5," Goodish said. "Then you'd look at the game sheet and see he had a goal and four assists, so you didn't have him under control at all."

Goodish joined the Knights with lofty credentials, but his junior career was undistinguished. In 264 games with the Knights, he collected 30 goals, 142 points and 387 penalty minutes. Though he was offered a tryout with the Colorado Rockies, he turned it down and spent three years playing hockey with the University of Western Ontario Mustangs while earning a business degree.

The player, once so highly regarded, had soured on hockey. A stockbroker until the crash of 1987, Goodish now owns FundEX Investments, a mutual fund dealership based in Markham, Ont. He said he is happy, fulfilled and has no regrets about not turning pro.

"I was a victim of junior hockey," Goodish said. "A lot of people took the fun out of the game for me, the way they treated people. The coaches, the managers, the owners, they're in it to make money. I understand that. The thing is, (we were) just kids." **99**

By JOHN HERBERT

The nickname was a natural: The Great Gretzky, or The Great One, as he later became known. Wayne Gretzky was great long before all those Stanley Cups, Art Ross Trophies and Hart Trophies. The nickname stuck simply because it fit.

Gretzky was only 16 when he arrived at the London Gardens in London, Ont., with the Sault Ste. Marie Greyhounds for an Ontario League game Dec. 6, 1977, against the London Knights.

The way he moved and played–silently, almost invisibly–was, simply, great. The game was a homecoming of sorts for Gretzky, the skinny kid from Brantford, just 50 miles west of London, when Muzz MacPherson's Greyhounds came to play the Knights.

The Gardens was packed to the rafters as it hadn't been for years. By then London had heard of Gretzky, but what really brought the fans out that night–more than 5,000–was the magic of his greatness. Everyone had heard about his 300-plus goals as a peewee. But

WAYNE PLAYED FOR THE VAUGHN NATIONALS BEFORE JOINING THE GREYHOUNDS.

periods against Dino Ciccarelli, who played for the Knights, in what turned out to be the highlight of the game.

First Gretzky scored. Then Ciccarelli. Then it was Gretzky's turn again, but he missed. As he skated back to center ice, Ciccarelli said something smart to him.

On it went until the last shot, the one which would have tied it up 3-3. Gretzky broke down the middle of the ice, but he lost control of the puck because the water from the flood had not quite frozen in that spot.

As Ciccarelli was celebrating his win he chirped at Gretzky and the pair soon found themselves in a shoving match. Off the benches came both teams and the goons paired off as The Great One and Dino watched. The headline in the London *Free Press* the next day blared out "Gretz-er-elli wins shootout."

From then on in my reports for the London *Free Press*, I referred to him as The Great Gretzky, which eventually became The Great One.

One of Gretzky's grade eight teachers at Greenbrier School in Brantford, Cam Martindale, recalled seeing the

The NICKNAME

nobody in London could quite understand what was so special about The Great Gretzky until that night. London won 6-5, but Gretzky recorded five assists–two of them on goals scored on plays in which he had left the ice before the puck entered the net.

He was everywhere. Yet he was nowhere to be found.

The Great Gretzky just vanished into thin air. He was not that fast. He was not that quick. He wore No. 99, but no one really knew why. But boy, could he play. He was the Great Gatsby and the Great Houdini rolled into one. He controlled the game like Bobby Orr. He had the hockey sense and passion of Gordie Howe. He had the playmaking skills of Stan Mikita.

Even then, Gretzky had the grace of Jean Béliveau and the determined look in his eye of Rocket Richard, who later said, "he's a natural scorer just like me."

There had never been anyone quite like Gretzky. All this at just 16.

Gretzky competed in a shootout that night between

name on the walls before he saw it in the papers. Leading up to the annual staff vs. senior boys basketball game, kids splashed nicknames on posters through the school: Tiger Taylor, Stompin' Stamer, Sogs Sovereign...and Great Gretzky.

One of my lasting memories of the Gretzky family came just a year ago. A friend of mine, Chris Goodwin, wanted to take his son, Russell, to see the shrine in the Gretzky basement in Brantford. As we pulled in front of Gretzky's home, his dad, Walter, came flying down his driveway to greet us.

"Which one is your son?" Walter asked, as he welcomed us to his home. "That's my son Tom," I said pointing to the smiling 11-year-old. Walter walked to Tom and put his arm on his shoulder, and without hesitation asked, "Do you know my son's nickname?" Tom replied: "The Great One."

"That's absolutely correct," Walter told my son.

"Do you know who gave it to him?" Walter asked.

"My dad," Tom said.

"That's absolutely right," Walter replied.

By ALEX MITCHELL

In less time than it takes to say Sault Ste. Marie, Angelo Bumbacco ignored a threat, added a phenom, created a fuss and carved out a place for himself in hockey history.

And all this for simply following the hockey executive's draft credo of "taking the best player available."

Of course, that player happened to be Wayne Gretzky, on whom Bumbacco–the Sault Ste. Marie Greyhounds'

Wayne's SOO-PER Season

THE GREYHOUNDS ROLLED THE DICE AND WON WHEN THEY PICKED GRETZKY.

GM–decided to take a calculated risk and make the third overall choice in the 1977 Ontario League draft.

The gamble wasn't so much a questioning of Gretzky's ability to play in the OHL, though there were many who doubted whether the 150-pound center was strong enough. (The Oshawa Generals took Tom McCarthy first overall, while the Niagara Falls Flyers opted for Jim Peters second.)

The real deterrent for Bumbacco should have been that the Gretzky camp made it clear prior to the draft Wayne wanted to play close to home. Sault Ste. Marie, located in Northern Ontario, is about 850 kilometers, an

$8\frac{1}{2}$-hour drive, from the Gretzky homestead in Brantford.

But after considerable dialogue, the Gretzkys agreed to a request from the Greyhounds to visit Sault Ste. Marie, take in the sights, visit the high school Wayne would attend and then offer their thoughts. By mid-summer, Gretzky was a Greyhound.

And what a Greyhound he was.

In his first regular season game, one in which the Greyhounds produced six goals in a win over the Generals, Gretzky had three goals and three assists. It was a harbinger of things to come. Gretzky scored, set up goals and killed penalties, but just as importantly, he put people in the seats and then lifted them out of them with his play. His exploits in the Sault Gardens became even greater, if not somewhat distorted, the next day when spectators told others what they witnessed from Gretzky the previous night.

And it wasn't just the fans who were amazed with Gretzky's play. Muzz MacPherson, the late Hounds' coach, formed a mutual admiration society with his phenom.

"He always comes to play," MacPherson said. "He gets as excited about a goal in practice as he does about one he scores in a game.

"Great anticipation, great puck sense. He'll tell you something he's going to do in a game–like Babe Ruth–and he'll go right out and do it."

Bumbacco could also talk for hours about his prized pick.

"This kid is amazing," he said, "all the ability plus he's a wonderful personality. Friendly, does well in school and he has show biz. You know what I mean?"

People tugged at Gretzky from many directions: the media was demanding; students in the hallways and classrooms at Sir James Dunn Secondary School viewed him as a celebrity; and people on the street wanted a piece of the action, whether it was an autograph or a few moments of conversation.

Gretzky took on everyone, dealing endlessly with the media while the team bus, loaded with tired players and

RECORD-BREAKING RESULTS: GRETZKY EQUALLED THE GREYHOUNDS' FRANCHISE RECORD FOR GOALS IN A SEASON (67) EN ROUTE TO A NEW STANDARD (70).

soggy equipment, waited for him outside the arena, often up to an hour. He dealt with the autograph-seekers, waiting outside the Hounds' dressing room door during road trips. And he fitted in those from the corporate world, people who wanted to do business with the phenom.

It's not that the Sault hadn't seen its share of great players pass through. Future NHLers such as Phil and Tony Esposito, Lou Nanne and Jerry Korab plied their trade as juniors for the Greyhounds. But none were in Gretzky's stratosphere in their rookie seasons.

Gretzky was such a spectacular first-year player he was able to raise the level of play of his teammates. Playing on a line with a pair of 19-year-old wingers, Gretzky turned Dan Lucas and Paul Mancini into dominant OHL performers, a level they hadn't achieved in previous seasons.

Lucas used his bulk to work the corners and a great wrist shot to finish off pinpoint Gretzky passes. Mancini, who showed signs of being an offensive threat the previous season in the Sault, had his numbers skyrocket once the phenom began looking his way.

Each member of the trio finished with 50 or more goals, while Gretzky, who had 70 goals and 182 points in 64

GRETZKY PLACED SECOND IN THE OHL SCORING RACE AS A ROOKIE.

games, chased Ottawa 67's center Bobby Smith to the wire in the league scoring race. Smith, three years Gretzky's senior, won the derby with 69 goals and 192 points.

How dominant was Gretzky? After scoring his first OHL goal in the Hounds' opener, he had 20 by Nov. 6 and 50 by Jan. 28, two days after his 17th birthday. Gretzky's 100th point was recorded against Niagara Falls three days into 1978. Assist No. 100 was produced two months later. And his goal total set a franchise record.

Big games? You bet. After getting six points on opening night, Gretzky collected another six less than a week later and went to town on Ottawa with a seven-point effort the following week. It was evident less than one month into the season that Gretzky was something special.

He also proved in his one and only major junior season he could dominate on the international stage. He led all scorers at the 1978 World Junior Championship with eight goals and 17 points. While the Canadians struggled as a team–they finished a disappointing third at the tournament–Gretzky excelled. The youngest player in the tournament, he was the only Canadian selected to the all-star team and named top forward.

His performance at the event made him feel comfortable that he could take the next step–into pro hockey. "That's when I realized I could make professional hockey a living," Gretzky later said.

That was good news for Gretzky, but bad news for fans in the Sault and junior hockey in general. When Bumbacco selected Gretzky, he was hoping to get four years from him, but had to settle for one.

Reality arrived in March when Gretzky beckoned a reporter to a table in a motel restaurant. Off the record, he told the reporter he was leaving at season's end, embarking on a pro career at 17, taking his act to Indianapolis of the World Hockey Association. No. 99's first and only major junior season ended when Ottawa knocked the Sault out of the playoffs.

News of his departure and signing with the Racers made headlines around North America. In Sault Ste. Marie, hockey fans bemoaned the loss of the city's greatest player. That loss was compounded several weeks later when team captain Craig Hartsburg left to become an underage player with the WHA's Birmingham Bulls.

It was a blow that took some time for the Hounds to overcome. "It was kind of devastating," said Brian Gualazzi, a member of the 1977-78 Greyhounds. "We had a good team in 1978 and we had a lot of guys coming back. Then in the summer, we lost Wayne Gretzky and Craig Hartsburg to the WHA. It was a big blow to the team."

But it was certainly fun while it lasted.

By REYN DAVIS

Wayne Gretzky made no bones about it as a kid growing up, Gordie Howe was his hockey hero. Never did he imagine he would line up with Mr. Hockey on the same line with the eyes of the hockey world upon them.

The occasion was the World Hockey Association's 1978-79 All-Star Series in Edmonton featuring the best players from the WHA against Moscow Dynamo. Gretzky, Howe and Howe's son Mark helped lead the WHA to a two-game sweep of the visitors.

"I didn't know for sure that I would even make the team," Gretzky said. "It was a tremendous thrill that I not only made the team, but Jacques Demers put me on a line with Gordie and Mark. That was especially exciting for an 18-

After one season of junior hockey in Sault Ste. Marie, Gretzky was signed to a seven-year, $1.75-million personal services contract by Nelson Skalbania, owner of the Indianapolis Racers, during the summer of 1978.

Indianapolis had no idea who he was or what he could do when Skalbania signed him. It took the skinny little kid from Brantford five games to score his first goal as a professional–against Edmonton, of all teams. And another four seconds to get his second.

He had his own fan club before he even suited up for his first regular season game. "The Great Gretzky Fan Club" was for those 17 and under. Gretzky's stay with the Racers only lasted eight games, though. He landed in Edmonton on the Oilers' doorstep, sold as property by Skalbania.

Neither Gretzky nor goaltender Ed Mio nor forward Peter

WHA
World Hockey Association Teen Sensation

year-old. I'm grateful to Demers for giving me that opportunity."

Indeed, it was a coming together of two special eras, one concluding and the other just beginning.

In fact, Gretzky's presence in the WHA spurred the merger that ushered the Edmonton Oilers, Winnipeg Jets, Quebec Nordiques and Hartford Whalers into the NHL. One year before his arrival, the WHA spent a third consecutive fruitless summer trying to convince the NHL the two parties should become one.

That same summer, Gretzky earned $200 a week as a laborer as part of a paving crew. Little did he know then his presence would pave the way for the WHA's entry into the NHL.

"I can hardly wait to see what happens when the big guys in the NHL see him," said Glen Sather, then coach and vice-president of hockey operations of the Oilers. "They'll think he's unbelievable, just as we do."

Driscoll knew precisely where their plane would land upon leaving Indianapolis. Both Mio and Driscoll had been recommended to Sather by Bill Goldsworthy who had been traded to Edmonton from Indianapolis the year before.

Winnipeg's Michael Gobuty and Barry Shenkarow were trying to buy Gretzky, too.

"I'm not here," Gobuty told two Winnipeg reporters in Indianapolis on the eve of the deal, begging for anonymity. "Neither is Barry."

Shenkarow apparently dropped out of the bidding when Jets' GM Rudy Pilous described Gretzky as "too scrawny" to be an impact player. It was the first and only time the Jets' owners listened to Pilous.

Another story had Shenkarow and Skalbania playing a game of high-stakes backgammon. If Skalbania won, the story goes, his prize would be the Winnipeg franchise; if Shenkarow won, he would get Gretzky.

The game never concluded.

What Gretzky did for Edmonton was perform magnificently for the WHA Oilers and go on to win four Stanley Cups, score 543 goals and engineer 977 others in nine NHL seasons. As part of the merger plan, each of the WHA teams was permitted to protect two skaters and two goalies. Gretzky was among those protected by the Oilers.

In his only WHA season in Edmonton, he scored 43 goals and drew 61 assists for 104 points. Add in his Indianapolis numbers, and he finished third in league scoring with 110 points. Real Cloutier of the Quebec Nordiques led the league in scoring with 75 goals and 129 points.

Gretzky concluded the season with seven goals in his last three games, earning WHA player-of-the-week honors. "He was in his infancy," said Joe Daley, the Winnipeg goaltender who led his team to the last WHA championship that year, beating the upstart Oilers in six games in the final.

"Wayne was a fuzzy-cheeked kid.

background

NHL'S CALDER TROPHY; THE ONE THAT GOT AWAY

Only a technicality kept Wayne Gretzky from a unique "three-peat." Gretzky was named the Ontario League's top rookie in 1977-78 and the WHA's top freshman in 1978-79. But players who joined the NHL from the WHA following the 1979 merger were ineligible for the 1980 NHL rookie prize. So, in spite of tying Marcel Dionne for the league lead in points, Gretzky wasn't a Calder candidate. Boston's Ray Bourque earned the 1979-80 honor instead.

Personally, I did not think he had the physical stature to last a long time. Nobody in his right mind could predict that."

Gretzky was only 17 when Skalbania signed him. And, yes, he did get tipsy when he drank his first beer at an Oilers' party. Indeed, he was the butt of many jokes by players, some of whom were old enough to be his father.

"He's one of the boys," they said. "We treat him the same way we treat everybody else on this team."

Edmonton, meanwhile, saw more good hockey in those 10 years than some cities will see in a century.

Gretzky was named the Oilers' most popular player and top rookie in his one WHA season. It was a sign of great things to come.

Today, the only former WHA team that remains is the Oilers. Gone are the Jets, Nordiques and Whalers, off to become Coyotes in Phoenix, Avalanche in Denver and Hurricanes in Carolina. **99**

A BIG DEAL: GRETZKY SIGNS A 21-YEAR CONTRACT WITH THE WHA OILERS IN FRONT OF HOMETOWN EDMONTON FANS AS HIS FATHER, WALTER (LEFT), LOOKS ON.

THE POWER & GLORY

GRETZKY BURST UPON THE NHL LIKE A SUPERNOVA AND BURNED BRIGHTLY FOR TWO DECADES

Bruce Bennett/BBS

By BOB McKENZIE

Wayne Gretzky was blessed with a vast array of talents, not the least of which was extraordinary vision, incredible touch and a sixth sense. Well, here are two more qualities that contributed to his greatness.

Rabbit ears and thin skin.

Perhaps no player in the NHL, certainly no superstar, was as acutely aware of everything that was being said and written about him as Gretzky. And no player used negative reviews to fuel an insatiable desire for success like No. 99. The Great Gretzky was one thing. To grate Gretzky was another.

"It got (instilled) in me from my dad," Gretzky said,

into positives. I would know. Gretzky has identified Game 7 of the 1993 Western Conference final–between his Los Angeles Kings and Doug Gilmour's Toronto Maple Leafs–at Maple Leaf Gardens as his finest NHL game. (Which is not to be confused with his best game ever, Game 2 of the 1987 Canada Cup final).

Gretzky scored three goals and two assists in a 5-4 win May 29 that eliminated the Leafs from the playoffs and quashed hopes of the Canadian dream series–Montreal versus Toronto.

The virtuoso performance at Gretzky's favorite NHL building came in the wake of a Toronto *Star* columnist suggesting, after Game 5 of the series, that Gretzky was "skating with a piano on his back."

PROVING
Them All Wrong

when asked about his sensitivities. "When I was a kid, there were a lot of things written about me. Most of them were nice, but there were criticisms–he's too small, wait until he plays under pressure–and none of it ever bothered me, but it would crush my dad, it would eat away at him."

At some point, though, probably once he became a pro player, Wayne and Walter swapped sensibilities.

"The funny thing was as I got older, (criticism) didn't bother my dad, but it

CRITICISM HELPED PUSH GRETZKY TO GREAT HEIGHTS DURING HIS CAREER.

started to eat away at me," Gretzky said. "I took his pain and all the things he worried about and I had it and he lost it. He was the guy who threw all that in my head. In some ways it made me a better player. In other ways it made me worry about things I shouldn't have been worried about."

More often than not, though, Gretzky turned negatives

Which, incidentally, he was, but then I should declare my bias: I wrote the column.

"That was you, you wrote that?" Walter Gretzky said with a laugh. "All I know is on that day (of Game 7), before Wayne went to the rink, he said, 'This is one piano that has another tune to play.' That kind of stuff always got him going. He liked to hear things like that. It made him play better."

What separated this criticism from the many other slings and arrows Gretzky suffered during his career was how personally and publicly he took it. Usually, when Gretzky was wounded by something said or written, he took great pains not to allow his critic any reflected glory. But not this time.

The "Piano Man" lines got good play in the media the next day. A couple of Leaf players went so far as to suggest

the only reason they lost to the Kings was because of my column.

And two days later in Montreal, at the Cup final introductory news conference, Gretzky went to the unusual length of mentioning me by name and discussing the merits of the column.

Gretzky seemed to interpret it as an assertion he was over the hill–which it wasn't–and was miffed that it came from someone with whom he'd had a good working relationship for 15 years.

Then and now, I find it difficult to believe the greatest player in the game required a critical column to light a fire under him in the deciding game of a series that would give Gretzky something he'd been looking for since he left Edmonton–a trip to the Cup final.

But there's also no disputing Gretzky calling Game 7 the best of his NHL career. And he did tell everyone he

sound bite

AGENT MIKE BARNETT ON 99'S DESIRE: RUN HIM AND RISK NIGHTMARE GAME

" If a player intentionally tried to take him into the boards hard...he would go out of his way to try to beat that player on a later shift. One night, we were driving back to Edmonton from Calgary. In the game, a particular Flames' defenseman decided early in the first period to rub out Wayne. I asked Wayne why he looked so motivated that night and what happened with the defenseman. 'I told him not to run me,' Wayne told me, 'and that's why (the defenseman) was minus-4.' "

was carrying the column with him during the Cup final for inspiration.

For what it's worth, the column was one of the best of my career and that was before Gretzky lit it up in Game 7. Childish as I am, once I heard Gretzky was carrying the column with him during the Cup final, I did the same.

As for the column itself, I wasn't present at the first four games of the Kings-Leafs series (a point Gretzky duly noted when taking issue with my words) as I was covering the Memorial Cup for television. I was looking for an angle in Game 5 and what stood out for me was how poorly Gretzky and Toronto winger Dave Andreychuk were playing in a critical game of a critical series.

Because I'd missed the first four games–I did see them on television–I

THE OPPOSITION MAY HAVE BEEN ABLE TO PUT THE GAME'S TOP SCORER ON HIS KNEES, BUT THEY COULD SELDOM KEEP GRETZKY OFF THE SCORESHEET.

surveyed a wide cross-section of media to ensure my theories were valid. The consensus was clear: to that point, Gretzky and Andreychuk had been series no-shows.

During the intermission before overtime, I wrote the first 10 paragraphs of a critical Gretzky column and the first 10 paragraphs of a critical Andreychuk piece. Whichever player lost would get roasted.

Toronto's Glenn Anderson scored in the final minute of the first overtime period.

The deadlines were tight. The rest of the Gretzky column was written within about 25 minutes and that included a visit to the dressing room to ask Gretzky two questions—was he injured or hurting in any way and was he frustrated at not having played to his usual level of excellence? No and no.

There was but one regret I had about that column and it was beyond my control. The column was widely perceived as a suggestion Gretzky was washed up when, in fact, it was nothing more or less than a critical evaluation of Gretzky's play, primarily in Game 5, but also Games 1 through 4.

It wasn't until after Gretzky scored the overtime winner in Game 6 in Los Angeles that I was even aware he was rankled by what had been written. The funny thing is, even though he scored the OT winner that night–Leafs' fans will tell you he shouldn't have been in the game after high-sticking Gilmour and not being tossed–his play wasn't considerably better in Game 6 than it was in Game 5.

But it was just the jumping off point Gretzky needed to set up the Game 7 heroics.

Once he got that goal and once I knew he was steaming over what I'd written–I was well aware of Gretzky's penchant for proving his critics wrong–I sensed Game 7 would be something to behold.

On the day of Game 7, a friend asked me how the Leafs would fare that night. I told him the Leafs would lose and Gretzky would light it up.

Light it up? It was unbelievable.

Maybe it was because I had something of a personal stake in it, but I can't recall any player playing any better or

PEOPLE WERE ALWAYS NIPPING AT GRETZKY'S HEELS AND THAT KEPT HIS MOTIVATION LEVEL HIGH.

taking over a game like Gretzky did that night at the Gardens. It was one of the most special nights from a most special player.

To what degree, if any, my words were a factor in making it happen I'll never truly know.

This much is certain, though. No player disliked criticism as much as Gretzky and no player was as capable of responding to it. **99**

Days of THUNDER

JANET JONES AND WAYNE GRETZKY
CELEBRATE THE 1988 STANLEY CUP

*"The biggest thrill of my career? It's no compari-
son. My first Stanley Cup in Edmonton."*
Wayne Gretzky, April 16, 1999

By JASON PAUL

In only five seasons, Wayne Gretzky
rewrote the NHL record book. He was
the owner of four Art Ross Trophies, five
Harts and one Lady Byng. But the prize
he really wanted his name engraved on
had eluded him.

As Gretzky and the Edmonton Oilers
closed to within one victory of winning
the 1984 Stanley Cup, he let his teammates
know this was the most important one.
"Wayne stood up in the dressing room
before (Game 5 against the New York
Islanders)," said Oilers' teammate Mark
Messier, "and said all the individual awards
he has won could never compare to winning the Stanley Cup. That got everyone
going and made us all realize how much it
means to win the Stanley Cup."

The Oilers, up 3-1 in the series, had been swept the previous year by the Islanders, and they were determined to beat the defending champs.

Gretzky had failed to score in the previous year's final and was held goal-less through Game 3 of '84. He finally solved Billy Smith with a pair in a 7-2 win in Game 4, and two more in a Cup-clinching 5-2 victory in Game 5.

The Oilers' triumph ended New York's four-year reign and began their own dynasty. Edmonton won three more Cups in the next four years, with Gretzky leading the league in playoff scoring each time.

In 1984-85, Gretzky added a new trophy to his collection–the Conn Smythe Trophy as playoff MVP after scoring an NHL record 47 post-season points.

In the Stanley Cup final, Gretzky was held pointless in a 4-1 loss to the Philadelphia Flyers in Game 1, but scored seven goals in the next four games. In what Gretzky calls his best game for the Oilers, he had a natural hat trick in Game 3 as Edmonton bounced back to win four straight.

A "three-peat" wasn't in the cards for 1986, however. Calgary halted the Oilers' dynasty in the Smythe Division final when young Oilers' defenseman Steve Smith bounced a clearing pass off goalie Grant Fuhr and into the net for the deciding goal in Game 7.

The Oilers roared back to the final the following year for another matchup against Philadelphia. The Flyers pushed the Oilers to a Game 7 in Edmonton, but the Oilers prevailed when Gretzky fed a pass to Jari Kurri, who snapped in the game-winning goal from 25 feet out in the second period.

The curtains closed on Gretzky's days as an Oiler in 1987-88, when he led the team to Cup No. 4 and earned his second Conn Smythe Trophy along the way.

Gretzky scored what he calls his greatest goal ever in his final appearance in the Battle of Alberta. While killing a penalty in overtime in Game 2 of the Smythe Division final in Calgary, Gretzky ripped a 40-foot slapshot over Mike Vernon's shoulder to win 5-4. The Oilers swept the series 4-0.

Gretzky broke his own NHL record of 30 assists in the playoffs by one and led all playoff performers with 43 points, including an NHL-record 13 points in the four-game final against the Boston Bruins.

In Game 4 in Edmonton, Gretzky and linemates Kurri and Esa Tikkanen collected eight points between them in a 6-3 win. Gretzky scored the winning goal.

Little did anyone realize it would be Gretzky's last sip from the Stanley Cup. A few months later, the city went into mourning when Gretzky was traded to the Los Angeles Kings. 🏒

A STATUE IN HONOR OF THE GREAT ONE STANDS OUTSIDE SKYREACH CENTRE.

GREAT PICKS
From The Great One

With countless highlights that span a 21-year career in the NHL, the WHA and international tournament play, picking the most memorable moments seems like an impossible task. But, like his ability to see and read the game like no other, Wayne Gretzky has little trouble recalling his most significant on-ice achievements. The Hockey News enlisted the help of The Great One himself to name his Five Greatest Goals and Five Greatest Games.

no. 1 goal
APRIL 21, 1988
OILERS 5 FLAMES 4

Gretzky scored the overtime winner, at 7:54 of the first extra period, to give the visiting Oilers a victory over the arch-rival Flames in Game 2 of the Smythe Division final. Edmonton went on to win the series 4-0 en route to a Cup victory over Boston. Gretzky's goal was a splendid shorthanded effort on a long slapper that beat Flames' goalie Mike Vernon.

no. 2 goal
DEC. 30, 1981
OILERS 7 FLYERS 5

An empty-netter for the books. It was the night Gretzky scored his 50th in 39 games to eclipse Montreal superstar Maurice "Rocket" Richard's 36-year mark of 50 in 50 games. Gretzky scored five goals on Philadelphia that night—four on goaltender Pete Peeters and No. 50 into an empty net. He finished the season with a record 92 goals.

no. 3 goal
FEB. 24, 1982
OILERS 6 SABRES 3

Just a couple of months after erasing Richard from the record book, Gretzky did the same to Boston's Phil Esposito, who held the single-season scoring record of 76 goals. Gretzky scored No. 77 in Buffalo against net-minder Don Edwards with 6:30 left in the game. For good measure, he added Nos. 78 and 79 before the game ended.

no. 4 goal
MARCH 23, 1994
KINGS 3 CANUCKS 6

Gretzky calls it the "most significant goal" of his career. Playing for the Los Angeles Kings at the Great Western Forum, Gretzky beat Vancouver goalie Kirk MacLean to score No. 802, eclipsing Gordie Howe to become the NHL's all-time leading goal scorer. Gretzky scored 802 goals in 1,117 regular season goals; Howe scored 801 in 1,767, 650 more games.

no. 5 goal
OCT. 14, 1979
OILERS 4 CANUCKS 4

It was his first NHL goal, a fanned shot that dribbled by Vancouver's Glen Hanlon. The shot resembled the one he took to score his first-ever pro goal a year earlier, when playing for Indianapolis against the WHA Oilers. Gretzky's 894th and last NHL regular season goal was scored March 29, 1999, against the New York Islanders.

no. 1 game
SEPT. 13, 1987
CANADA 6 SOVIET UNION 5

Game 2 versus the Soviet Union in the 1987 Canada Cup, best-of-three final in Hamilton. Gretzky set up five goals, including the double overtime winner by Mario Lemieux. "Because of the competition and level of skill, that was the best game I ever played." Canada won the series 2-1.

no. 2 game
MAY 29, 1993
KINGS 5 LEAFS 4

Game 7 of the Western Conference final, Los Angeles at Toronto. Gretzky scored his record eighth career playoff hat trick to all but singlehandedly lead the Kings to their first and his last Stanley Cup final appearance. "The best NHL game I ever played." L.A. lost to Montreal in the final.

no. 3 game
MAY 25, 1985
OILERS 4 FLYERS 3

Game 3 in Edmonton versus Philadelphia in the 1985 Stanley Cup final. After being held pointless in a 4-1 loss in Philadelphia in Game 1, Gretzky scored seven goals in the next four games, including a natural hat trick in Game 3. "That was my best game as an Oiler." Gretzky was named playoff MVP.

no. 4 game
MAY 19, 1984
OILERS 5 ISLANDERS 2

Game 5 of the 1984 final—his first Stanley Cup championship. The Oilers beat the defending champion New York Islanders, who had won four in a row, in five games. Upon retiring, Gretzky called winning his first Cup the biggest thrill of his career. "No comparison. The feeling never goes away."

no. 5 game
OCT. 10, 1979
OILERS 2 BLACKHAWKS 4

"My first NHL game, in Chicago, Oct. 10, 1979." The Oilers lost 4-2, with Gretzky recording one assist. Seventy-eight games later, Gretzky finished his first NHL season with 51 goals and 86 assists for 137 points. Marcel Dionne also scored 137 points, but won the scoring title based on goals (53).

By DICK CHUBEY

Then memory of Wayne Gretzky dabbing a tissue to his right eye lingers even today. Such was The Great One's tearful farewell to a town that had adopted him for the best 10 years of an incomparable hockey career.

No other television film clip has received such air time over the past 11 years in Edmonton as that scene on the darkest day in Edmonton's athletic annals.

The trade/selling of Gretzky to the Los Angeles Kings on Aug. 9, 1988, by Edmonton Oilers' owner Peter Pocklington left a city in a state of utter disbelief.

THE
BIG
Trade

Even today there are people who are far from over it, so just imagine the downer that engulfed the precinct at the time.

"That bleep Pocklington," cussed one lady caller to a media outlet. "Unfortunately, the sons-of-bitches got my money before they announced this. I will never set foot again in that building as long as I live."

She wasn't alone in bitterness.

"I'm from a small town," said another voice over the phone, "and it's like a funeral here. How many games has Gretzky pulled out for the Oilers? Who's going to do that for them when he's gone?"

The front page headline in the Edmonton *Sun* blared "99 Tears." Coverage and reaction appeared on pages 2, 3, 4, 5, 6, 10, 11, 18, 19, 23, 30, 36, 37, 38, 39, 40, 41, 42, 43, 46 and 47.

Gretzky's retirement from the New York Rangers and the NHL has led to more re-runs of the sombre press conference that afternoon at Molson House.

A mere 24 days after the wedding bells tolled only a few blocks away at St. Joseph's Basilica, Gretzky and his wife, Janet Jones, completed the elopement to Hollywood.

"The last three weeks have been a whirlwind for my wife and myself," said Gretzky in a brief address to the packed news conference in 1988. "But this was my own gut feeling and my own decision.

"I'm disappointed in having to leave Edmonton," he added prior to breaking down and weeping. "I promised 'Mess' (Mark Messier) I wouldn't do this."

"Wayne has an ego the size of Manhattan. I understand that, though. If people had told me how great I was day in and day out for 10 years, I'm sure my ego would be a pretty generous size, too."

There was no retracting Pocklington's words as he added that Edmonton fans shouldn't have been duped into thinking otherwise.

"It doesn't matter if they buy it or not, because that's the truth," he said. "All you can do is what Mark Twain says: When in doubt, tell the truth. If they don't buy it,

GRETZKY FACES A BANK OF MICROPHONES DURING AN EMOTIONAL FAREWELL AUG. 9, 1988, AS HE BIDS ADIEU TO THE OILERS AND GOES TO HOLLYWOOD.

While a city and even a country wept along with Gretzky, one man sneered.

"He's a great actor. I thought he pulled it off beautifully when he showed how upset he was, but he wants the big dream," Pocklington told a Los Angeles *Times* reporter on the day of the deal. "I call L.A. the land of the big trip and he wants to go where the trips are the biggest.

"All of a sudden, he figures, gee, I'll go and conquer that market. Not only that, but he'll conquer the United States. Wayne believes he can revive hockey in the U.S. or make it a sport to be watched by millions more.

that's their problem. If they think their king walked the streets of Edmonton without ever having a thought of moving, they are under a great delusion."

Later Gretzky's father revealed his son had spoken to him about purchasing a house in Edmonton with his marriage pending. But Walter Gretzky advised against it, confessing as early as the Stanley Cup final series two-plus months earlier he had been informed Pocklington was shopping No. 99.

Faced with leaving his teammates and friends, Gretzky chose Los Angeles as a destination and the NHL has, of course, subsequently flourished in a number of warm weather expansion sites as a direct result.

Yes, Peter, Gretzky did conquer the U.S.

However, moments prior to the press conference, Gretzky was taken aside by Oilers' GM Glen Sather. The Great One was asked by Sather if he was having second thoughts and should the deal be aborted. As far as Gretzky was concerned, he was past the point of return. Done deal. At 27, he was L.A.-bound in the company of Marty McSorley and Mike Krushelnyski. McSorley went at Gretzky's request and ironically returned to the Oilers as a free agent in 1998.

The Oilers, in turn, received 55-goal youngster Jimmy Carson, L.A. first-round draft pick Martin Gelinas, three first round picks (Corey Foster, Martin Rucinsky and Nick Stajduhar), plus $15 million (U.S.) cash.

Carson couldn't handle the pressure of playing in The Great One's shadow and was traded to the Detroit Red Wings in 1989.

The Gretzky-led Oilers lifted hockey to the No. 1 status when Edmonton joined the NHL. It was as though the Oilers were unbeatable with Gretzky & Co. Shock waves were felt throughout the league when the deal was made.

"If there was such a thing as an untouchable in this business, you'd think it was him," said then Washington Capitals' GM David Poile, now with the Nashville Predators.

Jari Kurri, Gretzky's right hand man, was tracked down in Finland when the deal came down.

"I couldn't think about it, it's a big shock," Kurri said. "I'm sad to see him go. You see a lot of trades in hockey and hear a lot of rumors, but this is something that I never expected to see happen."

Kurri later was to follow Gretzky to L.A., but only after he helped the Oilers win a fifth Stanley Cup in 1990.

"Thank God I believe in life after death," said Oilers' then co-coach John Muckler from his off-season home on Rhode Island. "Are the police on call out there?" Muckler,

perspective

KINGS' RETURN ON DEAL HALF AS MUCH AS GRETZKY

Los Angeles got quantity, not quality, when they traded free agent-to-be Wayne Gretzky to St. Louis Feb. 27, 1996. The Kings received forwards Craig Johnson, Patrice Tardif, Roman Vopat and two draft picks. In three-and-a-half years after the deal, Gretzky scored 77 goals (including playoffs). The three traded players combined for 39. Gretzky lasted just 2-1/2 months in St. Louis before signing with the New York Rangers.

GRETZKY SPENT 2½ MONTHS IN ST. LOUIS AFTER THE "OTHER" TRADE.

of course, was behind the Rangers' bench when Gretzky called it quits.

While Gretzky's career drew accolades from near and far, there was one dissenter in the crowd. When informed of Gretzky's retirement, Pocklington blurted: "Let's get this into perspective–it's a hockey player who's retiring, we're not curing cancer here."

Some things just never change. Like the city of Edmonton's affection for Gretzky. The Great One made a surprise appearance before Game 4 of the first round playoff series between the Oilers and Dallas Stars April 28, 1999. He was greeted by a two-minute standing ovation and the promise of more to come at a ceremony the next season. 🏒

FROM FRIEND TO FOE: GLENN ANDERSON OF THE EDMONTON OILERS GETS PHYSICAL WITH HIS FORMER TEAMMATE AFTER GRETZKY'S TRADE TO LOS ANGELES.

By STEVE DRYDEN *April 8, 1994*

Stretched out in matching black shirt and long underwear, the most striking thing about Wayne Gretzky is his size. He's not that small. After nearly two decades of watching him skate all scrunched up, it's easy to forget Gretzky is six feet tall.

When he sat down, rested his legs on a counter and contemplated hockey's most distinguished career, he was like a cat stretching to its full length.

Never has Gretzky stood so tall as March 23 when he established the league's most important individual record with the 802nd goal of his NHL career.

"You have always been The Great One," said league commissioner Gary Bettman, "but tonight you became the greatest."

There was never any doubt.

Gretzky, 33, has always been larger than life. But it took

Mich., staying up past midnight to watch the game on television and witness the fall of his gold mark.

"Shake his hand for me," Howe said during the third period. "It's a long reach from here."

Kings' left winger Luc Robitaille and defenseman Marty McSorley earned assists on the historic goal. Robitaille carried the puck into the Kings' zone and dropped it to Gretzky. No. 99 passed right to a late-arriving McSorley, who responded in kind with a return feed through the slot.

McLean was a prisoner of momentum, stranded on the left side of his crease.

"When I got (the puck) back, I saw the whole net," Gretzky said. "I couldn't believe I saw it."

One person stood in the way of hockey immortality. Canucks' defenseman Gerald Diduck was the last line of defense, the only person with a chance to stop Gretzky's one-timer.

The SHOT Heard Around The World

a second period power play goal against Vancouver Canucks' goalie Kirk McLean to further inflate Gretzky's status and fill him with his greatest sense of accomplishment.

"I don't think I've ever had a moment when I felt like that," Gretzky said.

Nor has the NHL. The game was stopped and a 10-minute ceremony marked Gretzky's passing of Gordie Howe on the all-time goal list.

A sellout crowd of 16,005–including Oscar winner Tom Hanks–saluted Gretzky with a thunderous ovation.

Hollywood wasn't out in full force, but in the aftermath Mary Hart leaned against a corridor wall and Goldie Hawn sashayed past the Los Angeles Kings' dressing room singing, "Oh, what a night."

One GH standing in for another?

Gordie Howe, as promised, didn't join a league caravan and follow Gretzky around California as The Great One played seven straight games in the Golden State.

The 66-year-old hockey legend was in Traverse City,

"I almost got a whack at it, but he put it in," Diduck said. "Now I'll be in the Hall of Fame forever."

The NHL gave Gretzky a bound volume containing official scoresheets of every game in which he scored a goal.

Gretzky came full circle with the goal. He first scored against the Canucks, Oct. 14, 1979, on Glen Hanlon. Hanlon is now the Canucks' goalie coach, but did not accompany the team to Los Angeles.

No. 99 said this record is tops among the 61 league marks he holds.

"By far," Gretzky said. "There is no comparison. The ones that are the best are the hardest ones to break. Somebody is going to have to play 16 years at 50 goals a year."

"That may happen. I think records are made to be broken. People like (Teemu) Selanne, (Sergei) Fedorov and (Eric) Lindros, if he stays healthy; those three guys have a strong chance."

He is being kind. All three, even Lindros, are well off Gretzky's early-career pace.

The record has been compared to everything from Hank Aaron's 715th home run to Kareem Abdul-Jabbar's basketball points record to Walter Payton's football rushing mark.

It belongs in a class of its own.

The sheer speed with which Gretzky erased the trio of Howe's major career offensive records (goals, assists and points) is the final piece of evidence to prove that No. 99 is the most statistically dominant athlete in the history of North American professional sport.

Gretzky scored 802 goals in 650 fewer regular season games than it took Howe to score 801 (1,117 to 1,767).

Still, Gretzky isn't sure how the record ranks with those in Major League Baseball, the National Football League and the National Basketball Association.

"It probably depends on where you live," Gretzky said. "Up in Canada, it might be up there with those records, but down here it's probably lower on the totem pole."

The miracle is not Howe many goals Gretzky has scored, but Howe he has scored them.

His first instinct has always been to pass. He doesn't strike fear into the hearts of goalies with the strength of his shot and the only thing overpowering about the lean scoring machine is his determination.

Gretzky doesn't rank himself among the game's purest goal-scorers. New York Islanders' great Mike Bossy was better in his estimation.

So is longtime teammate Jari Kurri.

"I'm better on breakaways, for sure," Kurri said, poking fun at No. 99's showdown shortcomings.

How, then, has Gretzky scored all those goals?

"He finds a spot," Kurri said. "He's a head-up shooter.

ARTURS IRBE IS BEATEN FOR THE GOAL THAT TIES GRETZKY WITH GORDIE HOWE.

HOWE, GRETZKY LINKED TOGETHER FROM THE START
The end was always clearly in sight for Wayne Gretzky. Forces of fate saw to that in the fall of 1979. One day before he scored on Oct. 14, 1979, against Glen Hanlon of the Vancouver Canucks to record his first NHL goal, Gordie Howe announced he would retire at the end of the 1979-80 season. Gretzky spotted Howe a 786-goal lead and then scored against Hanlon to begin a 15-year journey. He tied Howe's all-time NHL goal mark with No. 801 against San Jose Sharks' goalie Arturs Irbe March 20, 1994.

There are a lot of guys who just put their heads down and shoot."

Gretzky seldom buries goals. He deposits them past befuddled goalies, who are more likely to face backhanders and short slapshots than wrist shots.

"My stick's not designed to snap the puck like that," Gretzky said. "My stick is designed for more passes, slapshots and backhands."

Gretzky is a more dangerous playmaker than finisher, but he holds the most improbable scoring record of all: fastest 50 goals, 39 games in 1981-82.

Goal No. 802 completed Gretzky's triple jump past Howe. He had already passed Howe in career assists and points.

Gretzky is aiming for his 10th scoring championship, but said it wouldn't be "cool" to win another Art Ross Trophy if the Kings don't make the playoffs.

What's next for Gretzky?

A Stanley Cup in Los Angeles is the first priority.

But Gretzky has two more years to run on a contract valued at $25.5 million (U.S.) over three seasons and has not ruled out playing beyond the 1995-96 season.

Within his grasp are two unimaginable milestones: 900 goals and 1,851 assists (one more than Howe has NHL points).

Gretzky considered retirement last summer after returning from a serious back injury to lead Los Angeles to the Stanley Cup final, but he is back with renewed vigor.

"When I first got hurt last year and they told me I wasn't going to play," Gretzky said, "a couple of my friends immediately thought, 'You gotta come back for goal No. 801.' "

"I never really thought about it when I was told I probably wouldn't play again. I just said, 'Well, I'll finish second, but there's nothing I can do about it.' "

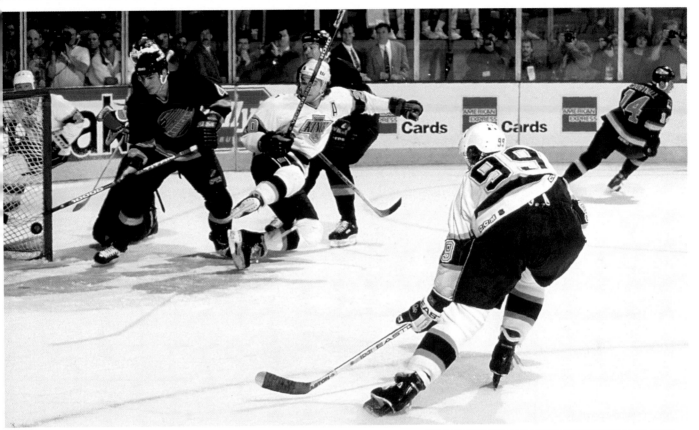

OBSCURED IN THE PICTURE IS OUT-OF-POSITION VANCOUVER GOALTENDER KIRK MCLEAN, WHO SURRENDERED HISTORIC GOAL 802 TO GRETZKY MARCH 23, 1994.

"When I started coming back and played so poorly at the beginning I didn't know what was going to happen. I think when I had the playoff run and we played well in the playoffs, I knew I was going to give it a good shot at 800."

The history-making goal against the Canucks was his 1,044th regular season and playoff goal since joining the Sault Ste. Marie Greyhounds of the Ontario League and, at least, the 2,204th since his rookie season as a six-year-old in 1967-68.

He scored 70 with the Greyhounds to run away with OHL rookie-of-the-year honors. The only major NHL award to elude him is the Calder Trophy, which goes to the NHL's top first-year player.

Gretzky shared the league scoring lead with Marcel Dionne that season, but wasn't eligible for the Calder because he was a WHA refugee.

Ray Bourque was voted top rookie.

Howe, who wanted fans to remember Gretzky was challenging his NHL record and not his combined NHL-WHA pro record (1,071 regular season and playoff goals), thinks the renegade league was equal because they paid comparable salaries to the NHL.

Few others do. A more plausible footnote to Gretzky's latest record was he scored his goals during an inflationary period in NHL scoring.

Gretzky said there should be an asterisk beside his record number of goals because his were scored in a different and higher-scoring era than Howe's. He said Howe would have scored many more goals had he played now.

As for Gretzky, 99 more goals would propel him past 900, his newest target.

"Tell him I think he's cutting his goals a little short," Howe said from Traverse City. "He could get 1,000. He's a young man yet. The older he gets, the tougher it will be to leave the game."

Gretzky was grateful for the words from his boyhood hero. "I've got a long way to go to 1,000," he said. "But I'll take it one step at a time. I'll shoot for 900 now."

Does he look forward to many more years in the NHL?

"The more you play," Gretzky said, "the more you realize you're closer to the end. When you're young, you think there are so many more things in your life you want to do, other things you want to accomplish. But when you get older, the biggest thing of all is you just want to play hockey. My life is hockey."

Postscript: Gretzky finished his career with 1,072 professional regular season and playoff goals, one more than Gordie Howe. Gretzky scored 894 NHL regular season and 122 playoff goals for a total of 1,016, plus 46 WHA regular season and 10 playoff goals for a total of 56. **99**

Ninety-Nine NUMBERS Of Distinction

0. Number of years Wayne Gretzky had to wait to be eligible for Hockey Hall of Fame. Customary three-year period waived April 29, 1999.

1. Named No. 1 NHL player of all-time by The Hockey News.

2. Won two Conn Smythe Trophies as playoff MVP.

3. Number of fighting opponents: Chicago's Doug Lecuyer March 14, 1980; Minnesota's Neal Broten Dec. 22, 1982; Chicago's Bob Murray March 7, 1984.

4. Number of times Gretzky lifted Stanley Cup above his head.

5. Number of times Gretzky led NHL in goals.

6. His height: 6 feet.

7. Most assists earned in one game.

8. Won eight consecutive Hart Trophies in first eight NHL seasons, winning ninth two years later.

9. Number he wore growing up.

10. Number of Art Ross Trophies as NHL's top scorer, including four 200-point seasons.

11. Number of professional coaches: Pat Stapleton, Glen Sather, Bryan Watson, John Muckler, Robbie Ftorek, Tom Webster, Barry Melrose, Rogie Vachon, Larry Robinson, Mike Keenan, Colin Campbell.

12. Playoff pucks put past goalie Mike Vernon, his most frequent post-season victim.

13. Number of consecutive seasons leading NHL in assists, beginning with rookie season.

14. Last number worn in Sault Ste. Marie before switching to No. 99.

15. Number of times leading NHL in assists.

16. Date on which Gretzky and Janet Jones wed, July 16, 1988.

NO. 16: GRETZKY-JONES, JULY 1988, WEDDING DAY.

17. Age he signed with Indianapolis of WHA.

18. Number of vehicles won in NHL.

19. Number of times leading team in scoring.

20. Number of NHL seasons.

21. Number of pro seasons.

22. Date of first pro goal: Oct. 22, 1978.

23. Ran up record 23-game assist streak in 1990-91.

24. Number of playoff game-winning goals in career. Only one came in overtime.

25. Record number of NHL all-star points. A goal and an assist earned Gretzky third MVP award in 1999 game. Holds records for goals (13) and assists (12).

26. Date of birth: Jan. 26, 1961, in Brantford, Ont.

27. Scored goal against all 27 NHL teams.

28. Mike Bossy scored 64 goals in 1981-82, but Gretzky had 28 more to capture first goal-scoring title.

29. Pucks put past goalie Richard Brodeur during the regular season, his favorite target.

30. Number of original scoresheets NHL presented Gretzky denoting league records.

31. Games played as a St. Louis Blue.

32. One record Gretzky didn't come close to–Gordie Howe's number of pro seasons.

33. Age when he won his 10th and last Art Ross Trophy as league's top scorer in 1993-94.

34. Had four points Dec. 18, 1983, against Winnipeg in 34th game of season, to reach 100 points.

35. Age when Gretzky became free agent for first time in career. He signed with Rangers July 21, 1996.

36. Number of goals scored with Seneca Young Nationals in 1976-77.

37. Number of points scored with Blues, including playoffs.

38. Number of goals scored in Winnipeg Arena, more than any other arena.

39. Number of games Gretzky needed to score 50 goals in 1981-82. He scored five goals in 39th game, including an empty netter for No. 50.

40. Points Gretzky scored in 1993 playoffs, leading Kings to their first and his last appearance in Stanley Cup final.

41. Number of questions Gretzky was asked at post-game media conference April 18, 1999, after final game.

42. Scored regular season goal in 42 different NHL arenas.

43. Number of hat tricks Gretzky scored as Oiler.

44. Number of assists earned in 31 games in five Canada Cup and World Cup tournaments.

45. Fewest games played in NHL season, missing 39 games in 1992-93 with herniated disc in back.

46. Number of goals in first pro season.

47. Points Gretzky scored in 1985 playoffs to break own record of 38.

48. Number of buildings in which Gretzky recorded at least one point as a professional. He was shut out in only one arena, the Springfield Civic Center.

49. Gretzky sparked growth south of 49th parallel. In 1988, there were 50 pro teams in four leagues. In 1999, there are 135 teams in seven leagues.

50. Number of career regular season hat tricks. His last came Oct. 11, 1997 against Vancouver.

51. Record number of consecutive games in which Gretzky had at least one point between Oct. 5, 1983, and Jan. 28, 1984.

52. Number of goals scored in 1985-86 when Gretzky collected record 163 assists and 215 points.

Ninety-Nine NUMBERS Of Distinction

53. Number of assists recorded in final NHL season. Last assist of career earned on Brian Leetch's goal April 18, 1999, giving him 1,963 assists.

54. Scored 54 goals in first season with Los Angeles (1988-89), the ninth and last time he reached 50-goal plateau.

55. Scored 55 goals against Toronto Maple Leafs in 63 games, his best success rate against any team.

56. Oilers won franchise-best 56 games in 1985-86.

57. Year Walter Gretzky met Phyllis Hockin. They married in 1960.

58. Number of points by which Gretzky outscored all 10 players he was traded for by Edmonton and Los Angeles.

59. Single-season high of 59 penalty minutes (1982-83).

60. Per cent of Kurri's career goals Gretzky assisted on (364 of 601 goals).

61. Number of NHL records Gretzky holds.

62. Goal total last time he surpassed 60 goals (1986-87).

63. Number of international games, resulting in 34 goals and 103 points.

64. Number of assists recorded in first pro season.

65. Age Gretzky is eligible to collect government pension.

66. Gretzky's only serious rival during career was Mario Lemieux, No. 66 for Pittsburgh.

67. Number of assists in 1997-98, tying him with Pittsburgh's Jaromir Jagr for league lead, the 16th and last time Gretzky led in assists.

68. No. 68, Jagr, was handed torch by Gretzky after The Great One played last game of career.

69. Number of assists in nine international competitions.

70. Number of times on cover of The Hockey News.

71. Year he scored 196 goals (as novice player), second-highest total of career.

72. Average number of goals Gretzky had over entire 32-year hockey career, peaking with 378 in 1971-72.

73. Number of goals scored to lead league in 1984-85, the last time he scored 70 goals.

74. Number of points by which Gretzky led runner-up Lemieux in scoring the year (1985-86) he set single season record of 215.

75. Number of inches of television presented to him by Ranger teammates as farewell gift.

76. Phil Esposito's 76-goal record was broken Feb. 24, 1982 when Gretzky scored a hat trick for No. 77.

77. The only major trophy not won by Gretzky was rookie of the year–won by No. 77 Ray Bourque in 1980-81.

NO. 53: GRETZKY'S HISTORIC LAST ASSIST.

78. His 1,963 career assists were 78 percent more than second-place Paul Coffey (1,102), the greatest differential in a major category of any pro sport.

79. Had 79 goals against Phoenix Coyotes-Winnipeg Jets–his highest total against any franchise.

80. Year he became youngest player (18) to score 50 goals.

81. Year he broke Esposito's points record (152, Gretzky 164) and Bobby Orr's assist record (102, Gretzky 109).

82. Most games he played in a season–1996-97 and 1997-98–his first two years with the Rangers.

83. Year of first appearance in Stanley Cup.

84. Year Oilers won first of four Stanley Cups over five years.

85. Year of Gretzky's first Conn Smythe Trophy and second Stanley Cup.

86. Number of assists recorded in first NHL season, the only time during the 1980s he didn't hit the century mark.

87. Year of greatest game ever–a five-assist performance against Soviet Union in Game 2 of 1987 Canada Cup.

88. Year of biggest trade in sports history. Gretzky is traded to Los Angeles Aug. 9, 1988, along with Mike Krushelnyski and Marty McSorley for Jimmy Carson, Martin Gelinas and the Kings' first round draft picks in 1989, 1991 and 1993, plus $15 million (U.S.).

89. Year Gretzky passed Howe (1,850) to become NHL's all-time leading scorer. He broke it in dramatic fashion Oct. 15, 1989, in Edmonton, scoring the tying goal for Los Angeles with 53 seconds left and the winner in overtime.

90. Number of goals scored in last year of minor hockey.

91. Kings' point total in Gretzky's first year in Los Angeles, a leap of 23 from previous year.

92. Number of goals in 1981-82, breaking Esposito's record by 26.

93. Scored 93rd playoff goal in 1991 to pass Jari Kurri as most prolific goal-scorer in post-season history. Gretzky finished with record 122 goals, 260 assists and 382 points.

94. Year Gretzky passed Howe with his 802nd regular season goal to become the NHL's all-time leading goal-scorer. Gretzky finished with 894.

95. Year of Gretzky's lowest point total (48) in 1994-95 lockout season.

96. Year he was traded to St. Louis–Feb. 27, 1996.

97. Number of regular season games missed over 20 NHL seasons.

98. Average attendance as percentage of capacity in buildings Kings visited in first season after trade to Los Angeles. Kings were a league-low 77 per cent in 1987-88.

99. Number no one will wear again in NHL.

THE BOYS ON THE BUS

GRETZKY AND FRIENDS KURRI, MESSIER, LOWE AND COFFEY WENT FOR THE RIDE OF THEIR LIVES

RIGHT
Hand Man

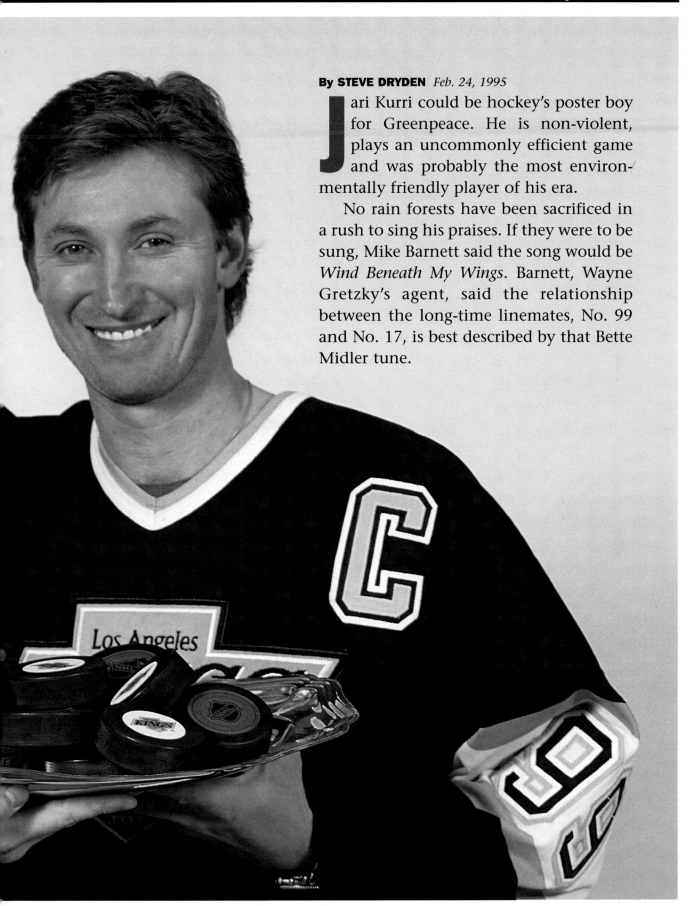

By **STEVE DRYDEN** *Feb. 24, 1995*

Jari Kurri could be hockey's poster boy for Greenpeace. He is non-violent, plays an uncommonly efficient game and was probably the most environ-/mentally friendly player of his era.

No rain forests have been sacrificed in a rush to sing his praises. If they were to be sung, Mike Barnett said the song would be *Wind Beneath My Wings*. Barnett, Wayne Gretzky's agent, said the relationship between the long-time linemates, No. 99 and No. 17, is best described by that Bette Midler tune.

"To get an opportunity to play with Jari has meant so much to my career both offensively and defensively," Gretzky said. "Jari is very unselfish. He would sacrifice himself for his teammates or the hockey team at any time."

The two worked well together from the moment they became full-time linemates early in Kurri's first season (1980-81) and have become on-ice soulmates.

Kurri. The all-time scoring leader's greatest gift–an ability to stop time with passes that float beyond defenders–was devastatingly effective throughout the 1980s because Kurri was in the same time warp through most of the decade.

The most memorable goal, though, isn't one of their many bang-bang goals. Rather, it illustrates the higher plane Gretzky and Kurri occupied for so long. Ask any long-

EDMONTON WAS REPRESENTED AT THE 1986 ALL-STAR GAME BY, FROM LEFT, ANDY MOOG, GRETZKY, GLENN ANDERSON, PAUL COFFEY, KEVIN LOWE, GLEN SATHER, MARK MESSIER, LEE FOGOLIN, JARI KURRI AND GRANT FUHR.

Previous page: Dan Hamilton/VPS

"Without Wayne, I don't know where I would be," Kurri said.

"We had the same feeling and the same kind of puck sense," Gretzky said. "From Day 1 it clicked. We think the same game. It's not easy to play with me. You've seen over the years it has been hard to find a guy who fits in with us."

During a trip to Toronto, Gretzky bought lunch for Kurri at The Great One's restaurant. Incontrovertible proof that Gretzky has been Kurri's meal ticket all along? Not a chance. The next day, Kurri bought a sandwich the two shared.

"We take care of each other," Gretzky said.

Gretzky and Kurri have combined for hundreds of goals, a large percentage of them Kurri's trademark one-timers.

No. 99 didn't need Kurri to change the game, but he would not have done so with such thoroughness if not for

time Gretzky-Kurri watcher for his favorite goal and the choice is obvious–a shorthanded goal against Chicago in Game 6 of the 1985 Campbell Conference Final.

"Wayne was dragging the puck through center ice and he ran out of room," recalled Dallas Stars' goalie Andy Moog, who was then with the Oilers. "He came over to our bench, just about stopped at the bench and he threw a backhand all the way across the ice. Jari was just streaking down the other side and he went in and beat (Murray Bannerman). I think Gretz was just sitting down and having a drink before Jari scored."

Postscript: Gretzky and Kurri combined for 560 goals over 12 NHL seasons together. Gretzky assisted on 364 Kurri goals; Kurri assisted on 196 Gretzky goals. Kurri retired after 1997-98 sitting ninth in all-time NHL goals (601) and 14th in all-time points (1,398) in 17 seasons. **99**

Bruce Bennett/BBS

By **DAN BARNES**

Separated as they have been by thousands of miles, the 49th parallel, a couple of years and their vastly different lifestyles, Wayne Gretzky and Mark Messier were bound to grow apart.

It happens, even to the closest of friends. And with a wistful sigh, Messier admitted that it happened to them. But at their very core there will always be the bond they built in Edmonton as the heart and soul of the raucous, upstart, unbelievable Oilers and rekindled together in New York as aging members of the Rangers.

"It was the ride. We were along for the same ride and a lot of amazing things happened," Messier said. "To be a

BROTHERS In Arms

part of it, to be the same age and play all those years was something I'll never forget. Wayne and I grew up together as 18-year-olds in Edmonton and going through all the things we did, it just cemented a bond. We're the next thing to brothers. It will be there forever."

Messier was on hand at Madison Square Garden April 18, 1999, to watch his buddy call it a glorious career. They hugged. They talked. They almost cried.

While Gretzky ended his record-shattering run in smashing style in New York and the friends spent time together on Broadway as high-profile Rangers, Messier's best memories are almost exclusively those they created together in Edmonton. They owned the town in the early 1980s and they would soon take possession of the NHL. As Edmonton teammates they won four Stanley Cups. There is no question the winning and the fame that it brought were part of their relationship, but that success didn't really begin until 1984 with their first Cup victory. Before that they were teammates and friends on a squad building momentum in the hinterland.

"I think what Mess taught me in life, more than anyone, I'm a person who believes in tomorrow, above all else," Gretzky said. "To me, tomorrow is everything. One of the few things I ever owned in Edmonton was my apartment. The cars were usually sponsorships. I put everything in the bank. Mess was the guy who taught me I might not be here tomorrow so you gotta enjoy it."

Messier has always lived in and for the moment. He was carefree and occasionally careless as a young adult in Edmonton.

Gretzky always had to be the responsible one, at least publicly. He could ill-afford a brush with the law or to be cast in a poor light by the media or fans. When the door of the Oilers' room closed, he was able to put on a different face. His own. Messier thinks that's why The Great One formed such lasting friendships with his fellow Oilers.

"There was so much pressure on him and he had some friends he was able to talk to when we were younger," Messier said. "He could be himself. He could be Wayne Gretzky inside that dressing room. Because of that and the championships, and the things we were able to do not only on the ice, but off the ice as well, the friendships were really cemented.

"Whether it's Kevin Lowe, who is one of my best friends, or Paul Coffey or whoever, all the guys, we've established a friendship, a bond, that's next to brotherhood and will be there forever."

Gretzky passed on the captaincy of the Oilers to Messier after the trade that rocked both their worlds on Aug. 9, 1988. More than that, he passed on a way of carrying himself and the game to new heights.

"He showed us a lot of class on and off the ice and showed us what it took to succeed not only as a team, but as an individual. How hungry he was to succeed rubbed off on us," Messier said.

The hunger is gone now for No. 99 and Gretzky's retirement has given his buddy pause. They are both 38 years old, born just eight days apart in 1961, Messier in Edmonton and Gretzky in Brantford. Messier thinks he wants to still keep playing. He thinks Vancouver can still be a good team. But the league won't be the same without his friend and that has made the Moose look inward.

"I would be lying to you if I said it didn't make me reflect on the past 20 years we spent together, my own career and where I stand now," Messier.

He stands as the man Wayne Gretzky called the best player he ever played with. High praise, indeed. But the fact Gretzky calls him a friend means far more to Messier. **99**

By JIM MATHESON

In his early Edmonton Oiler days, Kevin Lowe was called "Vicious" or "Vish," a play on his looking like punk rocker Sid Vicious. Maybe it also had something to do with the fact he sometimes snapped. He did break the odd string of ceiling lights on the way to the dressing room.

What Lowe never did was break under the stress of being Wayne Gretzky's roomie his first few years. Lowe, the Oilers' first draft pick in 1979, was 20 when Gretzky was 18.

Lowe did most of the cooking, helped open Gretzky's voluminous fan mail and even got their phone number changed several times, then had it unlisted. Lowe, who eventually moved into a condo that Gretzky bought, was always good-natured about it.

Neither roomie was quite ready for their NHL first season, though.

RECIPE
For Friendship

"The night before we went to Chicago for our first road trip, we still hadn't put our beds together," Lowe recalled. "We had just bought new ones and they sat there for awhile. Then the night before leaving, we were scrambling around, trying to get them together. They were waterbeds, of course, and we ended up waiting up half the night until the mattresses were filled."

Gretzky made no bones about knowing his way around the back of the net much better than a stove. Lowe, who co-owns one of the most popular sports bar/restaurants in Edmonton now, was the chef. "Steaks, fondue, roasts. He could make cheesecake," said Gretzky, wide-eyed.

"My wife (former Olympic skier Karen Percy) laughs when she hears stories about my cooking," Lowe said. "She thinks it has been blown out of proportion because she has never seen it. But with Wayne...how hard is it to throw a roast in the oven, cut up some potatoes and make a salad? Gretz couldn't do it, though. We used to share the duties of getting our pre-game meal ready. It usually consisted of T-bones, french fries, macaroni and cheese, perogies and maybe some broccoli. Guess which part he did?"

Would that be the perogies, Gretzky's favorite food?

It's not that Gretzky never tried. Oilers' equipment man Sparky Kulchisky recalls a time when he was at Paul Coffey's cottage in Ontario with Gretzky and Janet Jones, not long after the couple had met in 1988.

"(Gretzky) decided he was going to cook the entire meal. He wanted to impress Janet," Kulchisky said. "We had this day of (water) skiing, then Wayne got to work. Made the salad and said he wanted to fondue. He wouldn't take any help. I've got to tell you...it wasn't the best meal I ever had."

OK, so Gretzky's hands were those of a fourth-liner in the kitchen. Lowe could only do so much with what he had.

The only time Lowe ever showed Gretzky anything, with the puck, not a saucepan, was the first NHL game

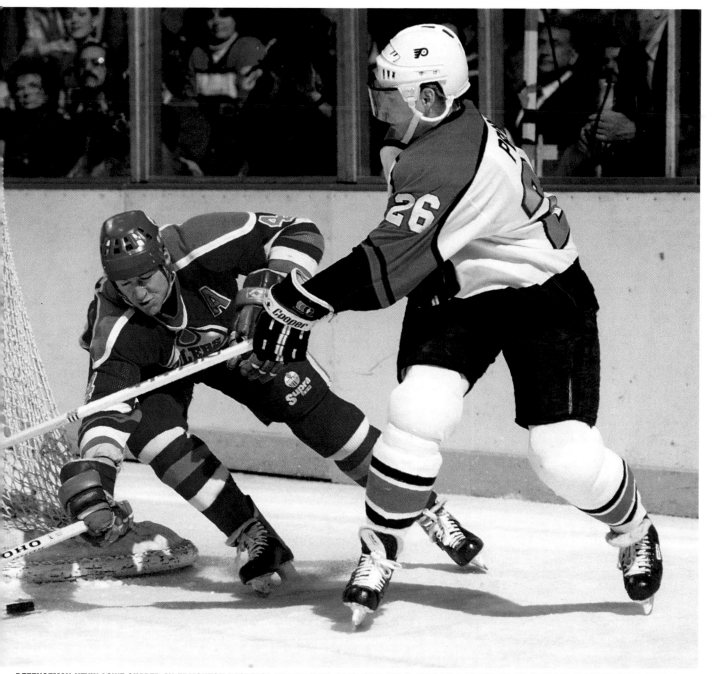

DEFENSEMAN KEVIN LOWE SHARED AN EDMONTON BACHELOR PAD WITH NO. 99 IN 1979 AND PROVED TO BE A MENTOR TO GRETZKY—IN THE KITCHEN, THAT IS.

Edmonton played–Oct. 10, 1979, at Chicago Stadium. Lowe scored on Tony Esposito on a feed from Gretzky. "He kept telling me the shot actually hit his stick," Lowe said, "but he wasn't even in the vicinity."

Lowe, to this day, has only one bad memory of Gretzky. That was playing against him for the first time after the 1988 trade to the Los Angeles Kings.

"I didn't say a thing to Wayne before the game while we were skating around. I didn't even look at him in the warmup. I didn't want to get caught up in the emotion of the moment," Lowe said. "I remember seeing Wayne after-

wards, seeing a picture of all the Oilers looking at Wayne...but not me. I didn't see him until the first shift."

Lowe threw a hit at Gretzky that night. Lowe couldn't play any other way. It was work as usual.

Still, the picture Wayne got from a local artist on the day they put the statue up in front of the Edmonton rink remained one of Gretzky's bittersweet moments. It showed a young boy playing hockey on the pond with a couple of buddies. He was going home after the game while the two friends were waving good-bye. "The boys were supposed to be Kevin and Mark (Messier)," said Gretzky, eyes misting. **99**

GRETZKY TRIES LIFE ON THE OTHER SIDE OF THE MICROPHONE, INTERVIEWING PALS PAUL COFFEY AND MARK MESSIER DURING THE OILERS' WILD HEYDAY.

By DAN BARNES

The Other KID

The voice of the Edmonton Oilers also had an eye and an ear on the team back in the glory days. And radio play-by-play man Rod Phillips remembers a sheepish Paul Coffey slinking up to him before practice one day in Edmonton, a confession on the tip of his tongue.

"He said, 'Rod, I've got to tell you something, but you can't tell any of the guys.' I said, 'Sure Coff, what is it?' He said, 'I was doing (donuts) in the parking lot and I hit your truck. But you can't tell the guys.' "

It was winter. There was a coat of new snow on the ground and an unparalleled joy of youth in Coffey's

actions. He was playing a man's game and doing it better than most, but he was a kid at heart.

"He was an 18-year-old (kid). Wayne, when he came to the team, was a mature 18-year-old, but Coff was a kid," Phillips said. "I don't think Wayne was ever an adolescent. He was mature the day we met."

But as different as Coffey and Gretzky were, there were similarities that drew them together and made The Great One an early supporter of the much-maligned, heavily talented defenseman.

"I think that because they come from similar parts of the country and Gretz was as misread in the early stages of his career as anyone in terms of his ability, he could see that in Coff," said Oilers' defenseman Kevin Lowe.

"He was one of the first guys to really be on Coff's side and to help him through the early years. People second-guessed him not for his ability, but where his ability was taking him."

That will be the book on Coffey, that he might have been the best defenseman the NHL has ever seen, but he never realized his potential after leaving Edmonton for stops with the Pittsburgh Penguins, Los Angeles Kings, Detroit Red Wings, Hartford Whalers, Philadelphia Flyers and Carolina Hurricanes. He was the first of the Oilers' big names to leave for big bucks in 1987.

"Coff was a hard guy to understand, very hard," Gretzky said. "And yet his heart is as good as gold. He's a great person. I guess the best way to describe how close we were, the six of us, really the whole team, is that when Paul had his contract problems, everyone was saying, 'Isn't that disrupting the team? He's hurting you guys.' But not once was anyone bitter toward him. We all wanted the best for Coff. No one phoned him and said, 'You idiot, get back here.' "

Oh sure, owner Peter Pocklington and GM Glen Sather were saying that back then, but teammates stood by him. That's what they did for one another. Coffey was the first to challenge team authority on many issues. He went public with his complaints. He went about things his own way, but everybody learned to respect the fact he would back up his words and truly believed in everything he did.

"He had a strong personality," said trainer Sparky Kulchisky, one of Coffey's best friends even today. "He stood up for what he believed in, whether it was right or wrong. That's what made him such a great player on the ice. He believed he could go through the whole team and he did it."

THE SIGHT OF SWIFT-SKATING PAUL COFFEY LEADING AN OILERS' RUSH STRUCK FEAR INTO FOES.

And you couldn't help but respect that kind of confidence, attitude, whatever you wanted to call it.

"Coff was friendly with everybody, but he liked his own time and own space," Lowe said. "He liked his music. He liked to kick back, sit in his own apartment and listen to music. Everyone learned to appreciate that about him."

And today, there are no traces of bitterness.

"The good memories are way, way stronger," Coffey said. "The relationships are way, way stronger than any disagreements we had. Glen and I laugh about our spats now, but we had some beauties. But with Slats you'd butt heads and then it would be over. He'd be the first guy to say hello the next morning. You don't get that in hockey anymore. He never did one thing that wasn't aimed at making you a better player. It just took me a long time to realize that."

Some would argue it took Coffey a while to grow up. Gretzky watched it from afar and figured out Coffey's strengths.

"People always wanted to come into the locker room. It's a big thrill for the kids. So I would take the kids into the room and the first person I would take them to was Paul," Gretzky said. "He would take them and make them feel as if they were his best friend. He had such a way with kids. He liked them so much.

"And yet, if I brought a businessman or older people, he wasn't comfortable with that. He's very shy. Kevin could handle those people, no problem. But kids, I'd take them straight to Paul."

Lowe remembers the sight of kids gathered around Coffey's dressing room stall.

"He could relate to kids. He could speak on their level. I don't know if that's good or bad. Does that sound bad?"

Not at all. **99**

THE UNBEATABLE FOE

MIKE LIUT, DENIS POTVIN AND IGOR LARIONOV WRITE INSIDE STORIES ON FACING 99

By MIKE LIUT with MARK BRENDER

There weren't many times when I knew what Wayne Gretzky was going to do. Funny thing is, there were even fewer when it mattered. For instance, Gretzky and Jari Kurri always attacked on a 2-on-1 from their off-wings. I can still see them so clearly, Wayne cradling the puck to my left, Kurri bearing down hard to my right.

Wayne carried it in a shooting position coming down the right wing, so I had to respect his shot. He had an extraordinary shot, not overpowering, but hard enough and deadly accurate. And he was so, so smart with it. I knew he had his eye on the top corner short

FACING 99: MIKE LIUT

Goalie Mike Liut played against Wayne Gretzky for 14 years in the WHA and NHL. They shared THN Player of the Year honors in 1980-81 after Liut had an all-star season with the St. Louis Blues. Gretzky finished ahead of Liut in league MVP voting that season. Liut, now 43, has a law degree and acts as a player agent.

on our team (St. Louis), but Wayne's passes were just that much better. He had the highest panic threshold of any player I ever faced. Peering back through the mesh, there was nothing I could do differently to defend against him. I only knew the Oilers would never lose a scoring chance because he couldn't make it happen.

I got used to that sensation quickly. Wayne had so many ways of making a goalie feel helpless, many more than I could ever figure out. People may compare Gretzky to Michael Jordan, but from how I saw Wayne on the ice, the comparison doesn't fit.

Bobby Orr, he was like Jordan: with both of them, you

Gretzky
MYSTERY
How Would He Beat You?

side, but because he shot left and had the puck in the middle of the ice, he was pushing me off the post with the threat of stick (far) side low. I had to be ready for either. I also knew the more likely outcome was that he wouldn't shoot at all.

Those passes over to Kurri were perfect, feathery soft and on the tape.

Kurri fired it a foot off the ice, above my pad, under the glove, but it was the perfect pass that scored the goal. Other guys would motion a pass with their arms or body. Wayne passed with his hands. Our only real chance was to make him dish off before the top of the circle, even if it meant the defenseman had to over-commit and give Kurri a partial breakaway. That way, at least, Kurri still had to gather the puck in and make a play.

The reality, though, was that if the two of them executed properly, the two of us–my defenseman and I–were virtually powerless to stop them.

It was the same thing when Wayne set up behind the net. Other guys worked behind the net, like Bernie Federko

knew they'd beat you, you knew exactly how they'd do it (by going right by you) and you knew you couldn't do a thing to stop it.

Wayne was like Larry Bird. You knew he'd beat you and you knew you wouldn't be able to stop it, only you didn't know what "it" was. Left side of the ice or right? Shot? A pass for a tap-in? Trailer No. 1 or No. 2? Cross-ice or behind the back?

Only Wayne knew on which front the troops were amassing.

Sometimes I'd look up to prepare for the rush and everything seemed normal to me. That's when I knew I was in trouble. If anyone else had the puck on a 3-on-2, with one of our backcheckers catching up, there wasn't a lot to worry about. When the puck-carrier was Wayne, I'd know something I'd never seen, never even contemplated, was going to happen between the red line and the top of the circle.

He was like a quarterback with too much time, only he was his own offensive line. He fended off pursuers with

GRETZKY PEERS OVER THE NET WHILE WHALERS' GOALIE MIKE LIUT REGAINS HIS BALANCE AFTER THWARTING AN OFFENSIVE ATTACK BY HIGH-FLYING EDMONTON.

those tight curls and turns, leaning in with his shoulders, coming out as fast as he went in, his head up, balanced perfectly. I'd scan the ice, trying to find the end game.

Then I'd fall behind the play and the defense would back in and the game would collapse around me like a house of crumbling bricks in an earthquake.

Wayne lived for this kind of chaos. I'm sure he sat on the bench, waiting to prey on an end-of-shift mismatch nobody else saw and then he'd get on the ice and instinctively raise his game to capitalize.

Everyone knows he had unnatural hockey sense, but it was driven home when I lived it, when I was victimized by it.

I remember him one night standing to my left below the goal line as the puck was fired into his corner. Our defenseman rushed at him. Wayne never looked back; he felt him coming. Just as the puck reached Wayne's stick–he had to wait for it to come across his body–he fired it on his forehand off the end boards. The defenseman missed it. Wayne spun clockwise and emerged in front of the goal line with the puck on his stick.

My pulse shot up like a champagne cork. I wanted to applaud. I had to come out at him; our other defenseman came over, too. A pass to an Oilers' teammate in front would have been a simple tip-in, but there was nobody there, probably because they'd never seen such a move either. He didn't score, but I never had any more respect for his genius than at that moment.

Often, though, Wayne scored even when I did everything right. One night in Edmonton, I took a slapshot from the point and directed it to my left, safely into the corner. That's what I thought, anyway. I knew Wayne was to my right. But what I didn't know was that when the puck had been passed up top from one defenseman to the other Wayne had swung around behind me. I directed the puck right onto his stick. We won the game 7-1 and that was the only goal scored against us.

I tried to expect the unexpected…really tried hard. If our defenseman threw the puck up the middle of the ice and it was picked off, that's where the trouble would be, so that's what I tried to anticipate. Wayne analyzed the game like a goalie. He saw what everyone else did, turned it on its head and used that insight to make the rest of us crazy. When he was supposed to headman the puck, he held it.

When he was supposed to make the easy pass to a linemate up the ice with him, he held on and found an even better pass–usually to an unguarded Paul Coffey joining the rush.

It amazed me how our defensemen would play Wayne so fundamentally wrong. I would watch them back in, though we knew that was the one thing he wanted to have happen. But you can't blame our guys. They had covered all the usual suspects; he simply didn't use them. You couldn't practice defending against him because nobody played the way he did.

In time, the Oilers all learned to play Wayne's way. Those Oiler teams played ball hockey on ice. They batted the puck out of mid-air, used caroms and bank shots, showed the kind of ingenuity that can't be diagrammed (or defended against) in a book or a between-periods chalk talk. Coffey would golf the puck out of his own zone cricket-style, knowing Wayne was already racing to center ice to pick it up wherever it landed. Wayne was always so quick to the puck. One step and he'd hook a defenseman's stick, strip the puck, get his body in front of him and be gone.

The Oilers were the rare monster equal to the myth. If I was in a funk coming into Edmonton, I knew I'd get shelled. But I never got angry when they ran up the score. They were relentless, that was their style. I never understood why some people wanted them to change their game because we were having a bad night or couldn't keep up.

I still have an old action shot of me and Wayne that ran in an Edmonton newspaper. He had intercepted a dump-in around the boards, came out front and caught everyone going the wrong way. I had to lunge to recover. In the picture I'm painfully off-balance. My goal stick looks like it's choking me and one skate blade is dug awkwardly into the ice. Fortunately, the other skate made it to the right spot. The puck is bouncing off my toe in front of a wide-open net. It might be the best save I ever made.

I remember what happened next. Wayne conceded nothing. He skated by and tapped me on the pads. "Great save, Mike," he said calmly. Then he skated to the faceoff circle and waited.

He was going to get another eight or nine chances that night, that's what he was telling me. Relentless, that was Wayne Gretzky. He had to make it known to both of us who was better. ❾❾

GRETZKY ON MIKE LIUT: NHL MVP COMPETITION

❝ He had an outstanding year (in 1980-81). I really thought that year we went head-to-head, I thought he was going to win the MVP. One, I'd won it (the year) before that and this was a chance for someone else to get it. And he'd taken a team (St. Louis) from the middle of the pack and took them to first or second place overall. I really thought he would have been a good choice for the MVP. If I would have lost, I wouldn't have been disappointed. As it turned out, I won it anyway. ❞

You Can't HIT What You Can't Find

**By DENIS POTVIN
with MARK BRENDER**

I weighed about 205 pounds in my playing days. Wayne Gretzky, full of pre-game pasta on a hungry afternoon, was 178. So the question itself made sense. The one where people would ask me, "Why didn't you just, you know, hit him?"

The answer is simple. I couldn't find him.

Trust me, there was nothing I wanted to do more than hit the guy. My brain always told me the same thing: "Hit first, then do something else." In the beginning I sat on the bench watching him and thought to myself, "Gee, this kid's awfully scrawny." I prepared to paste him. Pasting people was my game.

So I tried. I whiffed. Tried again. Whiffed. His game and mine didn't exactly mesh.

Hitting Gretzky was like wrapping your arms around fog. You saw him, but when you reached out to grab him your hands felt nothing, maybe just a chill. He had the strongest danger radar of anyone on the ice. I think he could sense me coming, the way you can sometimes look ahead and sense somebody watching you from behind. Randy Carlyle summed it up best when he said Wayne was like a deer. Anyone who hunts knows how graceful deer are. They look meek and mild, but

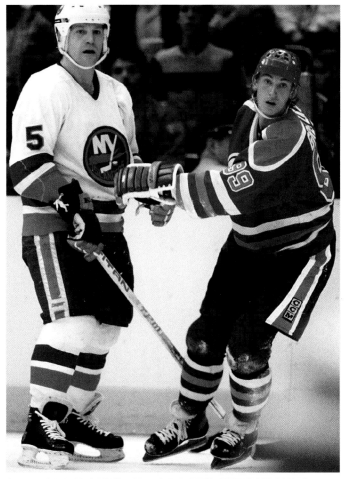

STANLEY CUP RIVALS DENIS POTVIN AND GRETZKY MEET AT THE BOARDS.

FACING 99: DENIS POTVIN

Denis Potvin was a three-time winner of the Norris Trophy as the game's best defenseman when Wayne Gretzky entered the NHL in 1979. They met in the 1983 and 1984 Cup finals. Edmonton ended the New York Islanders' four-year dynasty in the second meeting. Potvin, now 45 and a Hall of Famer, is a TV commentator for the Florida Panthers.

they're so hard to get at. That was Wayne. I can't remember one time in my career when I got a good piece of him.

It didn't help that he was a tough guy to dislike, too. I hit harder when I had a good hate going for somebody, but what was there to hate about Gretzky? It was like running into Gandhi in the corner. The most I could do when I managed to pin him to the boards was tell him to go away and not come back.

Wayne introduced totally new flow patterns to the game and because of that, I had to play him differently than anybody I ever faced. Hitting quickly gave way to the "do something else," which in his case was "avoid getting embarrassed."

Here's what I mean: offensive stars before Wayne had their individual strengths, but they attacked using the same principle, that being, the fastest way to the goal was the fastest way to a goal. Gilbert Perreault, Guy Lafleur, Bobby Orr, Marcel Dionne, Mario Lemieux, they all came at me full bore. They'd try to get by me, make a clear 1-on-1 challenge, *mano-a-mano*. I never got the sense that making that kind of challenge was important to Wayne. He had the moves to beat people in open ice and showed them from time to time, but taking on guys 1-on-1 wasn't his main interest. That one fact changed everything.

And when you think about it, Wayne's way made sense. Trying to beat me (or any physical defenseman) to the outside was a risk. That goes double for someone Wayne's size. Even assuming a player got by, he'd usually wind up in the corner having to cut back hard to the net. Even when Bobby Orr beat me, he'd often end up so deep that he'd have to circle the net.

So it was rare that winning a 1-on-1 battle in open ice resulted in a great position for the attacker. I think Wayne was the first guy to figure that out. If the idea was to get the puck behind the net, Wayne figured out a better way. If he gave up the puck, then skated behind the net–without the threat of being hit–the puck would find a way back to him. He used that principle, on either the giving or going end, all over the ice.

Whenever I did manage to track him down, I was invariably too late. The puck was already gone. The truly maddening part was that he never offered resistance. With players like Lemieux or Mark Messier, there was always physical resistance. With that battle came the chance for a little satisfaction. But Wayne was never there to be stronger or smarter than I was. He was there to get his play done and move on. Heck, he never even looked me in the eye the way other players did. He always looked beyond.

I was scared of his abilities the way you're scared of the unknown. I never understood him. I only knew enough to be afraid that something bad might happen if I didn't hold my position. I always found myself caught in-between with Wayne, wondering if I should keep my ground or charge him. He had such a great stutter step. He would come straight ahead at full speed, then all of a sudden he'd pull up, changing the gap between us from, say, three feet to eight in the blink of an eye. His hands would still be forward to make a pass, but his body would be leaning back out of harm's way. If I lunged, off-balance and out of position, he'd saunter by. He could play this game like a coiled snake rising out of a basket. I figure he must be a great fisherman, the way he laid the bait out, then pulled it away. Getting caught fishing at his line was something I tried to avoid.

My best memories of him come from the 1983 and '84

sound bite

GRETZKY ON DENIS POTVIN: OFFENSE VS. DEFENSE

" I just thought Denis was the consummate professional. He was great defensively, he'd never get caught out of position. Physically, he was pounding. If the puck was in the corner, you knew you were going to get hit by him and get hit hard. He was a clean player, but he could be really mean when he wanted to be. He was a big, strong man. I've said this before, (the Islanders) had so many great players on that team that it's hard to single out just one, but I think he was the guy who took them over the top. "

Stanley Cup finals. We were in opposite conferences, so we didn't play often in the season. Besides, I never put much stock in what a guy did over seven months. I wanted to know where he was going to be when I was in his face for five games over 10 nights in a playoff pressure cooker.

We managed to frustrate the Oilers in 1983 to win the last of our four Cups. Al Arbour designed our game plan against Gretzky. We tried to pressure him, force him to pass a little quicker than he wanted to. As soon as he made his trademark curl inside the blueline, it was my job to take off after him, hard. I didn't want to allow him time to find his pass. (One thing I didn't have to do was wince if he looked like he was going to shoot. Unlike most players, he knew exactly where he was putting the puck; my shin wasn't it). Then it was up to my teammates to shut off the passing lanes. The strategy worked well, though it was only a small part of why we won the series. Billy Smith's goaltending had a lot to do with it, too.

Going into the finals the next year, we had beaten the Oilers in 10 straight games. They got a boost of confidence with a 1-0 win in Game 1. We won two nights later 6-1, but back in Edmonton for Game 3 they had a look in their eyes that said, "Move over boys, we're taking over." The Oilers won 7-2. For us, that was the beginning of the end.

Wayne ended up leading playoff scorers with 35 points that year, but it was something he did off-ice a few weeks before our battles that really stunned me and earned my everlasting admiration. My father passed away two weeks before the 1984 final. We were in a quarterfinal series against the Washington Capitals at the time. I took a day and went home to Ottawa for the funeral. When I walked into the funeral home, there was an incredibly beautiful flower arrangement that caught my eye. The card read, "From Wayne Gretzky and the Edmonton Oilers."

It was one of the most touching gestures I ever saw in my career. When we were shaking hands at the end of the final, I leaned over and thanked him. Players on opposing teams just didn't do things like that. But that's Wayne; he understands everything about the game. He knew the only thing every 12-year-old kid growing up playing hockey wants to do is please his dad. It's all I ever wanted to do and it's a feeling that never left me. The last three seasons of my career after my dad died, I felt like I was playing in front of

THE HALL OF FAME DEFENSEMAN WAS TOUCHED WHEN GRETZKY SENT A FLOWER ARRANGEMENT ON BEHALF OF THE OILERS TO HIS FATHER'S FUNERAL SERVICE.

empty arenas. I'm convinced Wayne understood that. And it's just a guess on my part, but I'd bet that's the same feeling he had when his father Walter suffered an aneurysm a few years ago. He talked a little bit about retiring then. I think I understand what he might have been thinking.

But I don't want to push this similarity theme too far. Wayne gave us 20 years of unbelievable hockey, revolutionized the game and is idolized everywhere he goes. Me, I'm booed every time I enter an arena. Like I said, with Wayne it was just a whole different world. 99

By IGOR LARIONOV
with STEVE KETTMANN

I had never heard about Wayne Gretzky until I was 17 or 18. We were born on different sides of the ocean and we played in different hockey systems. The North American system was always tough and physical. For a guy his size to survive in that system and make all those incredible records took phenomenal vision and skating ability. He was just a super talented guy. Those guys are only born maybe once every 100 years. He's the best player I've ever seen, the greatest player ever, I'm sure.

He was a master. He was improvising all the time. It was always a treat to watch him play. Every time he took the ice, there was some spontaneous decision he would

FACING 99: IGOR LARIONOV

The careers and styles of Igor Larionov and Wayne Gretzky were mirror images for most of the 1980s and 1990s. Larionov, now 38 and with the Detroit Red Wings, has been called the "Russian Gretzky." In this excerpt from the upcoming book, *Thinking Forward: The Igor Larionov Story*, Larionov provides an international perspective on The Great One.

The first time I saw Wayne play was when the Soviet national team went to play in the 1981 Canada Cup, not long after I joined the team. The second day in Winnipeg we went to see Canada play an exhibition game against Sweden. I'd heard so much about Wayne by then, but that was the first time I'd seen him play and I was impressed. Usually the Canadian centers were big and strong guys who could shoot the puck well. There was not much thinking going on when they played. But Gretzky was skinny and the way he was doing things, scoring goals and making plays, you could tell from that first look he was a superstar. He was playing with Guy Lafleur on the same line and it was phenomenal. I had seen Lafleur play against the Red Army team in 1975

A Consummate ARTIST

make. That's what made him such a phenomenal player. You never knew what he was going to do. Other players would need maybe two seconds to make a decision. He would make it in half a second and it would always be the right decision.

He was like a great, talented actor who never failed his audience, just went to the stage every night and gave it everything he had. Wayne gave all of himself all those years. He was an artist.

In the Soviet Union, it was hard to get much information about what was happening in Canada, but I remember hearing about the 1978 World Junior Championship in Canada. Slava Fetisov was on that Soviet team because it was for players born in 1958 and 1959. Wayne played for Canada even though he was born in 1961. I heard about this 16-year-old playing great, but there was not much coverage of the tournament in Russia.

GRETZKY AND IGOR LARIONOV BATTLE FOR A LOOSE PUCK.

and here I had a chance to see Lafleur and Gretzky, the new superstar, playing together.

We didn't know what to do about Wayne. We played against Canada in the round robin a few days before the final and lost. Vladislav Tretiak didn't play, but we had a tough time and we had to figure out a way to play against Wayne. His style was so unusual for us. Usually in the Russian system, the center stays back and never goes deeper than the hash marks. But Wayne was playing behind the net. We had never seen anyone do that and it was big trouble for us. We didn't have any solution. Back in 1972, I saw Phil Esposito in the Summit Series and he was just a machine, scoring goals from the slot. Now in 1981, we saw a center playing behind the net.

So the day before the final against Canada, we had a meeting just talking about that certain play and I still wasn't sure what to do. Wayne was reading the game so well from back there. He could find any one of two or three guys and any of those decisions would be prime choices. The day of the final, we went over to the Montreal Forum before the game and the building was quiet. Nobody was there yet. So I walked around and I went right where the goal judge sat behind the net. I was standing there for five or 10 minutes, just thinking. An assistant coach came over and I asked him for ideas because I still wasn't sure what I could do. This was the biggest game of my career up to that point.

I spent maybe 20 minutes standing there trying to visualize how we could defend against him. Finally, I got an idea. There is a certain play, first of all, to try to anticipate the pass before it gets to Wayne, so he never gets the puck behind the net. Second, if he gets the puck, you can't pay much attention to him back there. You have to look at his passing options. So we made it the defense-man's responsibility to take Wayne if he tried a wrap-around. That ended up being a good idea. I scored twice in an 8-1 win. Gretzky was held off the scoresheet.

The first time I played directly against Wayne was when the Russian team went to Edmonton in 1982-83 and played against the Oilers. We lost that game 4-3 and Wayne scored a goal and had two or three assists. My line went against his line and he was excellent. The hockey was great, but we didn't get a chance to talk at all. Later that same season, the Oilers were out of the playoffs and so Wayne came to Finland to play in the World Championship. He missed some games that were played before he arrived and, still, he was the leading scorer.

FROM RED ARMY TO RED WINGS, LARIONOV HAS PLAYED NINE NHL SEASONS.

In those years, remember, it was the Cold War and the Russians were invading Afghanistan. There were cool relations between the Soviet Union and the Western world. Actually, at that time, the Russian players were not allowed to talk to anyone. We were locked in our rooms and there was a KGB guy stationed to make sure we didn't talk to anybody.

But after we lost to Canada in overtime in the semifinal of the 1984 Canada Cup, Wayne talked to some guy who was working for the NHL to invite me to join him at a nightclub in downtown Calgary. Once again, I was kind of locked in the hotel. The loss was big for us. In the Soviet Union in those years, every loss was like a big disaster for the whole country and the whole system. There was a big impact because of the politics involved. So I wasn't sure I could join Wayne at this nightclub. But around midnight, I escaped with another player, Alex Kozhevnikov.

We had a few drinks and I was trying to communicate in my abortive English. We were talking mostly about hockey. He asked me if I would like to play in the NHL and I said just what I thought: of course I would love to play. But I explained to him that it wasn't possible at that time. We spent maybe three or four hours together. Wayne was there and Larry Robinson, Michel Goulet, Mike Bossy and the rest of the guys. That was the first time we could talk. I was back in the hotel at around five in the morning.

Just to be around him was a huge thrill. It was an excellent time. I have never had any regrets about that, even though I wasn't able to travel outside the Soviet Union the next year. I don't know if it was related to that. I assume some people in the Russian embassy read the articles in the Canadian press that mentioned I was out with Gretzky until late that night and sent that back to the KGB in Moscow. But like I said, I have never had any regrets.

One of the best stories I can remember about Wayne was in 1987 when we went to Canada before the Canada Cup started. We were based for several days in Hamilton and played one exhibition game against Canada.

Before the game, Wayne asked if he could invite Slava Fetisov, Sergei Makarov and me to the house where he grew up in nearby Brantford. So after the game was over, Wayne's father, Walter, came to our hotel to tell us he was ready to take us to go see Wayne and his new girlfriend, Janet Jones. We had to go ask our coach, Viktor Tikhonov, and he said, "No, there are certain rules and you're not allowed to travel beyond a 40-kilometer radius around the rink."

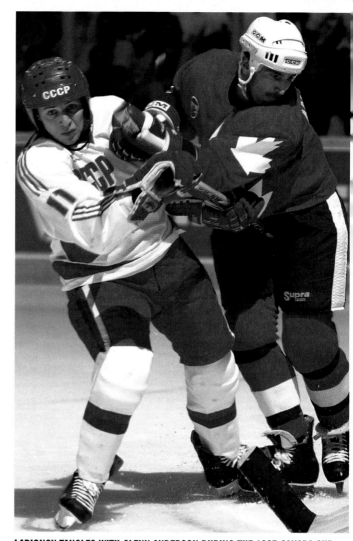

LARIONOV TANGLES WITH GLENN ANDERSON DURING THE 1987 CANADA CUP.

sound bite

GRETZKY ON IGOR LARIONOV: MIRROR IMAGES ON ICE

" We grew up playing against each other. He was a little older than me, but we started in 1981. When I started to get to know Igor a little, we would be able to communicate. Once I knew he spoke English, we would talk about hockey when we were alone...He was the first guy who communicated to me about Soviet hockey. Definitely, he saw the ice the same way as me, passing the puck, hockey sense, probably as similar to me as any player who has played the game. "

We told Walter that the answer from Tikhonov was no and then we explained there was only one solution. He had to invite Tikhonov along, too. So Walter went and asked him and Tikhonov said: "Yes, maybe we can go."

It was the three of us players along with Tikhonov and two other guys, including the equipment manager, who everyone knew worked for the KGB. We got to the house and Wayne showed us his trophy room in the basement. Wayne was there, his mom and dad, his grandfather, Dave Poulin and a couple of Wayne's other friends for the barbecue. Then we started the dinner, which was corn and salad and some good Canadian beef. They started serving wine and beer, but Russian players usually are not allowed to drink when the coach is around. So we said, "No, no, no, we're not going to drink."

Tikhonov said, "No, my guys aren't going to drink."

So they gave us Sprite or Coca-Cola to have with the steak.

It was kind of funny, really. Here we were, people from different sides of the ocean and everyone is having a good time and having a good, relaxing dinner and there is beer and wine being served, but we can't drink it.

Wayne understood why we couldn't partake. So we arranged it so that one by one we would get up from the table and go downstairs to the trophy room and there was Walter, who had some cold beers for us. You would kind of drink one or two beers and then go back upstairs. After that we were all on the same page, feeling good and loose.

The hockey that year was really something. Wayne played on a line with Mario Lemieux and they played incredibly. It was a treat to watch Wayne. It was a treat to be on the ice with him.

Of course I'm really sad to see him leave. I've been a big fan of his. I have never tried to copy his style. I have my own game. I came to the NHL and I was already an established player.

But he was always my idol, the way he played and carried himself with the media and the public and the kids. I'm just fortunate to have known this guy and played against him, but it's such a big loss for hockey. To not see him on the ice, that just makes me really sad. 99

SEASON
By Season

Legend of 99
- Gretzky's goals
- Gretzky's assists (points on far right)
- NHL leader or runner-up to Gretzky in points
- * NHL leader
- Seasons in red indicate Stanley Cup wins

Gretzky's Honors

Season	Goals	Assists	Points	Leader/Runner-up	Honors
1979-80 Edmonton	51	86*	137	Marcel Dionne *137	Hart, Lady Byng Second All-Star
1980-81 Edmonton	55	109*	*164	Marcel Dionne 135	Hart, Art Ross First All-Star
1981-82 Edmonton	92*	120*	*212	Mike Bossy 147	Hart, Art Ross First All-Star
1982-83 Edmonton	71*	125*	*196	Peter Stastny 124	Hart, Art Ross First All-Star
1983-84 Edmonton	87*	118*	*205	Paul Coffey 126	Hart, Art Ross First All-Star
1984-85 Edmonton	73*	135*	*208	Jari Kurri 135	Hart, Art Ross, Conn Smythe, First All-Star
1985-86 Edmonton	52	163*	*215	Mario Lemieux 141	Hart, Art Ross First All-Star
1986-87 Edmonton	62*	121*	*183	Jari Kurri 108	Hart, Art Ross First All-Star
1987-88 Edmonton	40	109*	149	Mario Lemieux *168	Conn Smythe Second All-Star
1988-89 Los Angeles	54	114*	168	Mario Lemieux *199	Hart Second All-Star
1989-90 Los Angeles	40	102*	*142	Mark Messier 129	Art Ross Second All-Star
1990-91 Los Angeles	41	122*	*163	Brett Hull 131	Art Ross, Lady Byng First All-Star
1991-92 Los Angeles	31	90*	121	Mario Lemieux *131	Lady Byng
1992-93 Los Angeles	16	49	65	Mario Lemieux *160	
1993-94 Los Angeles	38	92*	*130	Sergei Fedorov 120	Art Ross, Lady Byng Second All-Star
1994-95 Los Angeles	11	37	48	Jaromir Jagr *70	
1995-96 L.A./St.Louis	23	79	102	Mario Lemieux *161	
1996-97 Rangers	25	72*	97	Mario Lemieux *122	Second All-Star
1997-98 Rangers	23	67*	90	Jaromir Jagr *102	Second All-Star
1998-99 Rangers	9	53	62	Jaromir Jagr *127	Lady Byng

By KEN DRYDEN

I never played against Wayne Gretzky. He came into the NHL from the WHA with the Edmonton Oilers the October after I had played my last game in Montreal. I have met him and spoken with him a few times, but I know him mostly from the way you know him, from the thousands of impressions I have gotten of him from TV and newspapers during the last two decades.

I don't know if he's the greatest player ever. He is certainly the best player of a time when hockey has been exposed to more people in more different places. He may also be hockey's most important player.

He was, I think, the first Canadian forward to play a

KEN DRYDEN'S PERSPECTIVE

Ken Dryden has led a storied career on and off the ice and nobody has written a better story about hockey than *The Game*, Dryden's 1983 bestselling book. Now, the Hall of Fame goalie focuses on what Wayne Gretzky means to Canada, Gretzky's home and native land. Dryden, 51, is the president and GM of the Toronto Maple Leafs.

Gretzky made his opponents stop five players not one, and he made his teammates full partners to the game. He made them skate up to his level, pass and finish up to his level or be embarrassed.

He made them all better players. Not just statistically better players from riding his coattails. Bobby Orr had done the same a few years earlier, but as a defenseman, and while Orr's achievement may have been the more unexpected (imagine, a defenseman leading from behind), leading from in front is harder. Everything happens faster, there is less space and time to see the patterns and to make new ones, more reason to abandon the ideal and just do it for yourself.

A Canadian CULTURAL Icon

true team game. His predecessor superstars were always the focus of their team's strategy. The challenge was to get the puck to Howe or Richard or Hull or Mahovlich or Lafleur. Gretzky reversed that. He knew he wasn't big enough or strong enough, or even fast enough to do what he wanted to do if others focused on him.

Like a magician, he had to direct attention elsewhere, to his four teammates on the ice with him, to create the momentary distraction in order to move unnoticed into open ice where size and strength didn't matter. Then, he had to get the puck back, and accompanied by four players moving up the ice with him, and opponents backpedalling in sudden panic, to give it up again.

The irony is that Gretzky, the greatest scorer of all-time–by season with 92, and by career with 894–wasn't first of all a scorer. He was the artist who created the work of art and then left it to the artisan to finish it off.

His greatest contribution, however, may have come in other ways. This was never more apparent than in the days leading up to his retirement announcement. Happily for him, by the time the attention hit, he seemed genuinely to have his mind made up. For in that kind of clamor, you cannot discover your own mind. He was emotional, and conflicted, as one would be, but he seemed relaxed, at peace, almost serene.

As he has done so often on the ice, he managed to pull all his emotional/personal pieces together. Simply, he knew, it was time.

"I'm done," he said to his wife, Janet, the previous Sunday. So in the furor of his near week-long "death watch," he could just talk, openly, freely, with nothing to hide except his final words which, everyone knew, would come

GRETZKY HOLDS ALOFT THE CANADA CUP
AFTER CANADA WINS THE 1987 EVENT.

GRETZKY'S BRILLIANCE EXTENDED BEYOND THE NHL AND INTO INTERNATIONAL EVENTS SUCH AS THE 1991 CANADA CUP. HE LED THE TOURNAMENT WITH 12 POINTS.

soon enough. In Ottawa, after his last game in Canada, the next day in New York at his final press conference, there was no rushing off, and no reporters in a race to beat their deadlines.

Like after a season is over and the Cup is won, with all the pressure off and experiences to share, everyone seemed content to just hang around and talk. And Gretzky listened too. "Go ahead," he kept saying, encouraging the next questioner when it seemed to the media that they had already taken enough of his time. It's OK. He seemed utterly content with himself.

But he always has, and maybe that's what is behind his biggest achievement. If you were to put Wayne Gretzky in a room of ordinary people, he would not appear ordinary–his clothes, his hair, how he speaks about himself, his bearing and attitude–they would all set him apart. But if you were to put him in a room of superstars, he would stick out even more dramatically. There, he seems normal. Comfortably normal.

He is normal-sized. Every time he looks in the mirror, he knows he is not indestruc-

background

INTERNATIONAL STAGE SERVED GRETZKY WELL
Winning scoring titles was nothing new to Wayne Gretzky when he took his act into the international sphere. But it still came as a surprise when the 16-year-old phenom led the 1978 World Junior Championship in scoring. Canada finished third that year, but Gretzky was named best forward. He went on to earn scoring titles in his next five international events. Gretzky led Canada to three Canada Cup victories and was the most celebrated member of Canada's team at the 1998 Olympics.

tible, and he has known that all his life. He also possesses a rare perspective on the game and his place in it that can only come from being a lifelong fan.

He knows the names and records of all the great players. He has followed them, been inspired by their legends. Just watch him with Gordie Howe. Gretzky has caught up with and passed all of Howe's scoring records, and yet in his mind he knows he isn't Howe and he never will be. To his eight-year-old starry-eyed self, Howe was 10 feet tall, stronger than an ox, and able to skate and shoot faster than the wind. To the 20- or 38-year-old Gretzky, no matter what anyone else says, he can't match up. So Gordie Howe is the greatest of them all, and Wayne Gretzky is happily saddled with a humility he cannot deny.

It is a humility which comes when one has a sense of history. Gretzky knows that time didn't begin and end with him. It comes from being a working class kid for whom good things can never be assumed. He speaks about himself as if he is as mystified at the success he has had as everyone else is.

ORDINARY GUY, EXTRAORDINARY TALENT: GRETZKY'S ABILITY TO REMAIN HUMBLE DESPITE HIS LOFTY PLACE IN HOCKEY HISTORY IS A REMARKABLE ACHIEVEMENT.

The endless hours he spent as a young boy on his back-yard rink has somehow more to do with his father, Walter, who built the rink and found time for him; the passion that kept him there he sees as a "gift" that came from somewhere else. He is not today's ubiquitous self-made man who worships his creator.

Such self-image comes when one views one's immediate world as a burden and an obstacle to overcome. Gretzky doesn't see the world this way.

He didn't grow up resenting the limits of small-town, working class life, vowing to create a different future for himself. He likes what he is. He seems actually to like his father and mother, to like Brantford and Canada and hockey. So when he went to L.A. and New York, he loved L.A. and New York the way any normal kid would, but without feeling the need to hate Brantford, without needing to give up Canada.

It is not supposed to be that way. We want each of us to carve our own path, to be responsible for our own destiny, to be beholden to no one. When most people go from the small time to the big time, they reject utterly their former existence. They make fun of the person they once were. Not Gretzky.

He is the "Ordinary Superstar." Former Heisman Trophy winner and Montreal Alouette football player Johnny Rodgers hung that same phrase on himself, but wanting to elevate himself, he put the emphasis on "superstar." With Gretzky, it is on "ordinary."

99'S LAST INTERNATIONAL STAGE: THE '98 OLYMPICS.

Wayne Gretzky did not go out on top as a player. Michael Jordan did, so did Mario Lemieux and Jim Brown. No athlete who retires at 38 can expect to. But the power and appeal of sport is far more than just in its wins and losses.

Sport commands the attention of people with its compelling, unscripted, character-revealing dramas. I have at other times described hockey as Canada's national theatre. On its frozen stage, life lessons get played out, and millions watch and learn. And in the theatre, what counts is not just what happens, but how it happens. Great athletes, though they may not know it, get paid not just for what they do, but for how they do it. For how he played on the stage,

Gretzky, the superstar as person, clearly stepped down at the top of his game.

It is often said that Canadians love to lionize their stars and love even more to tear them down. There is some perverse sense of the democratic in Canadians that make us chop off any head that rises above the others. I don't think this is true, or at least not any more true than it is for Australians or Mexicans or Belgians or anyone else for whom center stage lies in some other country.

The standards of greatness in our world are established in New York or Paris or London or Hollywood. So people in smaller places wait for their stars to take to those stages, and then wait for the judgment of others. And to really make it, those homegrown stars often have to be so single-mindedly non-Canadian or a-Canadian that if they do succeed, we Canadians beat them up for not waving the flag when they get there.

To get to the top in hockey you have to live a Canadian life, one of ice and snow, struggle and physical pain, even if you grow up in Kazakhstan or Sweden. And to stay at the top, you cannot stray very far from that life. Even if Wayne Gretzky never lives in Canada again, deep in his bones he is Canadian. With him, Canadians feel a bond.

You could see it in the affection expressed towards him in those final days and in the ease of conversation he had with the Canadian people. Canadians had watched him grow up. He is the first superstar to be recorded in the making.

We could see for ourselves the mythic normalcy of his childhood. His size, strength, and skating stride all could have been us. He had no advantages–family money, influential friends–that made his experience different from our own as to set him apart. Even his hard work, his passion on the rink, looked to us like hard play, like the normal, natural passion we feel for this game.

He is the champion we all could have been. Hard working, hard playing, skilled, knowing what he is and what he isn't, what he can and cannot do, respectful and largely content, he is the face that Canadians would most like to present to the world. **99**

By BOB McKENZIE

It's only fitting No. 99 would decide to hang 'em up in 1999. Wayne Gretzky has always had a fascination with numbers and not just the ones on his back. Two hundred and fifteen, 92, 50 in 39, 802, 1,851…the list goes on. He has forced us all to become numerologists of sorts because no athlete has dominated the numbers of his game like The Great One has hockey.

"Hey, my dad just told me this," Gretzky said. "The first goal I ever scored was at 18:51 of the first period. 18:51, can you believe that?"

"I was six and I made the (10-year-old) travelling team (in Brantford)," Gretzky said. "There was this really good player on the team, I think his name was Brian Queley, and he wore No. 9. I took No. 11. I didn't play more than two shifts a game that year. The next year, Brian moved up and I got my No. 9. I wore it all the way through after that."

He wore it when he played lacrosse. And baseball, too, though Gretzky remembers there was a season or two when as a young pitcher he wore No. 1.

Gretzky was a No. 9 until he joined the Sault Ste. Marie Greyhounds as a 16-year-old. No. 9 wasn't available because it was being worn by Sault Ste. Marie, Ont., native Brian Gualazzi. "I always wore No. 9," said Gualazzi, now an assistant crown attorney in the Sault. "I didn't wear it because of Howe or Hull or any of those guys. I wore it because I was born on Nov. 9."

Registered
TRADEMARK 99®

The number is significant, of course, because it was Gretzky's 1,851st point–one more than Gordie Howe had in his NHL career–that made Gretzky the league's career scoring leader.

Gretzky's numbers are magical and he sees the magic in them. None have been more karmic than the one he wore on his back.

Why should we be surprised? The No. 9 has traditionally been a special one in hockey. The pantheon of greats who have worn it include Maurice Richard, Gordie Howe and Bobby Hull. And lest we forget Charlie Conacher, Teeder Kennedy, Johnny Bucyk, Clark Gillies and Lanny McDonald. Now, Paul Kariya of the Mighty Ducks of Anaheim is the standard bearer for the game's second-most special number.

Gretzky transformed No. 99 into its most special.

While many players will wear No. 9 as a tribute to one of the greats, you don't see anyone in the NHL, or just about anywhere else save kids' hockey, donning No. 99. The league made that issue moot when it retired the number across the board following Gretzky's retirement.

As a kid, No. 9 was always Gretzky's number.

"It was," he said, "for Gordie."

But it wasn't his first number in hockey.

And when Gualazzi joined the hometown Hounds as a rookie, he couldn't have it. Veteran Tim Coulis was wearing it. When Coulis left, Gualazzi snapped it up and was wearing it when a rookie Gretzky arrived on the scene.

The rest of the story has become hockey lore.

Gretzky wore No. 14 in training camp. Greyhounds' coach Muzz MacPherson suggested he switch to No. 19, which he did to start the 1977-78 Ontario League regular season.

"It was a few weeks into the season when Muzz and Angelo (Bumbacco, the Greyhounds' GM) came to me and suggested I wear two nines," Gretzky said.

"Phil Esposito was wearing No. 77 at the time, so double-digit numbers were being worn. At first, I said, 'No, that's too hot-doggish.' But they convinced me to wear it."

Gualazzi, a Minnesota North Stars' draftee who was recruited by Pierre Page for Dalhousie University, remembers it all well.

"No one ever asked me to give (No. 9) up," Gualazzi

Rocky Widner

NO. 99 ONCE THOUGHT ABOUT RETURNING TO HIS ORIGINAL NO. 11 SWEATER.

said. "Not that I would have. It was no issue. I was a veteran and Wayne was a rookie."

Gualazzi enjoyed his one season with Gretzky–they ended up on the same line in the playoffs–but Gualazzi flourished as a junior player the next season (Gretzky's first in the WHA) when he scored a then franchise-record 75 goals.

After kicking around briefly in the minors, Gualazzi put his efforts into getting a law degree. He moved back home and right into the Crown attorney's office. Beyond his hockey-playing days, the No. 9 hasn't held any special significance, though he still wears it when he plays pick-up hockey or with the Greyhound alumni team.

"They kept (No. 9) for me," Gualazzi said.

When Gretzky joined the WHA Edmonton Oilers early in 1978-79, coach-GM Glen Sather gave him the opportunity to discard No. 99. The late Bill Goldsworthy even offered to give up No. 9 if Gretzky wanted it.

"That was nice of Goldy, " Gretzky said. "And Slats said he was just trying to take the pressure off me. But I told him, 'I don't think it will matter much.' I knew then 99 would be my number."

It has become a trademark of sorts. No. 99 figures prominently in the logo for Gretzky's Toronto restaurant, the address of which was changed to 99 Blue Jays Way. Simply, the number and Gretzky have become synonymous.

A numerologist could have a field day with Gretzky. Numerology, not unlike astrology, can be manipulated to say just about anything you want.

But for what it's worth, Gretzky's full name (Wayne Douglas) gives him in numerology what's called a 'destiny' number of nine. Nines are generally regarded as multi-talented people, compassionate and global.

One wonders what might have unfolded for Gretzky if he hadn't resisted his urge to change numbers after Howe's retirement.

"When Gordie retired there for awhile and Gilbert Perreault came on the scene (with the Buffalo Sabres), I was tempted to go back to No. 11," Gretzky said. "I told my dad, 'I should have kept 11.' For kids of my era, No. 11 was a cool number because of Perreault.

"There have always been numbers more special than others–nine because of Gordie, four because of (Jean) Béliveau and (Bobby) Orr and seven because of (Esposito)."

And now 99, because of you know who, though when eight-year-old Ty Gretzky and his six-year-old brother Trevor play hockey at Chelsea Pier in New York, there's no No. 9 to be found on either of their backs. In fact, there's no last name either.

"We put their first names on the back of their sweaters," Gretzky said.

"They don't need that kind of pressure. I asked them what numbers they got. Trevor took No. 5 because that's his favorite. Ty got No. 14 because his favorite player is Brendan Shanahan." **99**

"He is great who is what he is from nature, and who never reminds us of others."

Ralph Waldo Emerson, *Uses of Great Men*

By JACK FALLA *Jan. 9, 1998*

Inside the New York Rangers' dressing room at the Playland Rink in Rye, N.Y., on this cold and drizzly Saturday morning, Wayne Gretzky, dressed in a white crew-neck T-shirt, black pants, black socks and brown Gucci horsebit buckle loafers, leans back in an overstuffed chair and, in answer to a question, contemplates the pantheon of 20th century sports immortals.

"Let's see...Muhammad Ali is pretty special...then there's Michael Jordan for what he has done for basketball..." He mentions Joe DiMaggio and Babe Ruth and then stops. "I'd be honored to be anywhere in the top 10," he says. "I think I'd vote for Ali."

And this is where Wayne Gretzky has brought us in the 20 years he has played hockey for a living. That he is the greatest NHL hockey player of all-time is a given, merely affirmed–not decided–by the voting of The Hockey News' 50-member committee. "How Great is Gretzky?" says committee member and Edmonton Oilers' president and GM Glen Sather, who coached Gretzky for 10 seasons. "There aren't enough adjectives. Just look at his records and longevity."

Gretzky's 61 NHL scoring records–and the sheer enormity of some of those numbers–make him the most statistically dominant athlete ever in North American team sports. And as Gretzky, now in the November of his career, rises above the worthy likes of Gordie Howe and Mario Lemieux, and inches past the once seemingly incomparable Bobby Orr, he draws ever nearer to Ali, Jordan, Pele and that elite hand-

Bruce Bennett/BBS

ful of others who make up the sporting patriciate of our fast passing century.

Congratulated on his election as the greatest hockey player ever, Gretzky at first slips into interview auto pilot–yes, it's "a great honor because of all the other great players" blah, blah–and then, as he often does after he gets beyond the first draft drift of his mind, he supplies a more revealing reaction. "As I get older I savor these things more. I enjoy the moment more. When I was younger things were happening so fast I hardly knew what I was doing."

It is a thought he will express in similar words the next night at Madison Square Garden though his enjoyment of that moment will be so obvious as to require no further

No.1 NHLer Of All-Time

expression. On his first shift in the third period of a game against the Mighty Ducks of Anaheim, Gretzky takes a pass from linemate Niklas Sundstrom and feeds Ulf Samuelsson, who scores, thus giving Gretzky his 1,851st assist or one more assist than second all-time scoring leader Gordie Howe has goals and assists combined. In the second period, Gretzky had tied the record, setting off a two-minute standing ovation. "Gret-SKI, Gret-SKI," they chanted, the accent on the wrong syllable, the sentiment on the right man, while on the Rangers' bench Gretzky smiled, waved a quick self-conscious acknowledgement and twice indulged in long cheek-puffing thank-God-that's-over exhalations. But now with the new standard set, the ovation is more restrained–not quite loud or long enough to drown out 2 Unlimited's "You All Ready 4 This?" pulsing out of the Garden's sound system. Yes, Gretzky is ready for this…

With the record not just equalled but broken, Gretzky grins broadly, waves more enthusiastically and this time mouths a "thank you" and when that brings up the volume of the ovation, he smiles again. This time it is the smile the writer has not seen since May 19, 1984, in Edmonton, the

night Gretzky kissed and lifted the first of his four Cups, the time he still calls, "my sweetest moment in hockey."

Now, in Manhattan, Gretzky is savoring the moment in which he pushed back one of hockey's last statistical frontiers. If the man never scored a goal he would still be the NHL's all-time leading scorer. It is almost unimaginable, as are so many of Gretzky's records because he does not merely extend by small increments the limits of what was once proven possible, but instead makes irrelevant previous standards, putting up numbers that belong on a pinball machine–career records in goals, assists and points. The philosopher Emerson wrote "great men exist that there be greater men," but it seems unlikely some of Gretzky's marks will ever be equaled. A few may not even be approached.

The day before ringing up assist No. 1,851, Gretzky reflects on some of his more compelling statistics.

"I think 163 assists in a season will be hard to beat. That and 215 points in a season," he says. He set both marks with Edmonton in 1985-86. "And the 51-game scoring streak will stand for awhile," the reference being to the 1983-84 feat that had sportswriters across North America comparing Gretzky's accomplishment to DiMaggio's 56-game hitting streak. Reminded of his 50 goals in 39 games,

Gretzky says, "I almost forgot about that one. Yeah. A guy could have 45 goals in 35 games and he'd still have to average better than a goal a game to beat it." He breaks into a bemused smile at the thought.

Indeed, of all Gretzky's records, scoring 50 goals in 39 games may be the most otherworldly. Fifty goals in 50 games had been one of hockey's mythical barriers since Maurice Richard set that standard in 1945. Mike Bossy equalled the mark in 1981. Then Gretzky simply destroyed it. It would be as if Roger Maris had not broken Babe Ruth's record of 60 home runs in a season by hitting 61, but had instead hit 73. Incomprehensible. Or if Roger Bannister had run the first sub four-minute mile not in 3:59.4, breaking the existing record by eight-tenths of a second, but had instead broken it by, say, four seconds. To find statistical comparisons to Gretzky, it is necessary to turn to rare events in other sports, to Bob Beamon breaking the world long jump record by nearly two feet at the Mexico City Olympics, to Secretariat, Ron Turcotte up, winning the 1973 Belmont by a super-equine 31 lengths, to Babe Ruth hitting a "dead ball era" baseball 579 feet in a 1919 spring training game in Tampa. Gretzky gave the NHL record book a torching that conjures up the memory of rocker Jerry Lee Lewis closing a set by playing "Great Balls of Fire" with his elbows and feet before setting his piano on fire with lighter fluid, walking off the stage and saying to the next act, "Top that." Were any of us ready 4 this?

Yet it is ironic the top goal-scorer of all time thinks it is his most famous record–92 goals in a season–that is most vulnerable. "Ninety-two goals can fall," he says of the record he set in 1981-82. Asked who among current players could do it, Gretzky says, "Paul Kariya. He takes a lot of shots…yeah, if a guy stays healthy and he's on the right team he could break that one."

But the operative phrase is "if a guy stays healthy," a difficult thing to do in a game played by athletes who are bigger, stronger and faster than ever. Staying healthy is one of Gretzky's more remarkable achievements and likely the key to his

sound bite

WAYNE GRETZKY ON HIS ERA AND THE STARS OF TODAY

" My timing was perfect. I played on the exact team I needed to be on. More offensive-minded than defensive-minded. Unfortunately for guys today, not only are the best players getting better, but everyone's getting better. Any of those guys, if you put them in the 1981 situation, (Teemu) Selanne could get 90 goals, (Paul) Kariya could get 170 points. (Jaromir) Jagr, (Eric) Lindros would do very well. "

selection as the No. 1 player ever. Put it this way: if Gretzky were a mountain range, he would not only be as high as the Himalayas, he would be as long as the Rockies. It is the heights he has reached that separate him from Howe, and it is the length of time he has occupied those heights (Gretzky has a league record 15 seasons with 100-or-more points and four seasons with 200-or-more) that separates him from the star-crossed Orr and Lemieux. Lemieux scored virtually the same number of goals as Gretzky over the same number of games (Gretzky had 616 to Lemieux's 613) and the transcendent Orr re-invented defense and was the first player to dominate a game over three zones. Lemieux, victim of a bad back and of Hodgkin's disease, never played a complete NHL season, and Orr played most of his nine full seasons on knees surgically repaired so many times writer George Plimpton described them as "looking like a bag of handkerchiefs."

REIJO RUOTSALAINEN OF THE NEW YORK RANGERS EXPERIENCES EVERY NHL DEFENSEMAN'S WORST NIGHTMARE: GOING 1-ON-1 WITH NO. 99 IN HIS PRIME.

"I've stayed healthy because I'm not a banger and a crasher," Gretzky says. "Guys who bang and crash wear down and I think the body can't keep repairing itself."

Early in his career Gretzky refused to follow off-ice weight training programs, sometimes glibly offering the non sequitur, "Show me a weight that ever scored a goal and I'll start lifting." That has changed.

"I train harder in the off-season now," he says. "Since I turned 28 or 29 I lift and work out about two hours a day in the summer. My No. 1 obligation is to be ready to play hockey." The weight work has re-shaped him slightly. Striding across the dressing room after a post-game shower and wearing only a towel, Gretzky reveals the trim lean body of a swimmer.

He appears to be slightly bigger through the chest and shoulders than he was in his Edmonton heyday. But back at the practice rink your eyes are drawn to the pipe cleaner thinness of his arms and the smallness of the

sound bite

JANET GRETZKY ON WAYNE THE DAD AND HIS FUTURE

❝ I'm bad cop, he's good cop...He brings a calmness in our home. When the door is closed and everything is behind him, everything's so easy for him, so relaxed. I think hockey is always going to be in Wayne's life. I know there are doors opening up. I mean, who better to be involved in an organization than Wayne Gretzky? It may not be in a year or three years, but I think it will be a part of his life. ❞

most gifted hands the game has ever seen. With his blond hair longer than he wore it last year and now swept back in a mane falling to mid-neck, Gretzky looks more like a dancer or rock singer than a professional athlete in a contact sport. Ask him for insight to his game and he doesn't talk of quickness (which he has in abundance) or his ability to know where the puck is going, a prescience acquired from his father, Walter, on the family's backyard rink in Brantford ("don't go where the puck is; go where it's going to be") or of unusual peripheral vision (a canard disproved early in his career by vision tests given to all Oilers' players). He talks of love.

"I still really, really love this game," he says. "I like playing it. I even like getting on the bus and talking about it."

And he loves talking about his children playing it. In a long conversation with Gretzky, nothing lights him up as much as the chance to talk about the three

Bruce Bennett/BBS

GRETZKY AND JANET JONES WERE MARRIED AT ST. JOSEPH'S BASILICA IN EDMONTON A LITTLE MORE THAN THREE WEEKS BEFORE THE TRADE TO LOS ANGELES.

children he has had with his wife, actress Janet Jones. "The two guys (Ty, 7, and Trevor, 5) play on the same team. Mike Richter's wife, Veronica, is the assistant coach." Ask him their positions and he looks at you incredulously. "Oh, they're both forwards. The little guy patterns himself after me, but Ty is more of a bull. He likes the physical contact. We don't push them, but they both just love the game. I guess it'll be harder on them as they get older." Then he laughs and says, "I hope they'll both be baseball players."

Gretzky's daughter, Paulina, 9, doesn't play hockey. "She's into piano and ballet. Just got accepted to the American Ballet Theater School. I guess that's like making an all-star team," he says. Paulina may be the hardest hitter in the Gretzky family. When the Philadelphia Flyers eliminated the Rangers from the 1997 playoffs and her father returned to the family's East Side Manhattan apartment, Gretzky recalls that "Paulina said I shouldn't worry about the loss. I said, 'Why shouldn't I worry about it?' She said, 'Because the Flyers are so young and you guys are so old.' "

GRETZKY BEATS DON EDWARDS FOR GOAL NO. 77 TO PASS PHIL ESPOSITO'S RECORD IN 1982.

(Give her an extra two minutes for intent to injure.)

Last summer Gretzky sent his sons to California where his father, Walter, runs a hockey camp. "They thought they were going to spend a nice week with Grandpa. Hah! Grandpa skated them into the ground."

Gretzky calls Walter and Glen Sather the two most important influences in his development as a hockey player. "It's as if my father raised me until age 17, then turned me over to Slats and said, 'You take him from here.' The one thing they had in common," Gretzky says, "is that they both pushed me. If I got 80 goals, Slats would tell me I could've had 85." Says Sather: "It would be a crime to have the God-given talent he has and not make the most of it because you didn't push hard enough." Sather's pushing caused some iciness between the two men during Gretzky's career in Edmonton, but Gretzky says that's meltwater under an old bridge. "No. We're fine. The best thing about Slats is that he always had faith in me."

Sather may have the best understanding of the Gretzkian

genius: "He does everything in the sweet spot," Sather says. "He's like the best golfers or tennis players or like Mickey Mantle. Every pass and every shot, right on the sweet spot."

Others can appreciate, but not comprehend. Says Boston GM Harry Sinden: "Gretzky sees a picture out there that no one else sees. It's difficult to describe because I've never seen the game he's looking at."

There is an almost Jesuitical quality–a confidence born of faith, works and insight–in Gretzky's game. "When he makes a pass you can't explain how he makes it," says Rangers' coach Colin Campbell, who played with Gretzky in 1979 in Edmonton. "It's not a Mark Messier pass or a Gil Perreault pass; it flutters over, under and around things and lands on the right stick blade too many times for it to be an accident. And he masquerades his intentions so well he mesmerizes everyone."

Not even Gretzky could argue that he's past his physical peak but, as Campbell says, "That's like saying my Rolls Royce is five years old. It's still a Rolls and it's still worth a lot."

That there was a whisper of the Rolls not being shipped to Nagano, Japan for the 1998 Olympics or, if shipped, being used as a kind of fourth line courtesy car, was absurd. Gretzky's presence at the Olympics, World Cup, Canada Cup, All-Star Game or any special event is hockey's gain because he is the world's greatest ambassador for his sport, its most recognized, promotable and evangelical athlete. It is a role he takes seriously and that he credits to Gordie Howe. "Growing up, my player role model was always Gordie. Later, as I got to know him, I noticed how he always had time for everyone. He'd go out of his way to talk to kids. He told me it was a responsibility and an obligation. It's not a problem for me. It's part of my hockey schedule."

❏ ❏ ❏ ❏ ❏

Back at Madison Square Garden, it is now 20 minutes after the game in which Gretzky recorded his 1,851st assist and a group of reporters has gathered in a corridor outside the Rangers' dressing room where Colin Campbell is holding an impromptu press conference. He is struggling to explain

TO HONOR GRETZKY'S STATUS AS THE NO. 1 NHL PLAYER OF ALL-TIME, THE HOCKEY NEWS SILVER-PLATED THE FIRST PAIR OF SKATES HE WORE IN THE NHL.

Gretzky's achievement. "How many assists is 1,851?" he asks rhetorically. "You can't even think of it. It's mind boggling. It's like how many stars are in the sky."

No it isn't, Colin. There are billions of stars in the sky; but Gretzky is more like the sun. And when the sun shines, the stars disappear.

Postscript: Mark McGwire broke Roger Maris' Major League Baseball record for home runs in 1998 by hitting 70. **99**

The TOP 50 Players of All-Time

Never before in the history of hockey has there been a more natural hat trick than that recorded by The Hockey News in balloting for the top 50 players in NHL history.

Wayne Gretzky, Bobby Orr and Gordie Howe could hardly be more different as players, but the difference between them in balloting to determine the best NHL player ever could hardly have been closer. Just 45 voting points–less than 2 per cent of Gretzky's winning total of 2,726–separate the three legends. While a clear-cut favorite didn't emerge, THN wholeheartedly endorses the selection of No. 99 as the NHL's No. 1 player.

(Goalie statistics are games, win-loss-tie record and goals-against average.)

	GP	G	A	Pts.
1. Wayne Gretzky	1,487	894	1,963	2,857
Center Edmonton, Los Angeles, St. Louis, Rangers				(1979-99)
2. Bobby Orr	657	270	645	915
Defenseman Boston, Chicago				(1966-78)
3. Gordie Howe	1,767	801	1,049	1,850
Right Winger Detroit, Hartford				(1946-80)
4. Mario Lemieux	745	613	881	1,494
Center Pittsburgh				(1984-97)
5. Maurice Richard	978	544	421	965
Right Winger Montreal				(1942-60)
6. Doug Harvey	1,113	88	452	540
Defenseman Montreal, Rangers, Detroit, St. Louis				(1947-69)
7. Jean Béliveau	1,125	507	712	1,219
Center Montreal				(1953-71)
8. Bobby Hull	1,063	610	560	1,170
Left Winger Chicago, Winnipeg, Hartford				(1957-80)
9. Terry Sawchuk	971	441-330-173		2.52
Goalie Detroit, Boston, Toronto, Los Angeles, Rangers				(1950-70)
10. Eddie Shore	553	105	179	284
Defenseman Boston, New York Americans				(1926-40)
11. Guy Lafleur	1,126	560	793	1,353
Right Winger Montreal, Rangers, Quebec				(1971-91)
12. Mark Messier	1,413	610	1,063	1,673
Center Edmonton, Rangers, Vancouver				(1979-present)
13. Jacques Plante	837	434-246-147		2.38
Goalie Montreal, Rangers, St. Louis, Toronto, Boston				(1953-73)
14. Ray Bourque	1,453	385	1,083	1,468
Defenseman Boston				(1979-present)
15. Howie Morenz	550	270	197	467
Center Montreal, Chicago, Rangers				(1923-37)
16. Glenn Hall	906	407-327-163		2.51
Goalie Detroit, Chicago, St. Louis				(1955-71)
17. Stan Mikita	1,394	541	926	1,467
Center Chicago				(1959-80)

	GP	G	A	Pts.
18. Phil Esposito	1,282	717	873	1,590
Center Chicago, Boston, Rangers				(1963-81)
19. Denis Potvin	1,060	310	742	1,052
Defenseman Islanders				(1973-88)
20. Mike Bossy	752	573	553	1,126
Right Winger Islanders				(1977-87)
21. Ted Lindsay	1,068	379	472	851
Left Winger Detroit, Chicago				(1944-65)
22. Red Kelly	1,316	281	542	823
Defenseman Detroit, Toronto				(1947-67)
23. Bobby Clarke	1,144	358	852	1,210
Center Philadelphia				(1969-84)
24. Larry Robinson	1,384	208	750	958
Defenseman Montreal, Los Angeles				(1972-92)
25. Ken Dryden	397	258-57-74		2.24
Goalie Montreal				(1971-79)
26. Frank Mahovlich	1,181	533	570	1,103
Left Winger Toronto, Detroit, Montreal				(1957-74)
27. Milt Schmidt	776	229	346	575
Center Boston				(1937-55)
28. Paul Coffey	1,322	385	1,102	1,487
Defenseman Edmonton, Pittsburgh, Los Angeles, Detroit, Hartford, Philadelphia, Chicago, Carolina				(1980-present)
29. Henri Richard	1,256	358	688	1,046
Center Montreal				(1955-75)
30. Bryan Trottier	1,279	524	901	1,425
Center Islanders, Pittsburgh				(1975-94)
31. Dickie Moore	719	261	347	608
Left Winger Montreal, Toronto, St. Louis				(1951-68)
32. Newsy Lalonde	99	124	27	151
Center Montreal, New York Americans				(1917-27)
33. Syl Apps	423	201	231	432
Center Toronto				(1936-48)

	GP	G	A	Pts.
34. Bill Durnan	383	208-112-62		2.36
Goalie Montreal				(1943-50)
35. Patrick Roy	778	412-243-95		2.66
Goalie Montreal, Colorado				(1985-present)
36. Charlie Conacher	459	225	173	398
Right Winger Toronto, Detroit, New York Americans				(1929-41)
37. Jaromir Jagr	662	345	517	862
Right Winger Pittsburgh				(1990-present)
38. Marcel Dionne	1,348	731	1,040	1,771
Center Detroit, Los Angeles, Rangers				(1971-89)
39. Joe Malone	125	146	21	167
Center Montreal, Quebec, Hamilton				(1917-24)
40. Chris Chelios	1,076	165	633	798
Defenseman Montreal, Chicago, Detroit				(1985-present)
41. Dit Clapper	833	228	246	474
Defenseman Boston				(1927-47)
42. Bernie Geoffrion	883	393	429	822
Right Winger Montreal, Rangers				(1950-68)
43. Tim Horton	1,446	115	403	518
Defenseman Toronto, Rangers, Pittsburgh, Buffalo				(1952-74)
44. Bill Cook	474	229	138	367
Right Winger Rangers				(1926-37)
45. Johnny Bucyk	1,540	556	813	1,369
Left Winger Detroit, Boston				(1955-78)
46. George Hainsworth	465	246-145-74		1.91
Goalie Montreal, Toronto				(1926-37)
47. Gilbert Perreault	1,191	512	814	1,326
Center Buffalo				(1970-87)
48. Max Bentley	646	245	299	544
Center Chicago, Toronto, Rangers				(1940-54)
49. Brad Park	1,113	213	683	896
Defenseman Rangers, Boston, Detroit				(1968-85)
50. Jari Kurri	1,251	601	797	1,398
Right Winger Edmonton, Los Angeles, Rangers, Anaheim, Colorado				(1980-98)

Don Dixon

BOBBY ORR AND WAYNE GRETZKY BOTH REVOLUTIONIZED THE GAME: THE ONE BIG DIFFERENCE IS THAT GRETZKY WON NINE HART TROPHIES TO ORR'S THREE.

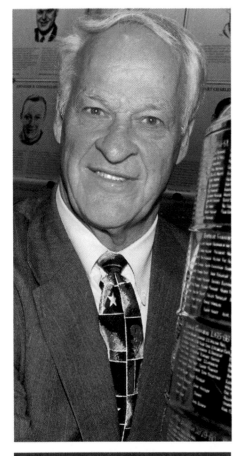

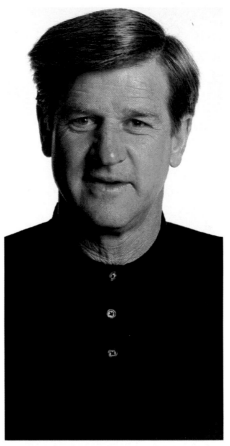

howe vs. gretzky

orr vs. gretzky

lemieux vs. gretzky

Wayne Gretzky eclipsed the majority of Gordie Howe's significant milestones, but Mr. Hockey still has a statistical edge in some categories of note. Below is a comparison of the pair's career numbers. All but the last five are restricted to their NHL careers. The final five are a combination of NHL and World Hockey Association regular season and playoffs.

Comparing the first nine seasons of Wayne Gretzky's and Bobby Orr's careers is more appropriate than some would think. The Great One played exactly nine seasons before being traded to Los Angeles. Orr left Boston for Chicago after nine full seasons and an injury-shortened 10-game 10th season. Below are the two megastars' totals after nine seasons each, including games, maximum number of games each could have played and what percentage that represents. Below that are the regular season standards set over that time. Only Orr's record for goals by a defenseman has been eclipsed (48 by Paul Coffey).

Mario Lemieux's career averages are superior to Gretzky's, but judged over the same number of games–the 745-game length of Mario's career–Gretzky edges Lemieux in goals and far exceeds him in points.

CATEGORY	Howe	Gretzky
Seasons	26	20
Games	1,767	1,487
Goals	801	894
Assists	1,049	1,963
Points	1,850	2,857
Penalty minutes	1,685	577
100-point seasons	1	15
50-goal seasons	0	9
40-goal seasons	5	12
30-goal seasons	14	14
Top five finishes in points	20	16
Stanley Cup	4	4
Hart Trophy	6	9
Conn Smythe Trophy	0	2
Art Ross Trophy	6	10
First All-Star	12	8
Second All-Star	9	7
Total All-Stars	21	15
NHL/WHA total seasons	32	21
NHL/WHA total games	2,421	1,788
NHL/WHA total goals	1,071	1,072
NHL/WHA total assists	1,518	2,297
NHL/WHA total points	2,589	3,369

REGULAR SEASON	Orr	Gretzky
Seasons	1966-75	1979-88
Games/NHL	621/688	696/720
Games Pct.	90%	97%
Stanley Cup	2	4
Hart Trophy	3	8
Conn Smythe Trophy	2	2
Art Ross Trophy	2	7
Norris Trophy	8	–
First All-Star	8	7
Second All-Star	1	2

GRETZKY'S REGULAR SEASON RECORDS

Category	Record	Previous	Increase	Pct.
Goals	92	76	16	21%
Assists	163	102	61	60%
Points	215	152	63	41%

ORR'S REGULAR SEASON DEFENSEMAN RECORDS

Category	Record	Previous	Increase	Pct.
Goals	46	24	22	92%
Assists	102	52	50	96%
Points	139	63	80	121%

REGULAR SEASON	Lemieux	Gretzky
Seasons	12	20
Games	745	1,487
Goals (per game)	613 (.823)	894 (.601)
Assists (per game)	881 (1.18)	1,963 (1.32)
Points (per game)	1,494 (2.01)	2,857 (1.92)
Hart Trophy	3	9
Art Ross Trophy	6	10
First 745 NHL GP	**Lemieux**	**Gretzky**
Goals	613	616
Assists	881	1,158
Points	1,494	1,774
Season Highs	**Lemieux**	**Gretzky**
Goals	85	92
Assists	114	163
Points	199	215
Goals per game	1.15	1.18
Assists per game	1.52	2.03
Points per game	2.67	2.77
PLAYOFFS	**Lemieux**	**Gretzky**
Stanley Cup	2	4
Games	89	208
Goals (per game)	70 (.797)	122 (.587)
Assists (per game)	85 (.955)	260 (1.25)
Points (per game)	155 (1.74)	382 (1.84)
Conn Smythe Trophy	2	2
Playoff Scoring Title	2	6

Who Is The ATHLETE Of The Century?

By MARK BRENDER

B y the eve of the 1999 playoffs and the historic first post-season game for the Carolina Hurricanes, a singularly uninterested newspaper columnist from Raleigh, N.C. had been subjected to all the hockey hype he could stand.

"The thing is, we have never liked hockey, we are not about to start liking hockey just because a pro team comes here, and we won't miss hockey if it moves on," wrote one Dennis Rogers of the Raleigh *News and Observer*. "We can't even get up enough passion to hate it. It simply bores us."

Mr. Rogers went on to denounce those fans who have some absurd "fixation" that hockey is the best of all possible games. "It's sounds as if some of you think we're a bunch of 'Hee Haw'-watchin', cousin-marryin', pickup truck drivin' rednecks too dumb to get it," he said. "*Au contraire*. We get it. We just don't want it."

And just think, that's 11 years after Wayne Gretzky moved to L.A. and opened up the South.

So it's safe to say even though Wayne is gone, his work as hockey missionary isn't done. It's also a safe bet none of the three other major professional sports would find a similar pocket of contempt anywhere in the continental United States. But Gary Bettman can take solace: if they aren't talking about you, you're not even on the map.

A generation from now, that may be Gretzky's lasting legacy, putting hockey on the map (Carolina excepted). And here's a related thought: only Gretzky, the ambassador,

GOAL NO. 984: THE LAST GOAL OF GRETZKY'S CAREER, MARCH 29, 1999. NO. 99'S CAREER GOAL TOTAL IS BUT ONE OF DOZENS OF NHL RECORDS THAT MAY NEVER BE SERIOUSLY CHALLENGED. GRETZKY IS THE MOST STATISTICALLY DOMINANT ATHLETE IN NORTH AMERICAN TEAM PRO SPORTS HISTORY.

could have created the climate for comparing Gretzky, the player, with his true sporting peers, legends like Michael Jordan, Babe Ruth and Jim Brown. That's because as much as Canadians loved their game before Gretzky their enthusiasm wasn't widely shared. They liked it that way, sure, but their heroes never received due acclaim outside the sport. Telling a Californian that Rocket Richard was no less a cultural beacon than Babe Ruth would have been akin to including for consideration the fellow who rewrote the team handball record books. Wasn't going to happen.

But 20 years after Gretzky entered the NHL, there's hockey all over North America. That has created legitimacy for the sport, which in turn makes comparisons possible and practical as well. Gretzky comes out of the lineup of legends looking pretty darn good.

He holds 61 NHL records, including most career goals, assists and points. He led his league in goals five times, points 11 times and assists 16 times (including from ages 19 to 31 inclusive). He won four Stanley Cups. He holds single-season records for goals, assists and points.

Between 1981-82 and 1986-87, his average margin of victory in the scoring race was 73. Before Gretzky came along, nobody had won by more than 26. He won the Hart Trophy eight years in a row. In comparison, nobody has ever won baseball's MVP for either the American or National League more than two years in a row. No wonder Gretzky wasn't allowed in hockey pools.

Now let's not kid ourselves, the competition for the title of North America's top professional team athlete of the century isn't chopped liver.

Jordan's six National Basketball Association championships, five MVP awards, six NBA Finals MVPs, 10 scoring titles and a record 31.5 career point-per-game average are nothing to sneeze at. When it came to crunch time, there was none better.

And as the premier baseball player and sporting icon of the 1920s, Ruth's swagger and swat were bigger than the game. His pitching record of $29^2/_3$ consecutive scoreless innings in the World Series lasted until 1961. As a hitter, he broke his own Major League Baseball home run record by 25 with 54 homers in 1920.

His 60-homer season in 1927 stood until Roger Maris knocked out 61 in 1961. Ruth's career home run record of 714 stood 39 years until Hank Aaron broke it in 1974. Ruth was walked a record 170 times in 1923. His mark of 457 total bases in 1921 has never been neared. For instance, in 1998, the year they both broke Maris' home run record, Sammy Sosa (416 total bases) and Mark McGwire (383), didn't come close.

Brown, for his part, was as dominant a player as the National Football League has ever known. He led the NFL in rushing eight seasons, five of them consecutively. Nobody else has led in more than four. He finished his career with a best-ever average gain of 5.22 yards.

Of course, there are other greats who wouldn't be out of place on this list. Among them are baseball's Ted Williams and Joe DiMaggio, football's John Elway, Walter Payton and Jerry Rice, and basketball's Wilt Chamberlain–and hockey's Gordie Howe and Bobby Orr.

But certainly it says something about Gretzky's status that he and baseball's Jackie Robinson are the only two athletes in North America, maybe the world, to have their numbers retired not just by their team, but by their entire profession.

Imagine Mount Rushmore marking the elite of professional team athletes. Jordan would be there, smiling, selling his shoes.

Brown would be there, maybe smiling, maybe growling, selling the world on his acting skills. Ruth would be there, selling cigars, looking for a whiskey and a light. And the blond-haired boy from Brantford would be there, too, smiling, selling his game.

So if you don't like his product and get called a redneck, Mr. Rogers, well, we're sorry. But there's not much to be done for the dinosaurs. **99**

the case for gretzky	the case for jordan	the case for ruth	the case for brown
Longevity	**Longevity**	**Longevity**	**Longevity**
20 NHL seasons, 1979-99	13 NBA seasons, 1985-98	22 MLB seasons, 1914-35	9 NFL seasons, 1957-65
Stats	**Stats**	**Stats**	**Stats**
Holds every NHL career and single-season regular season and playoff scoring record of significance, including 11 scoring titles.	Holds regular season (31.5) and playoff (33.4) records for career points-per-game average, 10 regular season scoring titles.	Held career home run record (714) for 39 years and single-season mark (60) for 34 years. Led American League in homers 12 times.	Led NFL in rushing eight seasons and touchdowns five seasons–both records. Average gain of 5.22 yards is all-time best.
Championships	**Championships**	**Championships**	**Championships**
Four Stanley Cups	Six NBA titles	Seven World Series	Two NFL titles
MVP	**MVP**	**MVP**	**MVP**
Nine regular season, Two playoffs	Five regular season, Six NBA Finals MVP	Most Valuable Player wasn't selected most of career	Two regular season
Can he be surpassed?	**Can he be surpassed?**	**Can he be surpassed?**	**Can he be surpassed?**
Next to impossible. No current player has a hope of knocking off his career marks and his single-season standards–92 goals, 163 assists and 215 points–are all but beyond reach.	Shaquille O'Neal entered his seventh season with a 27.2 PPG average. It's unlikely he or Allen Iverson will do it, though it's not inconceivable. Jordan's six NBA Finals MVP awards should be safe.	Ruth's two most significant marks—60 homers in a season and 714 in a career—have been topped. Roger Maris hit 61 in 1961 and Mark McGwire hit 70 in 1998. Hank Aaron finished with 755 all-time homers.	Someone may break Brown's mark of leading in rushing eight years...but not likely in nine seasons. No active NFL player is above a career mark of over five yards a carry.

THE FAREWELL

APRIL 18, 1999, MARKED THE END OF AN ERA, HIS ERA

THE NUMBERS

NOTHING DEFINES THE GREAT ONE'S CAREER BETTER THAN HIS OTHERWORLDLY STATS

The Record: Start to Finish

The most comprehensive statistical breakdown ever produced of Wayne Gretzky's numbers-filled career kicks off with a revelation. There is a mistake in No. 99's official scoring record–one that can be corrected now.

All biographies credit Gretzky with 64 regular season games with the Sault Ste. Marie Greyhounds of the Ontario Major Junior Hockey League (OMJHL) in 1977-78. But in responding to a request for Gretzky's major junior game-by-game scoring since playing three games with the Peterborough Petes in 1976-77, the Ontario League discovered he actually played only 63 games.

What's at the root of the mistake?

Gretzky missed five games, not four, of a 68-game regular season while starring for Canada at the World Junior Championship that year. Gretzky's 1977-78 bottom line properly reads: 63 games, 70 goals, 112 assists and 182 points. That means he played a total of 66 major junior games over two seasons, not 67, as long recorded.

What follows in this section is Gretzky's season-by-season, game-by-game goal, assist and point totals and each season's running tally, capped off by season and ongoing career totals (OHL, World Hockey Association, National Hockey League), including plus-minus (when available), penalty minutes, power play goals, shorthanded goals and game-winning goals.

Also listed are NHL playoff, All-Star Game and international competition totals. Single asterisks (*) indicate league- and tournament-leading totals and double asterisks (**) indicate NHL single and career regular season, playoff and All-Star Game records. Each season's package includes a context bar chart that relates a key Gretzky stat or fact to that (or those) of peers, plus a listing of milestone accomplishments and events.

Covered are Gretzky's one-plus seasons in the OHL, single season in the WHA and 20 in the NHL.

It all begins with a minor rewriting of history.

		REGULAR SEASON									PLAYOFFS							
Ontario Major Junior Hockey League	GP	G	A	Pts.	+/–	PIM	PP	SH	GW	GP	G	A	Pts.	PIM	PP	SH	GW
1976-77 Peterborough Petes	3	0	3	3	–	–	–	–	–	–	–	–	–	–	–	–	–
1977-78 Sault Ste. Marie Greyhounds	63	70	112	182	–	14	21	7	7	13	6	20	26	0	4	0	2
OHL TOTALS	**66**	**70**	**115**	**185**	**–**	**14**	**21**	**7**	**7**	**13**	**6**	**20**	**26**	**0**	**4**	**0**	**2**
World Hockey Association	GP	G	A	Pts.	+/–	PIM	PP	SH	GW	GP	G	A	Pts.	PIM	PP	SH	GW
1978-79 Indianapolis Racers	8	3	3	6	–	0	–	–	–	–	–	–	–	–	–	–	–
Edmonton Oilers	72	43	61	104	–	19				13	*10	10	*20	2	–	–	–
WHA TOTALS	**80**	**46**	**64**	**110**	**–**	**19**	**–**	**–**	**–**	**13**	**10**	**10**	**20**	**2**	**–**	**–**	**–**
National Hockey League	GP	G	A	Pts.	+/–	PIM	PP	SH	GW	GP	G	A	Pts.	PIM	PP	SH	GW
1979-80 Edmonton Oilers	79	51	*86	*137	+15	21	13	1	6	3	2	1	3	0	0	0	0
1980-81 Edmonton Oilers	80	55	**109	**164	+41	28	15	4	3	9	7	14	21	4	2	1	1
1981-82 Edmonton Oilers	80	**92	**120	**212	+81	26	18	6	12	5	5	7	12	8	1	1	1
1982-83 Edmonton Oilers	80	*71	**125	*196	+60	59	18	6	9	16	12	**26	**38	4	2	3	3
1983-84 Edmonton Oilers	74	*87	*118	*205	+76	39	20	12	11	19	13	*22	*35	12	2	0	3
1984-85 Edmonton Oilers	80	*73	**135	*208	+98	52	8	11	7	18	17	**30	**47	4	4	2	3
1985-86 Edmonton Oilers	80	52	**163	**215	+71	46	11	3	6	10	8	11	19	2	4	1	2
1986-87 Edmonton Oilers	79	*62	*121	*183	+70	28	13	7	4	21	5	*29	*34	6	2	0	0
1987-88 Edmonton Oilers	64	40	*109	149	+39	24	9	5	3	19	12	**31	*43	16	5	1	3
1988-89 Los Angeles Kings	78	54	*114	168	+15	26	11	5	5	11	5	17	22	0	1	1	0
1989-90 Los Angeles Kings	73	40	*102	*142	+8	42	10	4	4	7	3	7	10	0	1	0	0
1990-91 Los Angeles Kings	78	41	*122	*163	+30	16	8	0	5	12	4	11	15	2	1	0	2
1991-92 Los Angeles Kings	74	31	*90	121	–12	34	12	2	2	6	2	5	7	2	1	0	0
1992-93 Los Angeles Kings	45	16	49	65	+6	6	0	2	1	24	*15	*25	*40	4	4	1	3
1993-94 Los Angeles Kings	81	38	*92	*130	–25	20	14	4	0	–	–	–	–	–	–	–	–
1994-95 Los Angeles Kings	48	11	37	48	–20	6	3	0	1	–	–	–	–	–	–	–	–
1995-96 Los Angeles Kings	62	15	66	81	–7	32	5	0	2	–	–	–	–	–	–	–	–
St. Louis Blues	18	8	13	21	–6	2	1	1	1	13	2	14	16	0	1	0	1
Totals	80	23	79	102	–13	34	6	1	3	13	2	14	16	0	1	0	1
1996-97 New York Rangers	82	25	*72	97	+12	28	6	0	2	15	10	10	20	2	3	0	2
1997-98 New York Rangers	82	23	*67	90	–11	28	6	0	4	–	–	–	–	–	–	–	–
1998-99 New York Rangers	70	9	53	62	–23	14	3	0	3	–	–	–	–	–	–	–	–
NHL TOTALS	**1,487**	**894	**1,963	**2,857	**+518**	**577**	**204**	**73**	**91**	**208**	**122	**260	**382	**66**	**34**	**11**	**24**

1976-77, 1977-78: OMJHL Seasons

Member of 1976-77 Peterborough Petes

Date	Opponent	G	A	Pts.	G	A	Pts.
1. Nov. 27	Sault Ste. Marie	0	1	1	0	1	1
2. Dec. 9	Kingston	0	0	0	0	1	1
3. Jan. 8	Windsor	0	2	2	0	3	3

	GP	G	A	Pts.	+/–	PIM	PP	SH	GW
1976-77	3	0	3	3	–	0	0	0	0

	GP	G	A	Pts.	+/–	PIM	PP	SH	GW
Career	3	0	3	3	–	0	0	0	0

Member of 1977-78 Sault Ste. Marie Greyhounds

Date	Opponent	G	A	Pts.	G	A	Pts.
1. Sept. 24	Oshawa	3	3	6	3	3	6
2. Sept. 27	Sudbury	0	2	2	3	5	8
3. Sept. 29	Windsor	1	0	1	4	5	9
4. Sept. 30	London	3	3	6	7	8	15
5. Oct. 2	Oshawa	1	0	1	8	8	16
6. Oct. 7	Toronto	1	2	3	9	10	19
7. Oct. 9	Ottawa	1	6	7	10	16	26
8. Oct. 13	Kitchener	2	0	2	12	16	28
9. Oct. 16	London	1	2	3	13	18	31
10. Oct. 18	Hamilton	0	1	1	13	19	32
11. Oct. 21	Ottawa	1	2	3	14	21	35
12. Oct. 23	Peterborough	2	1	3	16	22	38
13. Oct. 27	Kingston	1	3	4	17	25	42
14. Oct. 28	Niagara Falls	1	2	3	18	27	45
15. Oct. 30	Kingston	0	2	2	18	29	47
16. Nov. 3	Toronto	0	3	3	18	32	50
17. Nov. 6	Windsor	2	3	5	20	35	55
18. Nov. 11	Niagara Falls	1	0	1	21	35	56
19. Nov. 13	Peterborough	3	4	7	24	39	63
20. Nov. 16	Sudbury	0	3	3	24	42	66
21. Nov. 18	Niagara Falls	1	0	1	25	42	67
22. Nov. 19	Toronto	1	3	4	26	45	71
23. Nov. 20	Kitchener	1	3	4	27	48	75
24. Nov. 24	Ottawa	0	0	0	27	48	75
25. Nov. 26	Oshawa	2	1	3	29	49	78
26. Nov. 27	Kingston	1	0	1	30	49	79
27. Nov. 29	Sudbury	2	1	3	32	50	82
28. Dec. 1	Windsor	0	1	1	32	51	83
29. Dec. 2	London	0	4	4	32	55	87
30. Dec. 9	Oshawa	0	0	0	32	55	87
31. Dec. 12	Niagara Falls	3	2	5	35	57	92
32. Dec. 15	Peterborough	1	2	3	36	59	95
33. Dec. 16	Ottawa	Did not play			36	59	95
34. Dec. 18	Sudbury	Did not play			36	59	95
35. Dec. 20	Toronto	Did not play			36	59	95
36. Dec. 21	Oshawa	Did not play			36	59	95
37. Dec. 30	Kingston	Did not play			36	59	95
38. Jan. 3	Niagara Falls	0	4	4	36	63	99
39. Jan. 5	Oshawa	2	1	3	38	64	102
40. Jan. 6	Ottawa	0	2	2	38	66	104
41. Jan. 7	Peterborough	1	1	2	39	67	106
42. Jan. 8	Hamilton	0	0	0	39	67	106
43. Jan. 13	Peterborough	2	2	4	41	69	110
44. Jan. 14	Hamilton	1	4	5	42	73	115
45. Jan. 19	Sudbury	2	4	6	44	77	121
46. Jan. 20	Sudbury	3	3	6	47	80	127
47. Jan. 22	Toronto	2	0	2	49	80	129
48. Jan. 28	Kitchener	1	0	1	50	80	130
49. Jan. 29	Hamilton	0	0	0	50	80	130
50. Jan. 31	Windsor	2	1	3	52	81	133
51. Feb. 2	Windsor	0	1	1	52	82	134
52. Feb. 3	London	2	2	4	54	84	138
53. Feb. 5	Peterborough	0	3	3	54	87	141
54. Feb. 9	Hamilton	2	0	2	56	87	143
55. Feb. 12	London	0	0	0	56	87	143
56. Feb. 16	Kitchener	3	1	4	59	88	147
57. Feb. 19	Ottawa	1	0	1	60	88	148
58. Feb. 25	Kitchener	2	2	4	62	90	152
59. Feb. 26	Hamilton	1	1	2	63	91	154
60. Mar. 3	Kingston	1	2	3	64	93	157
61. Mar. 4	Niagara Falls	0	2	2	64	95	159
62. Mar. 5	Toronto	1	1	2	65	96	161
63. Mar. 7	Sudbury	0	2	2	65	98	163
64. Mar. 10	Windsor	0	7	7	65	105	170
65. Mar. 12	Kitchener	0	2	2	65	107	172
66. Mar. 14	Sudbury	0	2	2	65	109	174
67. Mar. 17	Kingston	2	2	4	67	111	178
68. Mar. 19	London	3	1	4	70	112	182

	GP	G	A	Pts.	+/–	PIM	PP	SH	GW
1977-78	63	70	112	182	–	14	21	7	7

	GP	G	A	Pts.	+/–	PIM	PP	SH	GW
Career	66	70	115	185	–	14	21	7	7

playoffs

Date	Opponent	G	A	Pts.	G	A	Pts.
1. Mar. 21	Kingston	0	1	1	0	1	1
2. Mar. 23	Kingston	3	1	4	3	2	5
3. Mar. 25	Kingston	0	1	1	3	3	6
4. Mar. 26	Kingston	1	3	4	4	6	10
5. Mar. 27	Kingston	0	3	3	4	9	13
6. Mar. 28	Ottawa	1	0	1	5	9	14
7. Mar. 30	Ottawa	0	3	3	5	12	17
8. Mar. 31	Ottawa	0	0	0	5	12	17
9. Apr. 2	Ottawa	0	3	3	5	15	20
10. Apr. 4	Ottawa	0	2	2	5	17	22
11. Apr. 6	Ottawa	0	1	1	5	18	23
12. Apr. 7	Ottawa	0	2	2	5	20	25
13. Apr. 9	Ottawa	1	0	1	6	20	26

Totals

	GP	G	A	Pts.	PIM	PP	SH	GW
1977-78	13	6	20	26	0	4	0	2

	GP	G	A	Pts.	PIM	PP	SH	GW
Career	13	6	20	26	0	4	0	2

Legend GP games played, G goals, A assists, Pts. points, +/– plus minus, PIM penalty minutes, PP power play goals, SH shorthanded goals, GW game-winning goal, * league- or tournament-leading total, ** record total

1978-79: WHA Season

Date	Opponent	G	A	Pts.	G	A	Pts.
1. Oct. 14	Winnipeg	0	0	0	0	0	0
2. Oct. 15	Birmingham	0	0	0	0	0	0
3. Oct. 18	Quebec	0	1	1	0	1	1
4. Oct. 20	Edmonton	2	0	2	2	1	3
5. Oct. 22	New England	1	1	2	3	2	5
6. Oct. 27	Birmingham	0	1	1	3	3	6
7. Oct. 28	Winnipeg	0	0	0	3	3	6
8. Oct. 29	Winnipeg	0	0	0	3	3	6
Nov. 2	Sold to Edmonton						
9. Nov. 3	Winnipeg	1	0	1	4	3	7
10. Nov. 5	Quebec	0	0	0	4	3	7
11. Nov. 8	Quebec	0	1	1	4	4	8
12. Nov. 9	New England	1	0	1	5	4	9
13. Nov. 11	Birmingham	0	1	1	5	5	10
14. Nov. 12	Cincinnati	1	1	2	6	6	12
15. Nov. 17	Indianapolis	2	0	2	8	6	14
16. Nov. 19	Cincinnati	0	3	3	8	9	17
17. Nov. 21	Quebec	1	0	1	9	9	18
18. Nov. 24	Quebec	0	1	1	9	10	19
19. Nov. 28	Indianapolis	0	1	1	9	11	20
20. Dec. 1	New England	0	0	0	9	11	20
21. Dec. 3	New England	0	0	0	9	11	20
22. Dec. 6	Quebec	2	0	2	11	11	22
23. Dec. 7	New England	0	1	1	11	12	23
24. Dec. 9	Birmingham	1	0	1	12	12	24
25. Dec. 10	Indianapolis	0	0	0	12	12	24
26. Dec. 12	Cincinnati	3	0	3	15	12	27
27. Dec. 15	Soviet All-Stars	0	1	1	15	13	28
28. Dec. 19	Birmingham	1	0	1	16	13	29
29. Dec. 22	Winnipeg	0	2	2	16	15	31
30. Dec. 26	Winnipeg	0	0	0	16	15	31
31. Dec. 27	Winnipeg	1	0	1	17	15	32
32. Dec. 30	Czechoslovakia	0	2	2	17	17	34
33. Jan. 9	Winnipeg	0	1	1	17	18	35
34. Jan. 13	New England	3	0	3	20	18	38
35. Jan. 16	Winnipeg	0	1	1	20	19	39
36. Jan. 17	Winnipeg	0	1	1	20	20	40
37. Jan. 19	Birmingham	2	2	4	22	22	44
38. Jan. 21	Birmingham	0	0	0	22	22	44
39. Jan. 23	New England	1	1	2	23	23	46
40. Jan. 26	Cincinnati	0	1	1	23	24	47
41. Jan. 28	Cincinnati	1	0	1	24	24	48
42. Jan. 31	Winnipeg	0	1	1	24	25	49
43. Feb. 2	Winnipeg	0	0	0	24	25	49
44. Feb. 4	Quebec	0	0	0	24	25	49
45. Feb. 6	Birmingham	2	1	3	26	26	52
46. Feb. 7	Cincinnati	0	1	1	26	27	53
47. Feb. 9	Quebec	1	1	2	27	28	55
48. Feb. 11	Birmingham	0	2	2	27	30	57
49. Feb. 13	Quebec	1	2	3	28	32	60
50. Feb. 16	New England	1	0	1	29	32	61
51. Feb. 18	Birmingham	0	0	0	29	32	61
52. Feb. 20	New England	0	4	4	29	36	65
53. Feb. 23	Cincinnati	1	0	1	30	36	66
54. Feb. 25	Birmingham	1	1	2	31	37	68
55. Feb. 27	New England	0	0	0	31	37	68
56. Mar. 2	Cincinnati	0	2	2	31	39	70
57. Mar. 3	Cincinnati	0	2	2	31	41	72
58. Mar. 6	Quebec	1	1	2	32	42	74
59. Mar. 7	Quebec	1	0	1	33	42	75
60. Mar. 9	Birmingham	0	2	2	33	44	77
61. Mar. 11	Birmingham	0	3	3	33	47	80
62. Mar. 13	Cincinnati	0	0	0	33	47	80
63. Mar. 16	Quebec	0	0	0	33	47	80
64. Mar. 18	Quebec	0	1	1	33	48	81
65. Mar. 20	Finland	1	0	1	34	48	82
66. Mar. 21	Winnipeg	0	2	2	34	50	84
67. Mar. 23	Winnipeg	1	0	1	35	50	85
68. Mar. 25	Cincinnati	0	0	0	35	50	85
69. Mar. 28	Quebec	0	0	0	35	50	85
70. Mar. 30	New England	0	1	1	35	51	86
71. Apr. 1	New England	0	2	2	35	53	88
72. Apr. 3	Cincinnati	1	0	1	36	53	89
73. Apr. 4	Quebec	0	0	0	36	53	89
74. Apr. 6	New England	2	2	4	38	55	93
75. Apr. 8	Birmingham	0	2	2	38	57	95
76. Apr. 10	Winnipeg	3	1	4	41	58	99
77. Apr. 13	Birmingham	1	1	2	42	59	101
78. Apr. 14	Birmingham	0	3	3	42	62	104
79. Apr. 15	New England	3	1	4	45	63	108
80. Apr. 18	Winnipeg	1	1	2	46	64	110

	GP	G	A	Pts.	+/-	PIM	PP	SH	GW
1978-79	80	46	64	110	–	19	–	–	–
	GP	G	A	Pts.	+/-	PIM	PP	SH	GW
Career	80	46	64	110	–	19	–	–	–

context

WHA point totals by Gretzky and Messier as 17-year-olds

Wayne Gretzky	110
11 Mark Messier	

Messier

milestones

1. Oct. 18 Earns first pro assist on Richie Leduc's goal against Quebec's Richard Brodeur at 16:13 of first period

2. Oct. 20 Beats Edmonton's Dave Dryden at 6:37 of second period for first pro goal; gets second four seconds later

3. Nov. 2 Is sold to Edmonton along with Eddie Mio and Peter Driscoll in $850,000 deal

4. Dec. 12 Records first of four WHA hat tricks

5. April 18 Finishes regular season third overall in goals (46) and points (110), fifth in assists (64)

6. May 20 Finishes playoffs first in goals (10) and points (20), third in assists (10)

7. Named WHA rookie of the year

playoffs

Date	Opponent	G	A	Pts.	G	A	Pts.
1. Apr. 26	New England	0	1	1	0	1	1
2. Apr. 27	New England	1	3	4	1	4	5
3. Apr. 29	New England	1	0	1	2	4	6
4. May 1	New England	1	1	2	3	5	8
5. May 3	New England	3	0	3	6	5	11
6. May 5	New England	0	2	2	6	7	13
7. May 8	New England	2	0	2	8	7	15
8. May 11	Winnipeg	0	0	0	8	7	15
9. May 13	Winnipeg	0	0	0	8	7	15

Date	Opponent	G	A	Pts.	G	A	Pts.
10. May 15	Winnipeg	0	2	2	8	9	17
11. May 16	Winnipeg	1	1	2	9	10	19
12. May 18	Winnipeg	1	0	1	10	10	20
13. May 20	Winnipeg	0	0	0	10	10	20

Totals	GP	G	A	Pts.	PIM	PP	SH	GW
1979-80	13	10	10	20	2	–	–	–
	GP	**G**	**A**	**Pts.**	**PIM**	**PP**	**SH**	**GW**
Career	13	10	10	20	2	–	–	–

1979-80: NHL Season No. 1

Date	Opponent	G	A	Pts.	G	A	Pts.
1. Oct. 10	Chicago	0	1	1	0	1	1
2. Oct. 13	Detroit	0	1	1	0	2	2
3. Oct. 14	Vancouver	1	1	2	1	3	4
4. Oct. 19	Quebec	0	3	3	1	6	7
5. Oct. 21	Minnesota	1	1	2	2	7	9
6. Oct. 23	Islanders	0	1	1	2	8	10
7. Oct. 24	Rangers	0	0	0	2	8	10
8. Oct. 26	Atlanta	0	0	0	2	8	10
9. Oct. 28	Washington	0	0	0	2	8	10
10. Oct. 30	St. Louis	Did not play					
11. Nov. 2	Islanders	2	1	3	4	9	13
12. Nov. 4	Boston	0	1	1	4	10	14
13. Nov. 7	Detroit	1	1	2	5	11	16
14. Nov. 8	Boston	0	0	0	5	11	16
15. Nov. 11	Toronto	0	2	2	5	13	18
16. Nov. 13	Washington	1	1	2	6	14	20
17. Nov. 15	Philadelphia	0	2	2	6	16	22
18. Nov. 17	Hartford	0	0	0	6	16	22
19. Nov. 18	Buffalo	1	2	3	7	18	25
20. Nov. 21	Toronto	2	2	4	9	20	29
21. Nov. 24	Philadelphia	0	1	1	9	21	30
22. Nov. 28	Chicago	0	2	2	9	23	32
23. Nov. 30	Islanders	1	2	3	10	25	35
24. Dec. 5	Minnesota	0	0	0	10	25	35
25. Dec. 7	Winnipeg	0	0	0	10	25	35
26. Dec. 9	Hartford	1	1	2	11	26	37
27. Dec. 12	Atlanta	0	1	1	11	27	38
28. Dec. 14	Montreal	1	1	2	12	28	40
29. Dec. 16	Winnipeg	1	1	2	13	29	42
30. Dec. 19	Detroit	2	1	3	15	30	45
31. Dec. 21	Colorado	0	1	1	15	31	46
32. Dec. 22	Los Angeles	2	1	3	17	32	49
33. Dec. 26	Colorado	1	1	2	18	33	51
34. Dec. 28	Vancouver	1	0	1	19	33	52
35. Dec. 30	Quebec	0	1	1	19	34	53
36. Jan. 2	Hartford	0	1	1	19	35	54
37. Jan. 5	Los Angeles	2	0	2	21	35	56
38. Jan. 7	Montreal	0	0	0	21	35	56
39. Jan. 9	Quebec	1	0	1	22	35	57
40. Jan. 11	Rangers	0	1	1	22	36	58
41. Jan. 13	Buffalo	0	2	2	22	38	60
42. Jan. 16	Washington	1	1	2	23	39	62

Date	Opponent	G	A	Pts.	G	A	Pts.
43. Jan. 17	Boston	0	0	0	23	39	62
44. Jan. 19	Pittsburgh	2	2	4	25	41	66
45. Jan. 20	Buffalo	0	1	1	25	42	67
46. Jan. 23	Pittsburgh	1	1	2	26	43	69
47. Jan. 26	Toronto	0	2	2	26	45	71
48. Jan. 27	Philadelphia	1	1	2	27	46	73
49. Jan. 29	St. Louis	0	0	0	27	46	73
50. Jan. 30	Los Angeles	1	4	5	28	50	78
51. Feb. 1	Winnipeg	3	1	4	31	51	82
52. Feb. 3	Los Angeles	1	1	2	32	52	84
53. Feb. 6	St. Louis	1	2	3	33	54	87
54. Feb. 8	Atlanta	1	0	1	34	54	88
55. Feb. 10	Winnipeg	0	0	0	34	54	88
56. Feb. 13	Minnesota	0	1	1	34	55	89
57. Feb. 15	Washington	0	7	7	34	62	96
58. Feb. 17	St. Louis	1	2	3	35	64	99
59. Feb. 19	Hartford	0	0	0	35	64	99
60. Feb. 20	Rangers	0	0	0	35	64	99
61. Feb. 22	Colorado	0	0	0	35	64	99
62. Feb. 24	Boston	0	1	1	35	65	100
63. Feb. 27	Chicago	0	2	2	35	67	102
64. Feb. 29	Buffalo	0	1	1	35	68	103
65. Mar. 1	Vancouver	0	0	0	35	68	103
66. Mar. 4	Islanders	2	2	4	37	70	107
67. Mar. 6	Montreal	1	2	3	38	72	110
68. Mar. 8	Pittsburgh	1	1	2	39	73	112
69. Mar. 9	Philadelphia	0	1	1	39	74	113
70. Mar. 12	Quebec	2	0	2	41	74	115
71. Mar. 14	Chicago	0	0	0	41	74	115
72. Mar. 15	Montreal	1	0	1	42	74	116
73. Mar. 19	Rangers	0	1	1	42	75	117
74. Mar. 21	Pittsburgh	3	1	4	45	76	121
75. Mar. 25	Atlanta	2	2	4	47	78	125
76. Mar. 26	Detroit	0	2	2	47	80	127
77. Mar. 29	Toronto	2	4	6	49	84	133
78. Apr. 1	Vancouver	0	0	0	49	84	133
79. Apr. 2	Minnesota	1	0	1	50	84	134
80. Apr. 4	Colorado	1	2	3	51	86	137

	GP	G	A	Pts.	+/–	PIM	PP	SH	GW
1979-80	79	51	86*	137*	+15	21	13	1	6
	GP	G	A	Pts.	+/–	PIM	PP	SH	GW
Career	79	51	86	137	+15	21	13	1	6

context

NHL record point totals by 18-year-old first-year players

Wayne Gretzky '79-80 **137**
Dale Hawerchuk **103** '81-82

Hawerchuk

milestones

1. **Oct. 10** Records first assist on Kevin Lowe's goal against Chicago's Tony Esposito at 9:49 of first period
2. **Oct. 14** Scores first goal against Vancouver's Glen Hanlon at 18:51 of third period
3. **Feb. 1** Records first of 50 career NHL hat tricks
4. **Feb. 15** Has first of three seven-assist games, tying Billy Taylor's record for most in game
5. **April 2** Scores 50th goal against Buffalo's Don Edwards at 9:43 of second period, becoming youngest player to score 50 goals (19 years, two months)
6. **April 4** Ties Marcel Dionne for scoring title, but officially finishes second because Dionne has more goals (53-51); leads league in assists for first of 13 straight seasons
7. Named second all-star, league MVP, most gentlemanly player

playoffs

Date	Opponent	G	A	Pts.	G	A	Pts.
1. Apr. 8	Philadelphia	1	1	2	1	1	2
2. Apr. 9	Philadelphia	0	0	0	1	1	2
3. Apr. 11	Philadelphia	1	0	1	2	1	3

Totals

	GP	G	A	Pts.	PIM	PP	SH	GW
1979-80	3	2	1	3	0	0	0	0
	GP	**G**	**A**	**Pts.**	**PIM**	**PP**	**SH**	**GW**
Career	3	2	1	3	0	0	0	0

1980-81: NHL Season No. 2

	Date	Opponent	G	A	Pts.	G	A	Pts.
1.	Oct. 10	Quebec	2	1	3	2	1	3
2.	Oct. 12	Colorado	0	2	2	2	3	5
3.	Oct. 15	Buffalo	0	0	0	2	3	5
4.	Oct. 18	Islanders	2	1	3	4	4	8
5.	Oct. 19	Rangers	1	3	4	5	7	12
6.	Oct. 22	Calgary	0	2	2	5	9	14
7.	Oct. 24	Minnesota	0	0	0	5	9	14
8.	Oct. 26	Los Angeles	0	0	0	5	9	14
9.	Oct. 29	Toronto	0	2	2	5	11	16
10.	Nov. 1	Washington	0	0	0	5	11	16
11.	Nov. 3	Pittsburgh	2	0	2	7	11	18
12.	Nov. 5	Vancouver	0	2	2	7	13	20
13.	Nov. 7	Winnipeg	0	1	1	7	14	21
14.	Nov. 9	St. Louis	0	2	2	7	16	23
15.	Nov. 13	Philadelphia	0	0	0	7	16	23
16.	Nov. 15	Toronto	1	0	1	8	16	24
17.	Nov. 16	Chicago	1	2	3	9	18	27
18.	Nov. 19	Vancouver	0	2	2	9	20	29
19.	Nov. 23	Buffalo	0	1	1	9	21	30
20.	Nov. 25	Colorado	0	1	1	9	22	31
21.	Nov. 26	Chicago	1	4	5	10	26	36
22.	Nov. 28	Hartford	0	2	2	10	28	38
23.	Nov. 29	Boston	1	0	1	11	28	39
24.	Dec. 5	Rangers	1	0	1	12	28	40
25.	Dec. 7	Hartford	1	2	3	13	30	43
26.	Dec. 10	Islanders	0	0	0	13	30	43
27.	Dec. 13	Montreal	0	1	1	13	31	44
28.	Dec. 14	Quebec	0	1	1	13	32	45
29.	Dec. 16	Detroit	0	2	2	13	34	47
30.	Dec. 17	Washington	0	0	0	13	34	47
31.	Dec. 20	Montreal	0	1	1	13	35	48
32.	Dec. 23	Los Angeles	3	0	3	16	35	51
33.	Dec. 27	Detroit	0	3	3	16	38	54
34.	Dec. 29	Philadelphia	0	0	0	16	38	54
35.	Dec. 30	Calgary	1	1	2	17	39	56
36.	Jan. 2	Boston	0	1	1	17	40	57
37.	Jan. 3	Toronto	1	2	3	18	42	60
38.	Jan. 7	Washington	2	2	4	20	44	64
39.	Jan. 9	Hartford	0	1	1	20	45	65
40.	Jan. 11	Quebec	1	4	5	21	49	70
41.	Jan. 12	Montreal	0	0	0	21	49	70
42.	Jan. 14	Toronto	2	1	3	23	50	73
43.	Jan. 16	Buffalo	0	0	0	23	50	73
44.	Jan. 17	St. Louis	1	3	4	24	53	77
45.	Jan. 21	Vancouver	1	2	3	25	55	80
46.	Jan. 23	Rangers	0	2	2	25	57	82
47.	Jan. 24	Minnesota	0	1	1	25	58	83
48.	Jan. 28	Montreal	1	4	5	26	62	88
49.	Jan. 30	Chicago	1	2	3	27	64	91
50.	Feb. 1	Washington	0	2	2	27	66	93
51.	Feb. 3	St. Louis	0	0	0	27	66	93
52.	Feb. 4	Chicago	1	0	1	28	66	94
53.	Feb. 6	Winnipeg	3	3	6	31	69	100
54.	Feb. 8	Calgary	1	2	3	32	71	103
55.	Feb. 13	Quebec	1	0	1	33	71	104
56.	Feb. 15	Buffalo	0	1	1	33	72	105
57.	Feb. 18	St. Louis	5	2	7	38	74	112
58.	Feb. 20	Boston	0	0	0	38	74	112
59.	Feb. 21	Winnipeg	0	1	1	38	75	113
60.	Feb. 24	Los Angeles	1	0	1	39	75	114
61.	Feb. 25	Philadelphia	2	2	4	41	77	118
62.	Feb. 27	Detroit	1	1	2	42	78	120
63.	Feb. 28	Colorado	0	1	1	42	79	121
64.	Mar. 3	Islanders	2	2	4	44	81	125
65.	Mar. 4	Rangers	1	0	1	45	81	126
66.	Mar. 7	Philadelphia	4	0	4	49	81	130
67.	Mar. 8	Pittsburgh	0	1	1	49	82	131
68.	Mar. 12	Islanders	0	0	0	49	82	131
69.	Mar. 15	Calgary	1	0	1	50	82	132
70.	Mar. 16	Pittsburgh	0	3	3	50	85	135
71.	Mar. 18	Minnesota	0	4	4	50	89	139
72.	Mar. 20	Minnesota	1	0	1	51	89	140
73.	Mar. 21	Los Angeles	1	4	5	52	93	145
74.	Mar. 23	Boston	0	2	2	52	95	147
75.	Mar. 25	Hartford	1	3	4	53	98	151
76.	Mar. 28	Detroit	0	1	1	53	99	152
77.	Mar. 29	Pittsburgh	0	3	3	53	102	155
78.	Apr. 1	Colorado	0	2	2	53	104	157
79.	Apr. 3	Vancouver	1	1	2	54	105	159
80.	Apr. 4	Winnipeg	1	4	5	55	109	164

	GP	G	A	Pts.	+/–	PIM	PP	SH	GW
1980-81	80	55	**109	**164	+41	28	15	4	3
	GP	G	A	Pts.	+/–	PIM	PP	SH	GW
Career	159	106	195	301	+56	49	28	5	9

context

Timeline: NHL scoring records of more than 100 points in season

Wayne Gretzky
Phil Esposito

	'80-81	'81-82	'85-86
Wayne Gretzky	164	212	215

	'68-69	'70-71
Phil Esposito	126	152

Esposito

milestones

1. **Feb. 18** First of four career five-goal games; four goals in third period ties NHL record for most in period, shared by 10 others
2. **March 7** Fourth goal of game, an empty-netter, is 100th of career
3. **March 29** Breaks Phil Esposito's record of 152 points in season, set in 1970-71

4. **April 1** Breaks Bobby Orr's record of 102 assists in season, set in 1970-71
5. **April 4** Leads league in assists (109) and points (164) to win first of seven straight (10 altogether) Art Ross Trophies
6. Named first all-star, league MVP, starting stretch of seven consecutive seasons of winning both Hart and Art Ross Trophies

playoffs

	Date	Opponent	G	A	Pts.	G	A	Pts.
1.	Apr. 8	Montreal	0	5	5	0	5	5
2.	Apr. 9	Montreal	0	2	2	0	7	7
3.	Apr. 11	Montreal	3	1	4	3	8	11
4.	Apr. 16	Islanders	1	0	1	4	8	12
5.	Apr. 17	Islanders	0	1	1	4	9	13
6.	Apr. 19	Islanders	3	0	3	7	9	16
7.	Apr. 20	Islanders	0	2	2	7	11	18

	Date	Opponent	G	A	Pts.	G	A	Pts.
8.	Apr. 22	Islanders	0	2	2	7	13	20
9.	Apr. 24	Islanders	0	1	1	7	14	21

Totals

	GP	G	A	Pts.	PIM	PP	SH	GW
1980-81	9	7	14	21	4	2	1	1
	GP	G	A	Pts.	PIM	PP	SH	GW
Career	12	9	15	24	4	2	1	1

1981-82: NHL Season No. 3

Date	Opponent	G	A	Pts.	G	A	Pts.
1. Oct. 7	Colorado	0	1	1	0	1	1
2. Oct. 9	Vancouver	0	0	0	0	1	1
3. Oct. 10	Los Angeles	1	1	2	1	2	3
4. Oct. 14	Winnipeg	1	0	1	2	2	4
5. Oct. 16	Calgary	1	2	3	3	4	7
6. Oct. 18	Chicago	1	3	4	4	7	11
7. Oct. 20	Calgary	1	1	2	5	8	13
8. Oct. 21	Hartford	0	0	0	5	8	13
9. Oct. 23	Pittsburgh	1	1	2	6	9	15
10. Oct. 24	Colorado	1	1	2	7	10	17
11. Oct. 27	Islanders	0	1	1	7	11	18
12. Oct. 28	Rangers	2	2	4	9	13	22
13. Oct. 31	Quebec	4	1	5	13	14	27
14. Nov. 4	Toronto	2	0	2	15	14	29
15. Nov. 7	Colorado	0	0	0	15	14	29
16. Nov. 11	Hartford	2	1	3	17	15	32
17. Nov. 12	Boston	0	2	2	17	17	34
18. Nov. 14	Islanders	1	3	4	18	20	38
19. Nov. 15	Rangers	1	2	3	19	22	41
20. Nov. 17	St. Louis	2	1	3	21	23	44
21. Nov. 19	Minnesota	0	0	0	21	23	44
22. Nov. 21	Vancouver	2	2	4	23	25	48
23. Nov. 23	Detroit	1	1	2	24	26	50
24. Nov. 25	Los Angeles	4	1	5	28	27	55
25. Nov. 27	Chicago	2	3	5	30	30	60
26. Nov. 29	Winnipeg	1	3	4	31	33	64
27. Dec. 1	Montreal	0	3	3	31	36	67
28. Dec. 2	Quebec	0	2	2	31	38	69
29. Dec. 4	Vancouver	0	3	3	31	41	72
30. Dec. 5	Vancouver	0	2	2	31	43	74
31. Dec. 9	Los Angeles	1	0	1	32	43	75
32. Dec. 13	Islanders	1	3	4	33	46	79
33. Dec. 16	Colorado	1	2	3	34	48	82
34. Dec. 17	Calgary	1	0	1	35	48	83
35. Dec. 19	Minnesota	3	4	7	38	52	90
36. Dec. 20	Calgary	2	1	3	40	53	93
37. Dec. 23	Vancouver	1	3	4	41	56	97
38. Dec. 27	Los Angeles	4	1	5	45	57	102
39. Dec. 30	Philadelphia	5	1	6	50	58	108
40. Dec. 31	Vancouver	0	0	0	50	58	108
41. Jan. 2	Boston	1	1	2	51	59	110
42. Jan. 6	Colorado	2	2	4	53	61	114

Date	Opponent	G	A	Pts.	G	A	Pts.
43. Jan. 9	Calgary	1	4	5	54	65	119
44. Jan. 10	Calgary	0	0	0	54	65	119
45. Jan. 13	Washington	1	2	3	55	67	122
46. Jan. 14	Philadelphia	1	0	1	56	67	123
47. Jan. 16	Toronto	1	0	1	57	67	124
48. Jan. 17	Detroit	0	2	2	57	69	126
49. Jan. 20	St. Louis	3	2	5	60	71	131
50. Jan. 22	Vancouver	1	1	2	61	72	133
51. Jan. 24	Colorado	0	3	3	61	75	136
52. Jan. 26	St. Louis	1	1	2	62	76	138
53. Jan. 27	Chicago	1	1	2	63	77	140
54. Jan. 29	Buffalo	1	0	1	64	77	141
55. Jan. 31	Philadelphia	3	2	5	67	79	146
56. Feb. 3	Montreal	1	1	2	68	80	148
57. Feb. 6	Toronto	0	2	2	68	82	150
58. Feb. 7	Rangers	1	1	2	69	83	152
59. Feb. 12	Washington	1	2	3	70	85	155
60. Feb. 14	Boston	0	1	1	70	86	156
61. Feb. 17	Minnesota	2	3	5	72	89	161
62. Feb. 19	Hartford	3	2	5	75	91	166
63. Feb. 21	Detroit	1	4	5	76	95	171
64. Feb. 24	Buffalo	3	2	5	79	97	176
65. Feb. 27	Pittsburgh	1	1	2	80	98	178
66. Feb. 28	Washington	2	1	3	82	99	181
67. Mar. 2	Montreal	0	2	2	82	101	183
68. Mar. 3	Quebec	0	2	2	82	103	185
69. Mar. 6	Colorado	0	0	0	82	103	185
70. Mar. 10	Los Angeles	0	2	2	82	105	187
71. Mar. 12	Buffalo	0	0	0	82	105	187
72. Mar. 13	Vancouver	0	3	3	82	108	190
73. Mar. 15	Los Angeles	2	0	2	84	108	192
74. Mar. 17	Pittsburgh	3	2	5	87	110	197
75. Mar. 19	Calgary	1	1	2	88	111	199
76. Mar. 25	Calgary	2	2	4	90	113	203
77. Mar. 26	Colorado	1	2	3	91	115	206
78. Mar. 28	Los Angeles	1	1	2	92	116	208
79. Mar. 31	Los Angeles	0	3	3	92	119	211
80. Apr. 4	Winnipeg	0	1	1	92	120	212

	GP	G	A	Pts.	+/-	PIM	PP	SH	GW
1981-82	80	**92	**120	**212	+81	26	18	6	12
	GP	G	A	Pts.	+/-	PIM	PP	SH	GW
Career	239	198	315	513	+137	75	46	11	21

context

Three NHLers have scored 50 goals in fewer than 50 games*

Wayne Gretzky
Mario Lemieux and Brett Hull

	'80-81	'81-82		'85-86
Gretzky	39	42		49
Lemieux/Hull		46		49
		'88-89 Lemieux		'91-92 Hull

*50 team games from start of season. Alexander Mogilny reached 50 goals in his 46th game, but Buffalo's 53rd in 1993. Cam Neely reached 50 goals in his 44th game, but Boston's 66th in 1994.

Hull

milestones

1. **Dec. 30** Scores five goals–four on Flyers' Pete Peeters, plus an empty netter–to reach 50 goals in record-low 39 games
2. **Feb. 19** Breaks own record for most points in season (164)
3. **Feb. 24** Breaks Phil Esposito's record of 77 goals with natural hat trick against Buffalo's Don Edwards
4. **March 17** Breaks own record (109) for most assists in season; records 10th three-plus goal game, setting single season record

5. **March 25** Reaches 200-point mark first of four times during career, only player to do so
6. **March 28** Scores 92nd goal of season against Los Angeles' Mike Blake to complete NHL record goal-scoring season
7. **April 4** Leads league in goals (92), assists (120) and points (212)
8. Named first all-star, league MVP, NHLPA outstanding player

playoffs

	Date	Opponent	G	A	Pts.	G	A	Pts.
1.	Apr. 7	Los Angeles	1	3	4	1	3	4
2.	Apr. 8	Los Angeles	1	1	2	2	4	6
3.	Apr. 10	Los Angeles	2	2	4	4	6	10
4.	Apr. 12	Los Angeles	0	1	1	4	7	11
5.	Apr. 13	Los Angeles	1	0	1	5	7	12

Totals

	GP	G	A	Pts.	PIM	PP	SH	GW
1981-82	5	5	7	12	8	1	1	1
	GP	G	A	Pts.	PIM	PP	SH	GW
Career	17	14	22	36	12	3	2	2

1982-83: NHL Season No. 4

Date	Opponent	G	A	Pts.	G	A	Pts.
1. Oct. 5	Calgary	0	1	1	0	1	1
2. Oct. 8	Islanders	1	1	2	1	2	3
3. Oct. 9	Vancouver	2	1	3	3	3	6
4. Oct. 12	Calgary	1	2	3	4	5	9
5. Oct. 14	Hartford	1	2	3	5	7	12
6. Oct. 16	Boston	0	2	2	5	9	14
7. Oct. 17	Buffalo	1	2	3	6	11	17
8. Oct. 20	Hartford	0	1	1	6	12	18
9. Oct. 21	Boston	0	1	1	6	13	19
10. Oct. 24	Winnipeg	0	3	3	6	16	22
11. Oct. 27	Chicago	0	2	2	6	18	24
12. Oct. 29	Los Angeles	1	2	3	7	20	27
13. Oct. 31	Vancouver	1	0	1	8	20	28
14. Nov. 3	Winnipeg	1	1	2	9	21	30
15. Nov. 5	Rangers	1	1	2	10	22	32
16. Nov. 8	Quebec	0	4	4	10	26	36
17. Nov. 10	Pittsburgh	0	3	3	10	29	39
18. Nov. 11	New Jersey	1	0	1	11	29	40
19. Nov. 13	Philadelphia	1	0	1	12	29	41
20. Nov. 14	Rangers	2	2	4	14	31	45
21. Nov. 16	Islanders	0	1	1	14	32	46
22. Nov. 20	Vancouver	0	1	1	14	33	47
23. Nov. 21	Quebec	3	3	6	17	36	53
24. Nov. 24	Washington	1	1	2	18	37	55
25. Nov. 26	Winnipeg	2	2	4	20	39	59
26. Nov. 28	Detroit	0	4	4	20	43	63
27. Dec.1	Philadelphia	0	2	2	20	45	65
28. Dec. 4	Calgary	1	3	4	21	48	69
29. Dec. 5	Los Angeles	1	4	5	22	52	74
30. Dec. 7	St. Louis	2	0	2	24	52	76
31. Dec. 9	Los Angeles	0	0	0	24	52	76
32. Dec. 11	Minnesota	1	2	3	25	54	79
33. Dec. 17	New Jersey	1	3	4	26	57	83
34. Dec. 19	Montreal	0	1	1	26	58	84
35. Dec. 22	Minnesota	1	2	3	27	60	87
36. Dec. 23	Los Angeles	1	0	1	28	60	88
37. Dec. 26	Calgary	0	2	2	28	62	90
38. Dec. 29	Chicago	0	2	2	28	64	92
39. Dec. 31	Vancouver	2	1	3	30	65	95
40. Jan. 1	Winnipeg	0	0	0	30	65	95
41. Jan. 4	Calgary	1	0	1	31	65	96
42. Jan. 5	Winnipeg	2	3	5	33	68	101

Date	Opponent	G	A	Pts.	G	A	Pts.
43. Jan. 7	Pittsburgh	2	0	2	35	68	103
44. Jan. 9	Detroit	0	2	2	35	70	105
45. Jan. 11	St. Louis	0	2	2	35	72	107
46. Jan. 12	Chicago	2	1	3	37	73	110
47. Jan. 15	Minnesota	1	5	6	38	78	116
48. Jan. 18	Los Angeles	1	1	2	39	79	118
49. Jan. 19	Vancouver	1	3	4	40	82	122
50. Jan. 22	Vancouver	1	0	1	41	82	123
51. Jan. 23	Los Angeles	1	3	4	42	85	127
52. Jan. 26	Toronto	2	1	3	44	86	130
53. Jan. 29	Calgary	0	0	0	44	86	130
54. Jan. 30	Islanders	0	1	1	44	87	131
55. Feb. 3	Los Angeles	0	1	1	44	88	132
56. Feb. 4	Montreal	1	4	5	45	92	137
57. Feb. 11	Quebec	1	2	3	46	94	140
58. Feb. 14	Montreal	2	0	2	48	94	142
59. Feb. 17	Philadelphia	0	2	2	48	96	144
60. Feb. 19	Pittsburgh	2	1	3	50	97	147
61. Feb. 20	Buffalo	0	1	1	50	98	148
62. Feb. 22	Calgary	1	0	1	51	98	149
63. Feb. 23	Washington	2	1	3	53	99	152
64. Feb. 25	St. Louis	1	0	1	54	99	153
65. Feb. 27	Winnipeg	0	1	1	54	100	154
66. Mar. 1	New Jersey	1	1	2	55	101	156
67. Mar. 2	Washington	1	1	2	56	102	158
68. Mar. 5	Toronto	2	3	5	58	105	163
69. Mar. 6	Boston	1	0	1	59	105	164
70. Mar. 8	Hartford	3	1	4	62	106	168
71. Mar. 11	Rangers	0	0	0	62	106	168
72. Mar. 13	Buffalo	1	2	3	63	108	171
73. Mar. 16	Vancouver	1	2	3	64	110	174
74. Mar. 19	Detroit	1	4	5	65	114	179
75. Mar. 21	Toronto	1	2	3	66	116	182
76. Mar. 23	Winnipeg	0	1	1	66	117	183
77. Mar. 26	Los Angeles	2	1	3	68	118	186
78. Mar. 29	Vancouver	1	3	4	69	121	190
79. Apr. 1	Winnipeg	1	3	4	70	124	194
80. Apr. 3	Calgary	1	1	2	71	125	196

	GP	G	A	Pts.	+/–	PIM	PP	SH	GW
1982-83	80	*71	**125	*196	+60	59	18	6	9
	GP	G	A	Pts.	+/–	PIM	PP	SH	GW
Career	319	269	440	709	+197	134	64	17	30

context

NHL playoff points records and highs since 1981

		1983	1993	1988	1985
Wayne Gretzky		38	40	43	47
Mike Bossy and Mario Lemieux	35			44	
		1981 Bossy		1991 Lemieux	

Bossy

milestones

1. **Dec. 9** Compiles record 30-game point streak (24-52-76) from Oct. 5 to Dec. 7, breaking Guy Lafleur's mark of 28 (1976-77)

2. **Jan. 19** Beats Vancouver's Richard Brodeur for only regular season penalty shot goal

3. **Mar. 29** Breaks own assist record (120)

4. **April 3** Leads league in goals (71), assists (125) and points (196)

5. **May 12** Breaks Mike Bossy's record for points in playoff year (35)

6. Named first all-star, league MVP, NHLPA outstanding player

Date	Opponent	G	A	Pts.	G	A	Pts.
1. Apr. 6	Winnipeg	4	1	5	4	1	5
2. Apr. 7	Winnipeg	0	2	2	4	3	7
3. Apr. 9	Winnipeg	0	1	1	4	4	8
4. Apr. 14	Calgary	0	0	0	4	4	8
5. Apr. 15	Calgary	0	2	2	4	6	10
6. Apr. 17	Calgary	4	3	7	8	9	17
7. Apr. 18	Calgary	1	1	2	9	10	19
8. Apr. 20	Calgary	1	2	3	10	12	22
9. Apr. 24	Chicago	1	4	5	11	16	27
10. Apr. 26	Chicago	0	2	2	11	18	29

Date	Opponent	G	A	Pts.	G	A	Pts.
11. May 1	Chicago	0	2	2	11	20	31
12. May 3	Chicago	1	2	3	12	22	34
13. May 10	Islanders	0	0	0	12	22	34
14. May 12	Islanders	0	2	2	12	24	36
15. May 14	Islanders	0	1	1	12	25	37
16. May 17	Islanders	0	1	1	12	26	38

Totals	EDMONTON LOSES IN STANLEY CUP FINAL						
	GP	G	A	Pts.	PIM	PP	SH	GW
1982-83	16	12	**26	**38	4	2	3	3
	GP	G	A	Pts.	PIM	PP	SH	GW
Career	33	26	48	74	16	5	5	5

1983-84: NHL Season No. 5

Date	Opponent	G	A	Pts.	G	A	Pts.
1. Oct. 5	Toronto	1	1	2	1	1	2
2. Oct. 7	Winnipeg	2	1	3	3	2	5
3. Oct. 9	Minnesota	1	2	3	4	4	8
4. Oct. 12	Detroit	2	3	5	6	7	13
5. Oct. 15	Calgary	1	1	2	7	8	15
6. Oct. 16	Calgary	1	2	3	8	10	18
7. Oct. 19	Vancouver	2	0	2	10	10	20
8. Oct. 20	Los Angeles	1	0	1	11	10	21
9. Oct. 22	Vancouver	0	3	3	11	13	24
10. Oct. 26	Toronto	1	0	1	12	13	25
11. Oct. 29	Montreal	0	1	1	12	14	26
12. Oct. 30	Rangers	1	0	1	13	14	27
13. Nov. 2	Washington	2	3	5	15	17	32
14. Nov. 5	Pittsburgh	0	3	3	15	20	35
15. Nov. 6	Winnipeg	4	3	7	19	23	42
16. Nov. 8	Quebec	1	1	2	20	24	44
17. Nov. 9	Washington	1	3	4	21	27	48
18. Nov. 12	Detroit	3	2	5	24	29	53
19. Nov. 13	Chicago	0	1	1	24	30	54
20. Nov. 18	Buffalo	0	3	3	24	33	57
21. Nov. 19	New Jersey	3	5	8	27	38	65
22. Nov. 21	Winnipeg	1	0	1	28	38	66
23. Nov. 23	Los Angeles	0	2	2	28	40	68
24. Nov. 25	Minnesota	1	0	1	29	40	69
25. Nov. 26	St. Louis	0	5	5	29	45	74
26. Nov. 30	Philadelphia	1	1	2	30	46	76
27. Dec. 3	Los Angeles	0	3	3	30	49	79
28. Dec. 4	Islanders	0	1	1	30	50	80
29. Dec. 7	Vancouver	0	2	2	30	52	82
30. Dec. 10	Vancouver	0	1	1	30	53	83
31. Dec. 13	Islanders	1	1	2	31	54	85
32. Dec. 14	Rangers	3	2	5	34	56	90
33. Dec. 17	Quebec	1	5	6	35	61	96
34. Dec. 18	Winnipeg	2	2	4	37	63	100
35. Dec. 21	Winnipeg	3	2	5	40	65	105
36. Dec. 23	Calgary	1	1	2	41	66	107
37. Dec. 26	Calgary	1	2	3	42	68	110
38. Dec. 28	Vancouver	0	2	2	42	70	112
39. Dec. 30	Boston	0	1	1	42	71	113
40. Jan. 3	Calgary	1	3	4	43	74	117
41. Jan. 4	Minnesota	4	4	8	47	78	125
42. Jan. 7	Hartford	3	0	3	50	78	128

Date	Opponent	G	A	Pts.	G	A	Pts.
43. Jan. 9	Detroit	2	1	3	52	79	131
44. Jan. 11	Chicago	1	0	1	53	79	132
45. Jan. 13	Buffalo	0	1	1	53	80	133
46. Jan. 15	New Jersey	0	3	3	53	83	136
47. Jan. 18	Vancouver	3	2	5	56	85	141
48. Jan. 20	Los Angeles	2	3	5	58	88	146
49. Jan. 21	Los Angeles	0	2	2	58	90	148
50. Jan. 25	Vancouver	2	2	4	60	92	152
51. Jan. 27	New Jersey	1	0	1	61	92	153
52. Jan. 28	Los Angeles	0	0	0	61	92	153
53. Feb. 3	Calgary	Did not play					
54. Feb. 5	Washington	Did not play					
55. Feb. 7	Islanders	Did not play					
56. Feb. 9	Philadelphia	Did not play					
57. Feb. 11	Boston	Did not play					
58. Feb. 12	Hartford	Did not play					
59. Feb. 15	Winnipeg	2	2	4	63	94	157
60. Feb. 17	Boston	0	1	1	63	95	158
61. Feb. 19	Pittsburgh	2	1	3	65	96	161
62. Feb. 21	St. Louis	4	1	5	69	97	166
63. Feb. 22	Pittsburgh	4	1	5	73	98	171
64. Feb. 24	Calgary	0	0	0	73	98	171
65. Feb. 25	Toronto	2	0	2	75	98	173
66. Feb. 27	Winnipeg	1	1	2	76	99	175
67. Feb. 29	Philadelphia	0	2	2	76	101	177
68. Mar. 4	Montreal	2	1	3	78	102	180
69. Mar. 7	Chicago	0	3	3	78	105	183
70. Mar. 10	Rangers	1	0	1	79	105	184
71. Mar. 11	Vancouver	2	3	5	81	108	189
72. Mar. 13	Quebec	1	1	2	82	109	191
73. Mar. 15	Montreal	0	1	1	82	110	192
74. Mar. 17	Los Angeles	1	2	3	83	112	195
75. Mar. 18	Buffalo	0	0	0	83	112	195
76. Mar. 21	Hartford	0	1	1	83	113	196
77. Mar. 24	St. Louis	1	0	1	84	113	197
78. Mar. 25	Winnipeg	1	0	1	85	113	198
79. Mar. 27	Calgary	2	2	4	87	115	202
80. Mar. 31	Los Angeles	0	3	3	87	118	205

	GP	G	A	Pts.	+/–	PIM	PP	SH	GW
1983-84	74	*87	*118	*205	+76	39	20	12	11
	GP	G	A	Pts.	+/–	PIM	PP	SH	GW
Career	393	356	558	914	+273	173	84	29	41

context

NHL records for most consecutive games with point

	'82-83	'85-86	'83-84
Wayne Gretzky	30	39	51
Mario Lemieux and Mats Sundin	30	46	
	'92-93 Sundin	'89-90 Lemieux	

Sundin

milestones

1. **Nov. 19** Sets career high with eight points in 13-4 win; calls Devils a "Mickey Mouse operation"

2. **Jan. 4** Ties career high of eight points in game in 12-8 win

3. **Jan. 28** Sets record 51-game point streak (61-92-153) from Oct. 5 to Jan. 27, breaking own record (30)

4. **Feb. 22** Ties own record with 10th three-or-more goal game

5. **March 4** Sets record with 12th shorthanded goal of season;

Mario Lemieux breaks record with 13 (1988-89)

6. **March 18** Is held pointless for only third time in season

7. **March 31** Finishes with record highest points-per-game average in season (2.77) and goals-per-game average (1.18)

8. **May 19** Wins first of four Stanley Cups; leads playoffs in assists (22) and points (35)

9. Named first all-star, league MVP, NHLPA outstanding player

playoffs

Date	Opponent	G	A	Pts.	G	A	Pts.
1. Apr. 4	Winnipeg	0	3	3	0	3	3
2. Apr. 5	Winnipeg	1	1	2	1	4	5
3. Apr. 7	Winnipeg	0	0	0	1	4	5
4. Apr. 12	Calgary	2	2	4	3	6	9
5. Apr. 13	Calgary	1	1	2	4	7	11
6. Apr. 15	Calgary	0	1	1	4	8	12
7. Apr. 16	Calgary	0	1	1	4	9	13
8. Apr. 18	Calgary	0	0	0	4	9	13
9. Apr. 20	Calgary	0	2	2	4	11	15
10. Apr. 22	Calgary	1	2	3	5	13	18
11. Apr. 24	Minnesota	1	3	4	6	16	22
12. Apr. 26	Minnesota	1	1	2	7	17	24

Date	Opponent	G	A	Pts.	G	A	Pts.
13. Apr. 28	Minnesota	2	1	3	9	18	27
14. May 1	Minnesota	0	1	1	9	19	28
15. May 10	Islanders	0	0	0	9	19	28
16. May 12	Islanders	0	0	0	9	19	28
17. May 15	Islanders	0	1	1	9	20	29
16. May 17	Islanders	2	1	3	11	21	32
17. May 19	Islanders	2	1	3	13	22	35

Totals	EDMONTON WINS FIRST STANLEY CUP						
	GP	G	A	Pts.	PIM	PP	SH	GW
1984	19	13	*22	*35	12	2	0	3
	GP	G	A	Pts.	PIM	PP	SH	GW
Career	52	39	70	109	28	7	5	8

1984-85: NHL Season No. 6

Date	Opponent	G	A	Pts.	G	A	Pts.
1. Oct. 11	Los Angeles	0	1	1	0	1	1
2. Oct. 12	St. Louis	0	1	1	0	2	2
3. Oct. 14	Quebec	1	3	4	1	5	6
4. Oct. 16	Boston	2	1	3	3	6	9
5. Oct. 18	Minnesota	3	0	3	6	6	12
6. Oct. 19	Winnipeg	2	3	5	8	9	17
7. Oct. 21	Calgary	2	2	4	10	11	21
8. Oct. 24	Washington	0	2	2	10	13	23
9. Oct. 26	Los Angeles	0	4	4	10	17	27
10. Oct. 30	Vancouver	1	2	3	11	19	30
11. Nov. 2	Chicago	0	1	1	11	20	31
12. Nov. 4	Winnipeg	1	1	2	12	21	33
13. Nov. 6	Pittsburgh	1	0	1	13	21	34
14. Nov. 8	New Jersey	0	3	3	13	24	37
15. Nov. 9	Washington	2	4	6	15	28	43
16. Nov. 11	Philadelphia	2	2	4	17	30	47
17. Nov. 14	Montreal	0	0	0	17	30	47
18. Nov. 15	Calgary	1	0	1	18	30	48
19. Nov. 17	Vancouver	0	3	3	18	33	51
20. Nov. 21	Winnipeg	1	2	3	19	35	54
21. Nov. 24	St. Louis	2	3	5	21	38	59
22. Nov. 27	Toronto	3	2	5	24	40	64
23. Nov. 29	Boston	0	2	2	24	42	66
24. Nov. 30	Hartford	0	2	2	24	44	68
25. Dec. 5	Islanders	1	4	5	25	48	73
26. Dec. 7	Minnesota	1	2	3	26	50	76
27. Dec. 8	Vancouver	0	0	0	26	50	76
28. Dec. 13	Los Angeles	1	1	2	27	51	78
29. Dec. 15	St. Louis	5	1	6	32	52	84
30. Dec. 17	New Jersey	0	1	1	32	53	85
31. Dec. 19	Los Angeles	2	4	6	34	57	91
32. Dec. 21	Vancouver	0	0	0	34	57	91
33. Dec. 22	Calgary	2	2	4	36	59	95
34. Dec. 26	Calgary	0	4	4	36	63	99
35. Dec. 29	Detroit	3	3	6	39	66	105
36. Dec. 30	Vancouver	1	2	3	40	68	108
37. Jan. 2	Philadelphia	0	0	0	40	68	108
38. Jan. 4	Winnipeg	0	3	3	40	71	111
39. Jan. 6	Winnipeg	1	0	1	41	71	112
40. Jan. 8	Quebec	1	2	3	42	73	115
41. Jan. 10	Montreal	1	2	3	43	75	118
42. Jan. 12	Pittsburgh	0	3	3	43	78	121
43. Jan. 13	Buffalo	1	2	3	44	80	124
44. Jan. 16	Islanders	1	1	2	45	81	126
45. Jan. 18	Vancouver	1	0	1	46	81	127
46. Jan. 19	Vancouver	1	3	4	47	84	131
47. Jan. 21	Los Angeles	1	1	2	48	85	133
48. Jan. 25	New Jersey	1	2	3	49	87	136
49. Jan. 26	Pittsburgh	3	1	4	52	88	140
50. Jan. 28	Calgary	1	2	3	53	90	143
51. Jan. 29	Calgary	0	2	2	53	92	145
52. Feb. 2	Rangers	0	0	0	53	92	145
53. Feb. 3	Hartford	1	2	3	54	94	148
54. Feb. 6	Winnipeg	0	1	1	54	95	149
55. Feb. 8	Minnesota	0	2	2	54	97	151
56. Feb. 9	Detroit	0	2	2	54	99	153
57. Feb. 15	Rangers	2	2	4	56	101	157
58. Feb. 16	Philadelphia	0	2	2	56	103	159
59. Feb. 18	Buffalo	2	1	3	58	104	162
60. Feb. 19	Toronto	2	3	5	60	107	167
61. Feb. 22	Quebec	1	1	2	61	108	169
62. Feb. 23	Washington	0	1	1	61	109	170
63. Feb. 27	Montreal	1	0	1	62	109	171
64. Mar. 1	Los Angeles	0	3	3	62	112	174
65. Mar. 3	Winnipeg	1	1	2	63	113	176
66. Mar. 5	Calgary	0	1	1	63	114	177
67. Mar. 9	Rangers	1	0	1	64	114	178
68. Mar. 10	Vancouver	0	1	1	64	115	179
69. Mar. 13	Detroit	1	4	5	65	119	184
70. Mar. 15	Buffalo	0	1	1	65	120	185
71. Mar. 17	Los Angeles	0	1	1	65	121	186
72. Mar. 20	Chicago	0	2	2	65	123	188
73. Mar. 22	Toronto	1	0	1	66	123	189
74. Mar. 26	Islanders	1	1	2	67	124	191
75. Mar. 28	Boston	0	1	1	67	125	192
76. Mar. 29	Hartford	1	2	3	68	127	195
77. Mar. 31	Chicago	1	4	5	69	131	200
78. Apr. 2	Los Angeles	3	1	4	72	132	204
79. Apr. 5	Calgary	1	1	2	73	133	206
80. Apr. 6	Winnipeg	0	2	2	73	135	208

	GP	G	A	Pts.	+/-	PIM	PP	SH	GW
1984-85	80	*73	**135	*208	+98	52	8	11	7
	GP	G	A	Pts.	+/-	PIM	PP	SH	GW
Career	473	429	693	1,122	+371	225	92	40	48

context

Top marks for fewest games to reach 1,000 career points

Wayne Gretzky	424
Mario Lemieux and Mike Bossy	513 (Lemieux) 656 (Bossy)

Lemieux

milestones

1. Dec. 19 Registers 1,000th career point in record-low 424th game

2. Jan. 13 Scores 400th career goal against Sabres' Tom Barrasso at 19:05 of second period

3. March 29 Breaks own record (125) for most assists in season

4. April 2 Reaches 70-plus goals for record fourth straight season with hat trick against Kings' Bob Janecyk

5. April 6 Leads league in goals (73), assists (135) and points (208)

6. May 25 Breaks own record for most points (38) and assists (26) in one playoff; finishes with playoff-leading 30 assists and 47 points

7. May 30 Named playoff MVP

8. Named first all-star, league MVP, NHLPA outstanding player

Date	Opponent	G	A	Pts.	G	A	Pts.
1. Apr. 10	Los Angeles	0	2	2	0	2	2
2. Apr. 11	Los Angeles	0	1	1	0	3	3
3. Apr. 13	Los Angeles	0	2	2	0	5	5
4. Apr. 18	Winnipeg	1	2	3	1	7	8
5. Apr. 20	Winnipeg	1	0	1	2	7	9
6. Apr. 23	Winnipeg	1	1	2	3	8	11
7. Apr. 25	Winnipeg	3	4	7	6	12	18
8. May 4	Chicago	1	3	4	7	15	22
9. May 7	Chicago	0	3	3	7	18	25
10. May 9	Chicago	0	0	0	7	18	25
11. May 12	Chicago	1	2	3	8	20	28

Date	Opponent	G	A	Pts.	G	A	Pts.
12. May 14	Chicago	2	2	4	10	22	32
13. May 16	Chicago	0	4	4	10	26	36
14. May 21	Philadelphia	0	0	0	10	26	36
15. May 23	Philadelphia	1	0	1	11	26	37
16. May 25	Philadelphia	3	1	4	14	27	41
17. May 28	Philadelphia	2	0	2	16	27	43
18. May 30	Philadelphia	1	3	4	17	30	47

Totals	EDMONTON WINS SECOND STANLEY CUP						
	GP	G	A	Pts.	PIM	PP	SH	GW
1985	18	17	**30	**47	4	4	2	3
	GP	G	A	Pts.	PIM	PP	SH	GW
Career	70	56	100	156	32	11	7	11

1985-86: NHL Season No. 7

Date	Opponent	G	A	Pts.	G	A	Pts.
1. Oct. 10	Winnipeg	2	1	3	2	1	3
2. Oct. 13	St. Louis	0	2	2	2	3	5
3. Oct. 16	Islanders	0	1	1	2	4	6
4. Oct. 18	Boston	0	2	2	2	6	8
5. Oct. 20	Los Angeles	1	2	3	3	8	11
6. Oct. 23	Winnipeg	0	1	1	3	9	12
7. Oct. 25	Calgary	1	2	3	4	11	15
8. Oct. 28	Calgary	1	4	5	5	15	20
9. Oct. 30	Winnipeg	0	4	4	5	19	24
10. Nov. 1	Buffalo	0	0	0	5	19	24
11. Nov. 3	Toronto	3	0	3	8	19	27
12. Nov. 5	Vancouver	2	1	3	10	20	30
13. Nov. 6	Los Angeles	1	1	2	11	21	32
14. Nov. 8	Vancouver	0	4	4	11	25	36
15. Nov. 12	Washington	1	0	1	12	25	37
16. Nov. 14	Philadelphia	0	1	1	12	26	38
17. Nov. 16	Islanders	1	0	1	13	26	39
18. Nov. 17	Rangers	0	2	2	13	28	41
19. Nov. 19	Quebec	1	1	2	14	29	43
20. Nov. 20	Montreal	1	1	2	15	30	45
21. Nov. 23	New Jersey	0	1	1	15	31	46
22. Nov. 27	Vancouver	2	0	2	17	31	48
23. Nov. 30	Hartford	1	3	4	18	34	52
24. Dec. 1	Calgary	0	1	1	18	35	53
25. Dec. 3	Los Angeles	0	1	1	18	36	54
26. Dec. 5	Los Angeles	0	5	5	18	41	59
27. Dec. 7	Minnesota	1	4	5	19	45	64
28. Dec. 8	Chicago	0	1	1	19	46	65
29. Dec. 10	St. Louis	0	2	2	19	48	67
30. Dec. 11	Chicago	0	7	7	19	55	74
31. Dec. 13	Winnipeg	2	2	4	21	57	78
32. Dec. 15	Vancouver	0	3	3	21	60	81
33. Dec. 18	Washington	0	1	1	21	61	82
34. Dec. 20	Los Angeles	0	6	6	21	67	88
35. Dec. 22	Winnipeg	2	1	3	23	68	91
36. Dec. 29	Vancouver	0	2	2	23	70	93
37. Dec. 31	Philadelphia	3	0	3	26	70	96
38. Jan. 2	Calgary	1	1	2	27	71	98
39. Jan. 4	Hartford	0	2	2	27	73	100
40. Jan. 5	Calgary	1	2	3	28	75	103
41. Jan. 8	Toronto	3	3	6	31	78	109
42. Jan. 10	Quebec	0	3	3	31	81	112

Date	Opponent	G	A	Pts.	G	A	Pts.
43. Jan. 11	Montreal	1	3	4	32	84	116
44. Jan. 13	Boston	1	2	3	33	86	119
45. Jan. 15	Hartford	2	1	3	35	87	122
46. Jan. 18	Rangers	0	2	2	35	89	124
47. Jan. 22	Pittsburgh	1	1	2	36	90	126
48. Jan. 24	New Jersey	1	3	4	37	93	130
49. Jan. 25	Los Angeles	1	1	2	38	94	132
50. Jan. 27	Chicago	0	0	0	38	94	132
51. Jan. 29	St. Louis	0	3	3	38	97	135
52. Jan. 31	Calgary	0	4	4	38	101	139
53. Feb. 1	Calgary	0	3	3	38	104	142
54. Feb. 6	New Jersey	0	3	3	38	107	145
55. Feb. 8	Washington	0	2	2	38	109	147
56. Feb. 9	Buffalo	0	1	1	38	110	148
57. Feb. 11	Detroit	0	1	1	38	111	149
58. Feb. 14	Quebec	0	7	7	38	118	156
59. Feb. 16	Buffalo	1	3	4	39	121	160
60. Feb. 19	Toronto	2	0	2	41	121	162
61. Feb. 22	Boston	1	1	2	42	122	164
62. Feb. 24	Montreal	1	1	2	43	123	166
63. Feb. 26	Winnipeg	2	4	6	45	127	172
64. Mar. 2	Philadelphia	0	1	1	45	128	173
65. Mar. 4	Vancouver	0	4	4	45	132	177
66. Mar. 5	Los Angeles	2	2	4	47	134	181
67. Mar. 7	Pittsburgh	0	2	2	47	136	183
68. Mar. 9	Los Angeles	1	3	4	48	139	187
69. Mar. 11	Minnesota	0	0	0	48	139	187
70. Mar. 12	Winnipeg	0	2	2	48	141	189
71. Mar. 14	Detroit	1	4	5	49	145	194
72. Mar. 18	Winnipeg	1	2	3	50	147	197
73. Mar. 21	Winnipeg	0	1	1	50	148	198
74. Mar. 25	Detroit	0	3	3	50	151	201
75. Mar. 26	Pittsburgh	1	3	4	51	154	205
76. Mar. 28	Rangers	0	1	1	51	155	206
77. Mar. 29	Islanders	0	3	3	51	158	209
78. Apr. 2	Vancouver	1	1	2	52	159	211
79. Apr. 4	Calgary	0	3	3	52	162	214
80. Apr. 6	Vancouver	0	1	1	52	163	215

	GP	G	A	Pts.	+/-	PIM	PP	SH	GW
1985-86	80	52	**163	**215	+71	46	11	3	6
	GP	G	A	Pts.	+/-	PIM	PP	SH	GW
Career	553	481	856	1,337	+442	271	103	43	54

context

Timeline: NHL records and marks of 100-plus assists in season*

Wayne Gretzky ... '85-86 **163**

Bobby Orr and Mario Lemieux 102 | 114

Orr '70-71 ... Lemieux '88-89

*Wayne Gretzky earned more than 100 assists 11 times during his career

Orr

milestones

1. **Dec. 11** Ties Billy Taylor's record for most assists in road game with seven against Chicago in 12-9 win

2. **Dec. 20** Records only six-assist game of career; has three seven-assist games and 13 five-assist games

3. **Feb. 14** Records final seven-assist game of career in 8-2 win over Quebec

3. **March 7** Breaks own record (135) for most assists in season

4. **March 11** Is held pointless for only third time in season

5. **March 25** Records 200th point for third straight season

6. **March 29** Breaks own point record (212) with third assist; finishes with current record 215

7. **April 6** Leads league in assists (163) and points (215); finishes season with all-time highest average assists-per-game (2.04)

8. Named first all-star, league MVP

playoffs

Date	Opponent	G	A	Pts.	G	A	Pts.
1. Apr. 9	Vancouver	1	0	1	1	0	1
2. Apr. 10	Vancouver	1	1	2	2	1	3
3. Apr. 12	Vancouver	1	2	3	3	3	6
4. Apr. 18	Calgary	0	1	1	3	4	7
5. Apr. 20	Calgary	0	1	1	3	5	8
6. Apr. 22	Calgary	1	1	2	4	6	10
7. Apr. 24	Calgary	3	2	5	7	8	15

Date	Opponent	G	A	Pts.	G	A	Pts.
8. Apr. 26	Calgary	1	0	1	8	8	16
9. Apr. 28	Calgary	0	2	2	8	10	18
10. Apr. 30	Calgary	0	1	1	8	11	19

Totals

	GP	G	A	Pts.	PIM	PP	SH	GW
1986	10	8	11	19	2	4	1	2
	GP	**G**	**A**	**Pts.**	**PIM**	**PP**	**SH**	**GW**
Career	80	64	111	175	34	15	8	13

1986-87: NHL Season No. 3

	Date	Opponent	G	A	Pts.	G	A	Pts.
1.	Oct. 9	Philadelphia	0	0	0	0	0	0
2.	Oct. 11	Montreal	2	2	4	2	2	4
3.	Oct. 12	Winnipeg	1	0	1	3	2	5
4.	Oct. 15	Quebec	0	5	5	3	7	10
5.	Oct. 17	Detroit	0	4	4	3	11	14
6.	Oct. 19	Los Angeles	0	2	2	3	13	16
7.	Oct. 21	Chicago	2	3	5	5	16	21
8.	Oct. 22	Calgary	0	1	1	5	17	22
9.	Oct. 24	Boston	3	1	4	8	18	26
10.	Oct. 26	Vancouver	0	2	2	8	20	28
11.	Oct. 29	Washington	1	1	2	9	21	30
12.	Oct. 31	Vancouver	2	1	3	11	22	33
13.	Nov. 2	Los Angeles	0	3	3	11	25	36
14.	Nov. 5	Calgary	1	0	1	12	25	37
15.	Nov. 7	Calgary	1	1	2	13	26	39
16.	Nov. 8	Montreal	0	0	0	13	26	39
17.	Nov. 11	Islanders	0	1	1	13	27	40
18.	Nov. 13	Boston	1	0	1	14	27	41
19.	Nov. 15	Hartford	0	1	1	14	28	42
20.	Nov. 16	Rangers	1	2	3	15	30	45
21.	Nov. 19	Rangers	1	0	1	16	30	46
22.	Nov. 22	Vancouver	3	2	5	19	32	51
23.	Nov. 24	Calgary	1	1	2	20	33	53
24.	Nov. 26	Winnipeg	1	2	3	21	35	56
25.	Nov. 28	Chicago	0	2	2	21	37	58
26.	Dec. 3	Islanders	1	2	3	22	39	61
27.	Dec. 5	Pittsburgh	0	3	3	22	42	64
28.	Dec. 7	Philadelphia	1	0	1	23	42	65
29.	Dec. 9	Minnesota	1	1	2	24	43	67
30.	Dec. 10	Winnipeg	3	0	3	27	43	70
31.	Dec. 12	Winnipeg	0	3	3	27	46	73
32.	Dec. 14	Los Angeles	0	2	2	27	48	75
33.	Dec. 17	Quebec	4	1	5	31	49	80
34.	Dec. 19	Vancouver	2	0	2	33	49	82
35.	Dec. 20	Los Angeles	2	3	5	35	52	87
36.	Dec. 23	Winnipeg	0	0	0	35	52	87
37.	Dec. 28	Philadelphia	2	1	3	37	53	90
38.	Dec. 30	Vancouver	2	2	4	39	55	94
39.	Jan. 3	Los Angeles	1	2	3	40	57	97
40.	Jan. 7	Los Angeles	0	1	1	40	58	98
41.	Jan. 9	St. Louis	0	0	0	40	58	98
42.	Jan. 11	Calgary	0	2	2	40	60	100

	Date	Opponent	G	A	Pts.	G	A	Pts.
43.	Jan. 13	Detroit	1	2	3	41	62	103
44.	Jan. 15	Quebec	1	1	2	42	63	105
45.	Jan. 17	Toronto	1	3	4	43	66	109
46.	Jan. 18	Buffalo	0	2	2	43	68	111
47.	Jan. 21	Winnipeg	2	1	3	45	69	114
48.	Jan. 23	Rangers	2	2	4	47	71	118
49.	Jan. 24	Pittsburgh	1	3	4	48	74	122
50.	Jan. 27	Vancouver	0	2	2	48	76	124
51.	Jan. 28	Vancouver	0	4	4	48	80	128
52.	Jan. 30	Minnesota	1	0	1	49	80	129
53.	Feb. 1	Chicago	0	2	2	49	82	131
54.	Feb. 3	St. Louis	0	1	1	49	83	132
55.	Feb. 4	Minnesota	1	3	4	50	86	136
56.	Feb. 6	Islanders	0	2	2	50	88	138
57.	Feb. 8	St. Louis	2	2	4	52	90	142
58.	Feb. 15	Washington	0	0	0	52	90	142
59.	Feb. 18	Toronto	1	4	5	53	94	147
60.	Feb. 22	Winnipeg	1	1	2	54	95	149
61.	Feb. 24	Pittsburgh	0	1	1	54	96	150
62.	Feb. 25	New Jersey	0	0	0	54	96	150
63.	Feb. 27	Washington	0	0	0	54	96	150
64.	Mar. 4	Vancouver	1	2	3	55	98	153
65.	Mar. 6	Los Angeles	1	4	5	56	102	158
66.	Mar. 7	Montreal	0	2	2	56	104	160
67.	Mar. 11	Detroit	1	3	4	57	107	164
68.	Mar. 14	Buffalo	2	1	3	59	108	167
69.	Mar. 15	Hartford	1	1	2	60	109	169
70.	Mar. 17	New Jersey	0	3	3	60	112	172
71.	Mar. 19	Calgary	1	2	3	61	114	175
72.	Mar. 20	Calgary	0	1	1	61	115	176
73.	Mar. 23	New Jersey	0	3	3	61	118	179
74.	Mar. 25	Hartford	0	2	2	61	120	181
75.	Mar. 26	Boston	0	0	0	61	120	181
76.	Mar. 28	Toronto	0	0	0	61	120	181
77.	Mar. 29	Buffalo	0	0	0	61	120	181
78.	Mar. 31	Winnipeg	0	1	1	61	121	182
79.	Apr. 2	Calgary	1	0	1	62	121	183
80.	Apr. 4	Los Angeles	Did not play					

	GP	G	A	Pts.	+/–	PIM	PP	SH	GW
1986-87	79	*62	*121	*183	+70	28	13	7	4
	GP	G	A	Pts.	+/–	PIM	PP	SH	GW
Career	632	543	977	1,520	+512	299	116	50	58

milestones

1. Nov. 22 Third goal of game into empty net at 19:42 of third period is career 500th in 575th game

2. Dec. 10 Third of four 1986-87 hat tricks is 40th career, breaking Mike Bossy's record (39)

3. Dec. 17 Records last of nine career four-goal games, against Nordiques' Richard Sevigny

4. March 15 Reaches 60 goals for fifth and last time; ties with Mike Bossy for most career 60-goal seasons

5. April 4 Leads league in goals (62), assists (121) and points (183)

6. April 9 Surpasses Jean Béliveau (176) as all-time leading Stanley Cup playoff scorer with seven-point game

7. April 4 Leads playoffs in assists (29) and points (34)

8. Named first all-star, league MVP, NHLPA outstanding player

bruce bennett/bbs

playoffs

Date	Opponent	G	A	Pts.	G	A	Pts.
1. Apr. 8	Los Angeles	0	1	1	0	1	1
2. Apr. 9	Los Angeles	1	6	7	1	7	8
3. Apr. 11	Los Angeles	0	2	2	1	9	10
4. Apr. 12	Los Angeles	1	4	5	2	13	15
5. Apr. 14	Los Angeles	0	0	0	2	13	15
6. Apr. 21	Winnipeg	0	0	0	2	13	15
7. Apr. 23	Winnipeg	0	2	2	2	15	17
8. Apr. 25	Winnipeg	0	3	3	2	18	20
9. Apr. 27	Winnipeg	1	0	1	3	18	21
10. May 5	Detroit	0	0	0	3	18	21
11. May 7	Detroit	0	1	1	3	19	22
12. May 9	Detroit	0	0	0	3	19	22
13. May 11	Detroit	0	1	1	3	20	23

Date	Opponent	G	A	Pts.	G	A	Pts.
14. May 13	Detroit	0	0	0	3	20	23
15. May 17	Philadelphia	1	1	2	4	21	25
16. May 20	Philadelphia	1	1	2	5	22	27
17. May 22	Philadelphia	0	1	1	5	23	28
18. May 24	Philadelphia	0	3	3	5	26	31
19. May 26	Philadelphia	0	1	1	5	27	32
20. May 28	Philadelphia	0	1	1	5	28	33
21. May 31	Philadelphia	0	1	1	5	29	34

Totals	EDMONTON WINS THIRD STANLEY CUP						
	GP	**G**	**A**	**Pts.**	**PIM**	**PP**	**SH**	**GW**
1987	21	5	*29	*34	6	2	0	0
	GP	**G**	**A**	**Pts.**	**PIM**	**PP**	**SH**	**GW**
Career	101	69	140	209	40	17	8	13

1987-88: NHL Season No. 9

Date	Opponent	G	A	Pts.	G	A	Pts.
1. Oct. 9	Detroit	0	1	1	0	1	1
2. Oct. 11	Los Angeles	1	4	5	1	5	6
3. Oct. 14	Calgary	1	1	2	2	6	8
4. Oct. 16	Calgary	0	1	1	2	7	9
5. Oct. 17	Boston	1	2	3	3	9	12
6. Oct. 21	Los Angeles	2	1	3	5	10	15
7. Oct. 23	Vancouver	0	2	2	5	12	17
8. Oct. 24	Vancouver	2	3	5	7	15	22
9. Oct. 27	Quebec	0	0	0	7	15	22
10. Oct. 28	Montreal	0	1	1	7	16	23
11. Oct. 31	New Jersey	0	3	3	7	19	26
12. Nov. 1	Rangers	0	2	2	7	21	28
13. Nov. 4	Rangers	3	2	5	10	23	33
14. Nov. 5	Calgary	1	2	3	11	25	36
15. Nov. 7	Buffalo	2	0	2	13	25	38
16. Nov. 10	Los Angeles	0	1	1	13	26	39
17. Nov. 14	St. Louis	0	4	4	13	30	43
18. Nov. 15	Chicago	1	2	3	14	32	46
19. Nov. 18	Quebec	0	2	2	14	34	48
20. Nov. 20	Pittsburgh	0	2	2	14	36	50
21. Nov. 22	Winnipeg	2	0	2	16	36	52
22. Nov. 25	New Jersey	1	3	4	17	39	56
23. Nov. 27	Chicago	1	1	2	18	40	58
24. Nov. 29	Buffalo	0	2	2	18	42	60
25. Dec. 1	Washington	0	0	0	18	42	60
26. Dec. 2	Detroit	0	1	1	18	43	61
27. Dec. 5	Toronto	2	0	2	20	43	63
28. Dec. 6	Minnesota	5	1	6	25	44	69
29. Dec. 9	Winnipeg	0	1	1	25	45	70
30. Dec. 11	Vancouver	0	1	1	25	46	71
31. Dec. 12	Vancouver	2	1	3	27	47	74
32. Dec. 16	Los Angeles	1	1	2	28	48	76
33. Dec. 18	Winnipeg	0	2	2	28	50	78
34. Dec. 19	Hartford	0	0	0	28	50	78
35. Dec. 22	Los Angeles	0	2	2	28	52	80
36. Dec. 26	Calgary	1	0	1	29	52	81
37. Dec. 28	Vancouver	0	1	1	29	53	82
38. Dec. 30	Philadelphia	1	3	4	30	56	86
39. Jan. 2	Washington	Did not play					
40. Jan. 4	Boston	Did not play					
41. Jan. 6	Hartford	Did not play					
42. Jan. 8	Winnipeg	Did not play					
43. Jan. 9	Islanders	Did not play					
44. Jan. 11	Washington	Did not play					
45. Jan. 13	Calgary	Did not play					
46. Jan. 15	Winnipeg	Did not play					
47. Jan. 18	Montreal	Did not play					
48. Jan. 19	Quebec	Did not play					
49. Jan. 21	Philadelphia	Did not play					
50. Jan. 23	Islanders	Did not play					
51. Jan. 25	Pittsburgh	Did not play					
52. Jan. 29	Calgary	0	4	4	30	60	90
53. Jan. 30	Hartford	1	2	3	31	62	93
54. Feb. 3	New Jersey	1	2	3	32	64	96
55. Feb. 6	Los Angeles	1	1	2	33	65	98
56. Feb. 11	Vancouver	1	2	3	34	67	101
57. Feb. 12	Boston	0	2	2	34	69	103
58. Feb. 14	Vancouver	0	1	1	34	70	104
59. Feb. 17	Toronto	0	2	2	34	72	106
60. Feb. 19	Pittsburgh	0	0	0	34	72	106
61. Feb. 21	Winnipeg	Did not play					
62. Feb. 23	St. Louis	Did not play					
63. Feb. 24	Chicago	Did not play					
64. Feb. 28	Calgary	1	0	1	35	72	107
65. Mar. 1	Los Angeles	1	1	2	36	73	109
66. Mar. 4	Philadelphia	0	5	5	36	78	114
67. Mar. 5	Calgary	0	3	3	36	81	117
68. Mar. 7	Winnipeg	0	5	5	36	86	122
69. Mar. 9	Montreal	0	0	0	36	86	122
70. Mar. 12	Vancouver	0	2	2	36	88	124
71. Mar. 15	Buffalo	0	3	3	36	91	127
72. Mar. 18	Winnipeg	0	1	1	36	92	128
73. Mar. 20	Minnesota	1	2	3	37	94	131
74. Mar. 22	Detroit	0	3	3	37	97	134
75. Mar. 24	Rangers	0	0	0	37	97	134
76. Mar. 26	Islanders	1	2	3	38	99	137
77. Mar. 28	Toronto	1	3	4	39	102	141
78. Mar. 30	Minnesota	1	3	4	40	105	145
79. Apr. 1	St. Louis	0	3	3	40	108	148
80. Apr. 3	Los Angeles	0	1	1	40	109	149

	GP	G	A	Pts.	+/−	PIM	PP	SH	GW
1987-88	64	40	*109	149	+39	24	9	5	3
	GP	G	A	Pts.	+/−	PIM	PP	SH	GW
Career	696	583	1,086	1,669	+551	323	125	55	61

context

NHL record for career assists and runner-up total

Wayne Gretzky	1,963
Paul Coffey	1,102

Coffey

milestones

1. Nov. 4 Records 1,000th career assist on Esa Tikkanen's goal at 2:57 of third period, becoming second player to reach milestone

2. March 1 Records 1,050th assist on Jari Kurri's goal at 12:44 of first period to pass Gordie Howe as NHL's all-time assists leader

3. April 3 Leads league in assists (109), finishes second to Mario Lemieux in points (168); fails to score 50 goals for first time

5. May 26 Leads playoffs in assists (31) and points (43); named playoff MVP.

6. Named second all-star

7. August 9 Traded to Los Angeles with Mike Krushelnyski and Marty McSorley for $15 million (U.S.), Jimmy Carson, Martin Gelinas and L.A.'s first round draft picks in 1989 (acquired by New Jersey, who select Jason Miller), 1991 (Martin Rucinsky) and 1993 (Nick Stajduhar)

Bruce Bennett/BBS

playoffs

Date	Opponent	G	A	Pts.	G	A	Pts.
1. Apr. 6	Winnipeg	0	2	2	0	2	2
2. Apr. 7	Winnipeg	0	0	0	0	2	2
3. Apr. 9	Winnipeg	0	1	1	0	3	3
4. Apr. 10	Winnipeg	0	3	3	0	6	6
5. Apr. 12	Winnipeg	1	4	5	1	10	11
6. Apr. 19	Calgary	1	0	1	2	10	12
7. Apr. 21	Calgary	2	0	2	4	10	14
8. Apr. 23	Calgary	0	2	2	4	12	16
9. Apr. 25	Calgary	1	0	1	5	12	17
10. May 3	Detroit	0	3	3	5	15	20
11. May 5	Detroit	1	2	3	6	17	23
12. May 7	Detroit	2	0	2	8	17	25

Date	Opponent	G	A	Pts.	G	A	Pts.
13. May 9	Detroit	0	2	2	8	19	27
14. May 11	Detroit	1	2	3	9	21	30
15. May 18	Boston	1	0	1	10	21	31
16. May 20	Boston	1	2	3	11	23	34
17. May 22	Boston	0	4	4	11	27	38
18. May 24	Boston	0	2	2	11	29	40
19. May 26	Boston	1	2	3	12	31	43

Totals	EDMONTON WINS FOURTH STANLEY CUP						
	GP	G	A	Pts.	PIM	PP	SH	GW
1988	19	12	**31	*43	16	5	1	3
	GP	G	A	Pts.	PIM	PP	SH	GW
Career	120	81	171	252	56	22	9	16

1988-89: NHL Season No. 10

	Date	Opponent	G	A	Pts.	G	A	Pts.
1.	Oct. 6	Detroit	1	3	4	1	3	4
2.	Oct. 8	Calgary	2	2	4	3	5	8
3.	Oct. 9	Islanders	1	1	2	4	6	10
4.	Oct. 12	Boston	2	0	2	6	6	12
5.	Oct. 15	Philadelphia	0	1	1	6	7	13
6.	Oct. 17	Calgary	1	1	2	7	8	15
7.	Oct. 19	Edmonton	0	2	2	7	10	17
8.	Oct. 22	Minnesota	2	0	2	9	10	19
9.	Oct. 25	Edmonton	0	2	2	9	12	21
10.	Oct. 28	Winnipeg	0	2	2	9	14	23
11.	Oct. 30	Winnipeg	1	0	1	10	14	24
12.	Nov. 1	Quebec	1	0	1	11	14	25
13.	Nov. 2	Montreal	0	3	3	11	17	28
14.	Nov. 5	Toronto	0	2	2	11	19	30
15.	Nov. 6	Chicago	2	1	3	13	20	33
16.	Nov. 10	Hartford	0	2	2	13	22	35
17.	Nov. 12	Pittsburgh	0	1	1	13	23	36
18.	Nov. 15	Vancouver	2	0	2	15	23	38
19.	Nov. 17	Rangers	0	3	3	15	26	41
20.	Nov. 19	Buffalo	1	0	1	16	26	42
21.	Nov. 22	Philadelphia	0	2	2	16	28	44
22.	Nov. 23	Detroit	1	5	6	17	33	50
23.	Nov. 26	Calgary	1	0	1	18	33	51
24.	Nov. 27	Vancouver	0	0	0	18	33	51
25.	Nov. 29	New Jersey	2	2	4	20	35	55
26.	Dec. 1	Toronto	0	5	5	20	40	60
27.	Dec. 3	Chicago	1	3	4	21	43	64
28.	Dec. 6	Winnipeg	1	1	2	22	44	66
29.	Dec. 8	Winnipeg	1	3	4	23	47	70
30.	Dec. 10	Islanders	0	1	1	23	48	71
31.	Dec. 12	Rangers	1	0	1	24	48	72
32.	Dec. 14	Pittsburgh	Did not play					
33.	Dec. 16	Detroit	1	2	3	25	50	75
34.	Dec. 17	Minnesota	0	0	0	25	50	75
35.	Dec. 20	Calgary	0	2	2	25	52	77
36.	Dec. 21	Minnesota	1	0	1	26	52	78
37.	Dec. 23	Vancouver	2	2	4	28	54	82
38.	Dec. 27	Montreal	0	1	1	28	55	83
39.	Dec. 29	Vancouver	1	2	3	29	57	86
40.	Jan. 5	Calgary	0	2	2	29	59	88
41.	Jan. 6	Winnipeg	0	0	0	29	59	88
42.	Jan. 8	Winnipeg	1	0	1	30	59	89

	Date	Opponent	G	A	Pts.	G	A	Pts.
43.	Jan. 10	Edmonton	0	4	4	30	63	93
44.	Jan. 12	St. Louis	0	1	1	30	64	94
45.	Jan. 14	Hartford	2	1	3	32	65	97
46.	Jan. 17	St. Louis	0	0	0	32	65	97
47.	Jan. 19	Islanders	0	1	1	32	66	98
48.	Jan. 21	Hartford	1	3	4	33	69	102
49.	Jan. 24	Washington	0	2	2	33	71	104
50.	Jan. 26	Vancouver	0	1	1	33	72	105
51.	Jan. 28	Edmonton	0	3	3	33	75	108
52.	Jan. 31	Calgary	1	3	4	34	78	112
53.	Feb. 2	New Jersey	1	0	1	35	78	113
54.	Feb. 4	Buffalo	3	1	4	38	79	117
55.	Feb. 9	Boston	0	0	0	38	79	117
56.	Feb. 10	Washington	1	2	3	39	81	120
57.	Feb. 12	Chicago	3	0	3	42	81	123
58.	Feb. 15	Boston	0	1	1	42	82	124
59.	Feb. 18	Quebec	2	5	7	44	87	131
60.	Feb. 20	Toronto	2	1	3	46	88	134
61.	Feb. 22	Washington	0	1	1	46	89	135
62.	Feb. 24	Edmonton	0	0	0	46	89	135
63.	Feb. 26	New Jersey	0	0	0	46	89	135
64.	Feb. 27	Rangers	0	3	3	46	92	138
65.	Mar. 1	Buffalo	1	1	2	47	93	140
66.	Mar. 2	St. Louis	1	1	2	48	94	142
67.	Mar. 4	Philadelphia	2	4	6	50	98	148
68.	Mar. 7	Pittsburgh	0	2	2	50	100	150
69.	Mar. 10	Vancouver	1	0	1	51	100	151
70.	Mar. 12	Edmonton	1	1	2	52	101	153
71.	Mar. 14	Quebec	0	1	1	52	102	154
72.	Mar. 15	Montreal	0	1	1	52	103	155
73.	Mar. 18	Calgary	0	2	2	52	105	157
74.	Mar. 21	Edmonton	0	2	2	52	107	159
75.	Mar. 23	Calgary	0	1	1	52	108	160
76.	Mar. 25	Edmonton	0	1	1	52	109	161
77.	Mar. 28	Winnipeg	1	2	3	53	111	164
78.	Mar. 29	Winnipeg	1	0	1	54	111	165
79.	Apr. 1	Vancouver	0	3	3	54	114	168
80.	Apr. 2	Vancouver	Did not play					

	GP	G	A	Pts.	+/–	PIM	PP	SH	GW
1988-89	78	54	*114	168	+15	26	11	5	5
	GP	G	A	Pts.	+/–	PIM	PP	SH	GW
Career	774	637	1,200	1,837	+566	349	136	60	66

context

Seven NHLers have won more than two Hart Trophies

Wayne Gretzky
MVP Winners

Bobby Clarke, Mario Lemieux, Howie Morenz, Bobby Orr	3		
Eddie Shore	4		
Gordie Howe	6		
			9

Howe

milestones

1. Oct. 6 Makes Forum debut as Los Angeles King, scoring on first shot en route to four-point night in 8-2 win

2. Nov. 23 Scores 600th career goal, beating Red Wings' Greg Stefan at 8:23 of first period; adds five assists for one of 20 career six-point games

3. Jan. 10 Sets up Bernie Nicholls' goal at 9:24 of first period to pass Gordie Howe for career regular season and playoff points (2,011)

4. Jan. 21 Sets up Luc Robitaille's goal at 14:57 of second period for fourth point of game to pass Marcel Dionne into second place on all-time scoring list with 1,771st career point; Dionne adds one more point later in season to finish with 1,771 career points

5. March 4 Scores twice to reach 50 goals for last time, tying Mike Bossy for most career 50-goal seasons (nine)

6. Named second all-star, league MVP

Graphic Artists/HHOF

Date	Opponent	G	A	Pts.	G	A	Pts.
1. Apr. 5	Edmonton	0	1	1	0	1	1
2. Apr. 6	Edmonton	1	1	2	1	2	3
3. Apr. 8	Edmonton	0	0	0	1	2	3
4. Apr. 9	Edmonton	0	3	3	1	5	6
5. Apr. 11	Edmonton	1	2	3	2	7	9
6. Apr. 13	Edmonton	0	1	1	2	8	10
7. Apr. 15	Edmonton	2	1	3	4	9	13
8. Apr. 18	Calgary	0	2	2	4	11	15

Date	Opponent	G	A	Pts.	G	A	Pts.
9. Apr. 20	Calgary	0	3	3	4	14	18
10. Apr. 22	Calgary	0	1	1	4	15	19
11. Apr. 24	Calgary	1	2	3	5	17	22

Totals

	GP	G	A	Pts.	PIM	PP	SH	GW
1989	11	5	17	22	0	1	1	0
	GP	G	A	Pts.	PIM	PP	SH	GW
Career	131	86	188	274	56	23	10	16

1989-90: NHL Season No. 11

	Date	Opponent	G	A	Pts.	G	A	Pts.
1.	Oct. 5	Toronto	0	1	1	0	1	1
2.	Oct. 7	Edmonton	2	0	2	2	1	3
3.	Oct. 8	Detroit	0	3	3	2	4	6
4.	Oct. 11	Islanders	1	2	3	3	6	9
5.	Oct. 13	Vancouver	0	3	3	3	9	12
6.	Oct. 15	Edmonton	2	1	3	5	10	15
7.	Oct. 17	Boston	0	0	0	5	10	15
8.	Oct. 21	St. Louis	1	0	1	6	10	16
9.	Oct. 22	Chicago	0	2	2	6	12	18
10.	Oct. 25	Calgary	0	0	0	6	12	18
11.	Oct. 27	Winnipeg	0	2	2	6	14	20
12.	Oct. 29	Winnipeg	0	0	0	6	14	20
13.	Oct. 31	Pittsburgh	3	3	6	9	17	26
14.	Nov. 2	Boston	0	0	0	9	17	26
15.	Nov. 4	Hartford	0	1	1	9	18	27
16.	Nov. 5	Buffalo	0	2	2	9	20	29
17.	Nov. 8	Calgary	1	2	3	10	22	32
18.	Nov. 11	Montreal	0	3	3	10	25	35
19.	Nov. 14	Calgary	0	4	4	10	29	39
20.	Nov. 15	Edmonton	0	1	1	10	30	40
21.	Nov. 18	Washington	0	2	2	10	32	42
22.	Nov. 22	Chicago	1	2	3	11	34	45
23.	Nov. 25	Vancouver	0	2	2	11	36	47
24.	Nov. 26	Vancouver	0	3	3	11	39	50
25.	Nov. 30	Edmonton	1	1	2	12	40	52
26.	Dec. 2	Rangers	0	3	3	12	43	55
27.	Dec. 6	Vancouver	0	2	2	12	45	57
28.	Dec. 8	Edmonton	1	1	2	13	46	59
29.	Dec. 10	Quebec	0	4	4	13	50	63
30.	Dec. 11	Montreal	0	1	1	13	51	64
31.	Dec. 13	Hartford	1	1	2	14	52	66
32.	Dec. 15	New Jersey	1	0	1	15	52	67
33.	Dec. 16	Philadelphia	0	0	0	15	52	67
34.	Dec. 19	Winnipeg	2	4	6	17	56	73
35.	Dec. 21	Quebec	1	1	2	18	57	75
36.	Dec. 23	Vancouver	0	1	1	18	58	76
37.	Dec. 27	Calgary	1	1	2	19	59	78
38.	Dec. 30	Philadelphia	0	2	2	19	61	80
39.	Jan. 1	Washington	2	1	3	21	62	83
40.	Jan. 2	Islanders	0	2	2	21	64	85
41.	Jan. 4	New Jersey	0	1	1	21	65	86
42.	Jan. 6	Toronto	1	1	2	22	66	88

	Date	Opponent	G	A	Pts.	G	A	Pts.
43.	Jan. 9	St. Louis	1	0	1	23	66	89
44.	Jan. 11	Edmonton	1	0	1	24	66	90
45.	Jan. 13	Hartford	0	2	2	24	68	92
46.	Jan. 16	Buffalo	1	1	2	25	69	94
47.	Jan. 18	Detroit	2	2	4	27	71	98
48.	Jan. 23	Vancouver	0	0	0	27	71	98
49.	Jan. 25	Edmonton	0	0	0	27	71	98
50.	Jan. 27	Rangers	1	0	1	28	71	99
51.	Jan. 30	New Jersey	0	2	2	28	73	101
52.	Feb. 1	Chicago	1	1	2	29	74	103
53.	Feb. 3	Calgary	0	2	2	29	76	105
54.	Feb. 6	Calgary	0	1	1	29	77	106
55.	Feb. 8	Winnipeg	0	0	0	29	77	106
56.	Feb. 10	Pittsburgh	0	1	1	29	78	107
57.	Feb. 12	Toronto	0	0	0	29	78	107
58.	Feb. 14	Detroit	2	1	3	31	79	110
59.	Feb. 15	Minnesota	0	1	1	31	80	111
60.	Feb. 17	Quebec	2	3	5	33	83	116
61.	Feb. 19	Washington	1	0	1	34	83	117
62.	Feb. 21	Minnesota	1	2	3	35	85	120
63.	Feb. 24	Vancouver	0	2	2	35	87	122
64.	Feb. 28	Edmonton	1	2	3	36	89	125
65.	Mar. 2	Winnipeg	0	2	2	36	91	127
66.	Mar. 4	Winnipeg	0	1	1	36	92	128
67.	Mar. 5	Calgary	0	0	0	36	92	128
68.	Mar. 7	Montreal	1	1	2	37	93	130
69.	Mar. 10	Pittsburgh	1	2	3	38	95	133
70.	Mar. 12	Rangers	0	2	2	38	97	135
71.	Mar. 14	Buffalo	1	2	3	39	99	138
72.	Mar. 17	Boston	1	2	3	40	101	141
73.	Mar. 18	Philadelphia	Did not play					
74.	Mar. 20	Minnesota	Did not play					
75.	Mar. 22	Islanders	0	1	1	40	102	142
76.	Mar. 24	St. Louis	Did not play					
77.	Mar. 27	Winnipeg	Did not play					
78.	Mar. 29	Winnipeg	Did not play					
79.	Mar. 31	Vancouver	Did not play					
80.	Apr. 1	Calgary	Did not play					

	GP	G	A	Pts.	+/-	PIM	PP	SH	GW
1989-90	73	40	*102	*142	+8	42	10	4	4
	GP	G	A	Pts.	+/-	PIM	PP	SH	GW
Career	847	677	1,302	1,979	+574	391	146	64	70

context

NHL record for career points and totals for the runners up

Wayne Gretzky		2,857
Marcel Dionne and Gordie Howe	1,771 | 1,850	
	Dionne Howe	

Dionne

milestones

1. Oct. 15 In Edmonton, Gretzky sets up Bernie Nicholls' goal at 4:32 of first period to tie Gordie Howe as NHL's all-time leading scorer at 1,850 points, beats Bill Ranford at 19:07 of third period to become all-time leader, then adds OT winner at 3:24
2. Nov. 4 Gretzky receives 10-minute misconduct and game misconduct at 20:00 of third period, setting career game high with 20 penalty minutes

3. Dec. 10 Earns 1,900th career point on fourth assist of game
4. April 1 Leads league in assists (102) and points (142)
5. Named second all-star

Bruce Bennett/BBS

playoffs

Date	Opponent	G	A	Pts.	G	A	Pts.
1. Apr. 4	Calgary	Did not play					
2. Apr. 6	Calgary	Did not play					
3. Apr. 8	Calgary	0	1	1	0	1	1
4. Apr. 10	Calgary	1	4	5	1	5	6
5. Apr. 12	Calgary	0	0	0	1	5	6
6. Apr. 14	Calgary	1	2	3	2	7	9
7. Apr. 18	Edmonton	0	0	0	2	7	9

Date	Opponent	G	A	Pts.	G	A	Pts.
8. Apr. 20	Edmonton	0	0	0	2	7	9
9. Apr. 22	Edmonton	1	0	1	3	7	10
10. Apr. 24	Edmonton	Did not play					

Totals

	GP	G	A	Pts.	PIM	PP	SH	GW
1990	7	3	7	10	0	1	0	0
	GP	G	A	Pts.	PIM	PP	SH	GW
Career	138	89	195	284	56	24	10	16

1990-91: NHL Season No. 12

Date	Opponent	G	A	Pts.	G	A	Pts.
1. Oct. 4	Islanders	2	1	3	2	1	3
2. Oct. 6	Vancouver	0	0	0	2	1	3
3. Oct. 9	Vancouver	0	1	1	2	2	4
4. Oct. 11	Edmonton	1	4	5	3	6	9
5. Oct. 13	Boston	2	2	4	5	8	13
6. Oct. 14	St. Louis	0	1	1	5	9	14
7. Oct. 17	Minnesota	1	2	3	6	11	17
8. Oct. 19	Hartford	1	0	1	7	11	18
9. Oct. 23	Calgary	0	2	2	7	13	20
10. Oct. 26	Winnipeg	0	1	1	7	14	21
11. Oct. 28	Winnipeg	0	2	2	7	16	23
12. Oct. 30	Islanders	1	1	2	8	17	25
13. Oct. 31	Rangers	1	0	1	9	17	26
14. Nov. 2	Washington	1	1	2	10	18	28
15. Nov. 4	Chicago	0	1	1	10	19	29
16. Nov. 8	Detroit	1	1	2	11	20	31
17. Nov. 10	Edmonton	1	1	2	12	21	33
18. Nov. 14	Buffalo	1	1	2	13	22	35
19. Nov. 17	Pittsburgh	0	0	0	13	22	35
20. Nov. 20	New Jersey	1	2	3	14	24	38
21. Nov. 22	Calgary	0	2	2	14	26	40
22. Nov. 24	Montreal	0	3	3	14	29	43
23. Nov. 25	Quebec	1	1	2	15	30	45
24. Nov. 27	Detroit	0	1	1	15	31	46
25. Nov. 29	St. Louis	1	1	2	16	32	48
26. Dec. 1	Toronto	0	1	1	16	33	49
27. Dec. 5	Winnipeg	1	1	2	17	34	51
28. Dec. 8	Winnipeg	0	2	2	17	36	53
29. Dec. 11	Rangers	2	0	2	19	36	55
30. Dec. 13	Calgary	0	0	0	19	36	55
31. Dec. 15	Edmonton	1	4	5	20	40	60
32. Dec. 18	Edmonton	0	1	1	20	41	61
33. Dec. 20	Calgary	1	1	2	21	42	63
34. Dec. 22	Vancouver	0	2	2	21	44	65
35. Dec. 27	Philadelphia	0	2	2	21	46	67
36. Dec. 29	Montreal	1	0	1	22	46	68
37. Dec. 31	Minnesota	0	2	2	22	48	70
38. Jan. 2	Rangers	0	0	0	22	48	70
39. Jan. 3	Islanders	3	0	3	25	48	73
40. Jan. 5	Toronto	0	2	2	25	50	75
41. Jan. 6	Chicago	0	1	1	25	51	76
42. Jan. 8	Hartford	0	2	2	25	53	78

Date	Opponent	G	A	Pts.	G	A	Pts.
43. Jan. 10	Buffalo	0	4	4	25	57	82
44. Jan. 12	Vancouver	1	1	2	26	58	84
45. Jan. 14	New Jersey	1	2	3	27	60	87
46. Jan. 16	Hartford	0	2	2	27	62	89
47. Jan. 17	Boston	1	1	2	28	63	91
48. Jan. 22	Edmonton	Did not play					
49. Jan. 25	Vancouver	1	1	2	29	64	93
50. Jan. 26	Vancouver	3	2	5	32	66	98
51. Jan. 30	New Jersey	0	2	2	32	68	100
52. Feb. 2	Vancouver	1	2	3	33	70	103
53. Feb. 4	Detroit	0	3	3	33	73	106
54. Feb. 5	Philadelphia	0	0	0	33	73	106
55. Feb. 8	Buffalo	0	1	1	33	74	107
56. Feb. 9	St. Louis	0	1	1	33	75	108
57. Feb. 12	Calgary	0	2	2	33	77	110
58. Feb. 14	Edmonton	0	2	2	33	79	112
59. Feb. 16	Boston	0	1	1	33	80	113
60. Feb. 18	Washington	1	2	3	34	82	116
61. Feb. 20	Quebec	1	1	2	35	83	118
62. Feb. 22	Winnipeg	1	4	5	36	87	123
63. Feb. 24	Winnipeg	1	2	3	37	89	126
64. Feb. 26	Pittsburgh	0	3	3	37	92	129
65. Feb. 28	Winnipeg	0	1	1	37	93	130
66. Mar. 2	Winnipeg	0	3	3	37	96	133
67. Mar. 5	Washington	0	3	3	37	99	136
68. Mar. 7	Pittsburgh	1	1	2	38	100	138
69. Mar. 9	Quebec	0	2	2	38	102	140
70. Mar. 10	Montreal	0	3	3	38	105	143
71. Mar. 12	Philadelphia	0	3	3	38	108	146
72. Mar. 14	Chicago	0	1	1	38	109	147
73. Mar. 16	Calgary	0	2	2	38	111	149
74. Mar. 17	Vancouver	0	2	2	38	113	151
75. Mar. 20	Toronto	0	4	4	38	117	155
76. Mar. 23	Calgary	0	3	3	38	120	158
77. Mar. 24	Edmonton	0	1	1	38	121	159
78. Mar. 26	Edmonton	2	0	2	40	121	161
79. Mar. 28	Minnesota	1	1	2	41	122	163
80. Mar. 31	Calgary	Did not play					

	GP	G	A	Pts.	+/−	PIM	PP	SH	GW
1990-91	78	41	*122	*163	+30	16	8	0	5

	GP	G	A	Pts.	+/−	PIM	PP	SH	GW
Career	925	718	1,424	2,142	+604	407	154	64	75

context

Most career playoff points

| Wayne Gretzky | 122 |
| Jari Kurri | 109 |

Kurri

milestones

1. Oct. 26 Records 2,000th career point with assist on Tomas Sandstrom's goal at 14:32 of first period

2. Jan. 3 Beats Islanders' Glenn Healy at 11:48 of first period for 700th career goal, becoming fourth player to reach mark

3. March 26 Scores twice to reach 40 goals for record 12th consecutive season; 12 seasons of 40-plus goals also record

4. March 7 Records 100th assist for record 11th straight season;

11 seasons of 100-plus assists is record

5. March 26 Sets record 23-game assist streak (48 assists) from Feb. 8 to March 24, breaking own record (17)

6. April 10 Scores 93rd playoff goal, beating Canucks' Kirk McLean at 13:11 of first period, to pass Jari Kurri as all-time playoff goal leader

7. Named first all-star

Dan Hamilton/VPS

Dan Hamilton/VPS

playoffs

	Date	Opponent	G	A	Pts.	G	A	Pts.
1.	Apr. 4	Vancouver	1	1	2	1	1	2
2.	Apr. 6	Vancouver	1	0	1	2	1	3
3.	Apr. 8	Vancouver	1	0	1	3	1	4
4.	Apr. 10	Vancouver	1	1	2	4	2	6
5.	Apr. 12	Vancouver	0	4	4	4	6	10
6.	Apr. 14	Vancouver	0	0	0	4	6	10
7.	Apr. 18	Edmonton	0	2	2	4	8	12
8.	Apr. 20	Edmonton	0	0	0	4	8	12

	Date	Opponent	G	A	Pts.	G	A	Pts.
9.	Apr. 22	Edmonton	0	0	0	4	8	12
10.	Apr. 24	Edmonton	0	2	2	4	10	14
11.	Apr. 26	Edmonton	0	0	0	4	10	14
12.	Apr. 28	Edmonton	0	1	1	4	11	15

Totals

	GP	G	A	Pts.	PIM	PP	SH	GW
1990	12	4	11	15	2	1	0	2
	GP	G	A	Pts.	PIM	PP	SH	GW
Career	150	93	206	299	58	25	10	18

1991‑92: NHL Season No. 13

Date	Opponent	G	A	Pts.	G	A	Pts.
1. Oct. 4	Winnipeg	0	2	2	0	2	2
2. Oct. 6	Edmonton	0	0	0	0	2	2
3. Oct. 8	Edmonton	0	1	1	0	3	3
4. Oct. 10	Calgary	0	0	0	0	3	3
5. Oct. 12	Winnipeg	0	2	2	0	5	5
6. Oct. 16	San Jose	Did not play					
7. Oct. 19	Minnesota	Did not play					
8. Oct. 22	New Jersey	Did not play					
9. Oct. 23	Rangers	Did not play					
10. Oct. 26	Islanders	Did not play					
11. Oct. 28	Detroit	0	1	1	0	6	6
12. Oct. 30	Hartford	1	1	2	1	7	8
13. Oct. 31	Boston	1	1	2	2	8	10
14. Nov. 2	Toronto	2	2	4	4	10	14
15. Nov. 7	Vancouver	0	0	0	4	10	14
16. Nov. 9	Edmonton	0	2	2	4	12	16
17. Nov. 11	Winnipeg	0	0	0	4	12	16
18. Nov. 12	Vancouver	1	0	1	5	12	17
19. Nov. 14	Buffalo	0	0	0	5	12	17
20. Nov. 16	Detroit	0	0	0	5	12	17
21. Nov. 19	San Jose	0	2	2	5	14	19
22. Nov. 21	Rangers	1	0	1	6	14	20
23. Nov. 23	San Jose	3	1	4	9	15	24
24. Nov. 26	Toronto	1	3	4	10	18	28
25. Nov. 28	Calgary	0	3	3	10	21	31
26. Nov. 30	New Jersey	0	1	1	10	22	32
27. Dec. 3	San Jose	1	1	2	11	23	34
28. Dec. 5	Chicago	0	2	2	11	25	36
29. Dec. 7	Quebec	0	2	2	11	27	38
30. Dec. 12	Winnipeg	1	0	1	12	27	39
31. Dec. 14	Vancouver	1	2	3	13	29	42
32. Dec. 17	Minnesota	0	1	1	13	30	43
33. Dec. 21	Detroit	1	0	1	14	30	44
34. Dec. 26	San Jose	1	2	3	15	32	47
35. Dec. 28	Edmonton	1	3	4	16	35	51
36. Dec. 29	Calgary	0	0	0	16	35	51
37. Dec. 31	Vancouver	0	1	1	16	36	52
38. Jan. 2	Edmonton	0	0	0	16	36	52
39. Jan. 4	Philadelphia	1	2	3	17	38	55
40. Jan. 7	Pittsburgh	0	1	1	17	39	56
41. Jan. 9	Philadelphia	1	0	1	18	39	57
42. Jan. 10	Washington	0	2	2	18	41	59

Date	Opponent	G	A	Pts.	G	A	Pts.
43. Jan. 12	New Jersey	0	2	2	18	43	61
44. Jan. 14	San Jose	0	1	1	18	44	62
45. Jan. 16	Washington	0	1	1	18	45	63
46. Jan. 22	Minnesota	0	0	0	18	45	63
47. Jan. 23	St. Louis	0	2	2	18	47	65
48. Jan. 25	Calgary	0	2	2	18	49	67
49. Jan. 28	St. Louis	1	1	2	19	50	69
50. Jan. 30	Rangers	0	0	0	19	50	69
51. Feb. 1	Chicago	1	1	2	20	51	71
52. Feb. 4	Islanders	0	1	1	20	52	72
53. Feb. 6	Hartford	0	3	3	20	55	75
54. Feb. 8	Pittsburgh	2	0	2	22	55	77
55. Feb. 9	Buffalo	0	1	1	22	56	78
56. Feb. 11	St. Louis	0	1	1	22	57	79
57. Feb. 13	Chicago	0	0	0	22	57	79
58. Feb. 15	Washington	0	3	3	22	60	82
59. Feb. 17	Boston	2	2	4	24	62	86
60. Feb. 19	Edmonton	1	1	2	25	63	88
61. Feb. 21	Calgary	1	2	3	26	65	91
62. Feb. 23	Winnipeg	0	3	3	26	68	94
63. Feb. 25	Vancouver	0	1	1	26	69	95
64. Feb. 27	Quebec	Did not play					
65. Feb. 29	Montreal	1	3	4	27	72	99
66. Mar. 3	Philadelphia	0	1	1	27	73	100
67. Mar. 4	San Jose	0	3	3	27	76	103
68. Mar. 7	Pittsburgh	1	2	3	28	78	106
69. Mar. 9	Toronto	0	1	1	28	79	107
70. Mar. 11	Hartford	0	0	0	28	79	107
71. Mar. 14	Montreal	0	1	1	28	80	108
72. Mar. 15	Boston	0	1	1	28	81	109
73. Mar. 17	Winnipeg	0	1	1	28	82	110
74. Mar. 19	Buffalo	0	0	0	28	82	110
75. Mar. 21	Calgary	2	1	3	30	83	113
76. Mar. 26	Calgary	1	0	1	31	83	114
77. Mar. 27	Winnipeg	0	3	3	31	86	117
78. Mar. 29	Edmonton	0	0	0	31	86	117
79. Apr. 4	Vancouver	0	4	4	31	90	121
80. Apr. 5	Vancouver	0	0	0	31	90	121

	GP	G	A	Pts.	+/–	PIM	PP	SH	GW
1991-92	74	31	*90	121	-12	34	12	2	2
	GP	**G**	**A**	**Pts.**	**+/–**	**PIM**	**PP**	**SH**	**GW**
Career	999	749	1,514	2,263	+592	441	166	66	77

context

Most consecutive seasons with 100‑plus points

Wayne Gretzky
100‑Point Men   **6**   **13**

Mike Bossy, Guy Lafleur, Mario Lemieux, Bobby Orr, Peter Stastny, Steve Yzerman

Yzerman

milestones

1. **Dec. 21** Scores 732nd career goal, beating Red Wings' Tim Cheveldae at 8:59 of first period, to move past Marcel Dionne into second in all-time career goals
2. **March 3** Records assist to reach 100 points for NHL-record 13th straight season
3. **April 5** Leads league in assists (90) for 13th straight season;

streak of 11-straight 100-plus assist seasons ends; finishes as minus player (minus-12) for first time in career
4. **April 20** Sets up Paul Coffey at 0:46 of first period to record 300th playoff point, extending NHL post-season points record
5. Named most gentlemanly player

playoffs

Date	Opponent	G	A	Pts.	G	A	Pts.
1. Apr. 18	Edmonton	0	0	0	0	0	0
2. Apr. 20	Edmonton	0	4	4	0	4	4
3. Apr. 22	Edmonton	0	0	0	0	4	4
4. Apr. 24	Edmonton	0	1	1	0	5	5
5. Apr. 26	Edmonton	2	0	2	2	5	7

Date	Opponent	G	A	Pts.	G	A	Pts.
6. Apr. 28	Edmonton	0	0	0	2	5	7

Totals

	GP	G	A	Pts.	PIM	PP	SH	GW
1992	6	2	5	7	2	1	0	0
	GP	G	A	Pts.	PIM	PP	SH	GW
Career	156	95	211	306	60	26	10	18

1992-93: NHL Season No. 14

Date	Opponent	G	A	Pts.	G	A	Pts.
1. Oct. 6	Calgary	Did not play					
2. Oct. 8	Detroit	Did not play					
3. Oct. 10	Winnipeg	Did not play					
4. Oct. 13	San Jose	Did not play					
5. Oct. 15	Calgary	Did not play					
6. Oct. 17	Boston	Did not play					
7. Oct. 20	Calgary	Did not play					
8. Oct. 23	Winnipeg	Did not play					
9. Oct. 24	Minnesota	Did not play					
10. Oct. 27	Islanders	Did not play					
11. Oct. 29	Boston	Did not play					
12. Oct. 31	Hartford	Did not play					
13. Nov. 5	New Jersey	Did not play					
14. Nov. 7	Buffalo	Did not play					
15. Nov. 8	San Jose	Did not play					
16. Nov. 10	Winnipeg	Did not play					
17. Nov. 12	Vancouver	Did not play					
18. Nov. 14	Edmonton	Did not play					
19. Nov. 16	Vancouver	Did not play					
20. Nov. 17	San Jose	Did not play					
21. Nov. 19	Chicago	Did not play					
22. Nov. 21	Toronto	Did not play					
23. Nov. 25	Edmonton	Did not play					
24. Nov. 27	Detroit	Did not play					
25. Nov. 28	Toronto	Did not play					
26. Dec. 1	Chicago	Did not play					
27. Dec. 3	Pittsburgh	Did not play					
28. Dec. 5	Hartford	Did not play					
29. Dec. 8	Montreal	Did not play					
30. Dec. 10	Quebec	Did not play					
31. Dec. 12	St. Louis	Did not play					
32. Dec. 15	Tampa Bay	Did not play					
33. Dec. 18	Edmonton	Did not play					
34. Dec. 19	Calgary	Did not play					
35. Dec. 22	Vancouver	Did not play					
36. Dec. 26	San Jose	Did not play					
37. Dec. 29	Philadelphia	Did not play					
38. Dec. 31	Vancouver	Did not play					
39. Jan. 2	Montreal	Did not play					
40. Jan. 6	Tampa Bay	0	2	2	0	2	2
41. Jan. 8	Winnipeg	2	0	2	2	2	4
42. Jan. 10	Chicago	0	2	2	2	4	6
43. Jan. 12	Ottawa	0	1	1	2	5	7
44. Jan. 14	New Jersey	0	0	0	2	5	7

Date	Opponent	G	A	Pts.	G	A	Pts.
45. Jan. 16	Winnipeg	0	1	1	2	6	8
46. Jan. 19	Edmonton	0	1	1	2	7	9
47. Jan. 21	Vancouver	0	2	2	2	9	11
48. Jan. 23	Rangers	0	0	0	2	9	11
49. Jan. 26	San Jose	0	2	2	2	11	13
50. Jan. 28	Calgary	0	1	1	2	12	14
51. Jan. 30	Chicago	0	0	0	2	12	14
52. Feb. 2	Quebec	0	0	0	2	12	14
53. Feb. 3	Montreal	0	0	0	2	12	14
54. Feb. 9	Edmonton	0	2	2	2	14	16
55. Feb. 11	Detroit	0	2	2	2	16	18
56. Feb. 13	Washington	0	0	0	2	16	18
57. Feb. 15	Vancouver	0	1	1	2	17	19
58. Feb. 17	Minnesota	1	4	5	3	21	24
59. Feb. 18	Chicago	0	0	0	3	21	24
60. Feb. 20	Washington	0	1	1	3	22	25
61. Feb. 22	Tampa Bay	1	3	4	4	25	29
62. Feb. 25	St. Louis	0	0	0	4	25	29
63. Feb. 27	Toronto	0	0	0	4	25	29
64. Mar. 2	Calgary	2	0	2	6	25	31
65. Mar. 4	Ottawa	0	4	4	6	29	35
66. Mar. 6	Edmonton	1	2	3	7	31	38
67. Mar. 9	Rangers	0	2	2	7	33	40
68. Mar. 11	Pittsburgh	1	1	2	8	34	42
69. Mar. 15	Buffalo	1	2	3	9	36	45
70. Mar. 16	Winnipeg	1	2	3	10	38	48
71. Mar. 18	Islanders	1	0	1	11	38	49
72. Mar. 20	St. Louis	0	1	1	11	39	50
73. Mar. 24	Vancouver	0	0	0	11	39	50
74. Mar. 26	Edmonton	1	0	1	12	39	51
75. Mar. 28	Winnipeg	0	0	0	12	39	51
76. Mar. 29	Detroit	2	2	4	14	41	55
77. Mar. 31	Toronto	0	2	2	14	43	57
78. Apr. 1	Philadelphia	0	2	2	14	45	59
79. Apr. 3	Minnesota	0	0	0	14	45	59
80. Apr. 6	Calgary	0	0	0	14	45	59
81. Apr. 8	San Jose	0	1	1	14	46	60
82. Apr. 10	San Jose	1	1	2	15	47	62
83. Apr. 13	Vancouver	0	0	0	15	47	62
84. Apr. 15	Vancouver	1	2	3	16	49	65

	GP	G	A	Pts.	+/–	PIM	PP	SH	GW
1992-93	45	16	49	65	+6	6	0	2	1
	GP	G	A	Pts.	+/–	PIM	PP	SH	GW
Career	1,044	765	1,563	2,328	+598	447	166	68	78

context

Most 50-goal seasons
Wayne Gretzky	**9**
Mike Bossy	**9**

Bossy

milestones

1. Jan. 6 After missing first 39 games of season with herniated disc in back, returns to play in 1,000th career game, recording two assists in 6-3 loss

2. May 7 Becomes first player to score 100 playoff goals when he beats Canucks' Kirk McLean at 9:03 of third period

3. May 29 Sets NHL record with eighth career playoff hat trick in 5-4 win over Toronto in conference final, passing Maurice Richard and Jari Kurri (seven)

4. June 9 Leads playoffs in goals (15), assists (25) and points (40)

Bruce Bennett/BBS

Robert Laberge/BBS

playoffs

Date	Opponent	G	A	Pts.	G	A	Pts.
1. Apr. 18	Calgary	0	1	0	0	1	1
2. Apr. 21	Calgary	0	1	1	0	2	2
3. Apr. 23	Calgary	0	1	1	0	3	3
4. Apr. 25	Calgary	0	0	0	0	3	3
5. Apr. 27	Calgary	1	3	4	1	6	7
6. Apr. 29	Calgary	1	2	3	2	8	10
7. May 2	Vancouver	1	0	1	3	8	11
8. May 5	Vancouver	1	2	3	4	10	14
9. May 7	Vancouver	2	1	3	6	11	17
10. May 9	Vancouver	0	2	2	6	13	19
11. May 11	Vancouver	1	0	1	7	13	20
12. May 13	Vancouver	1	2	3	8	15	23
13. May 17	Toronto	0	1	1	8	16	24
14. May 19	Toronto	0	1	1	8	17	25

Date	Opponent	G	A	Pts.	G	A	Pts.
15. May 21	Toronto	0	1	1	8	18	26
16. May 23	Toronto	1	1	2	9	19	28
17. May 25	Toronto	0	0	0	9	19	28
18. May 27	Toronto	1	0	1	10	19	29
19. May 29	Toronto	3	1	4	13	20	34
20. June 1	Montreal	1	3	4	14	23	37
21. June 3	Montreal	0	0	0	14	23	37
22. June 5	Montreal	1	1	2	15	24	39
23. June 7	Montreal	0	1	1	15	25	40
24. June 9	Montreal	0	0	0	15	25	40

Totals	LOS ANGELES LOSES IN STANLEY CUP FINAL						
	GP	G	A	Pts.	PIM	PP	SH	GW
1993	24	*15	*25	*40	4	4	1	3
	GP	G	A	Pts.	PIM	PP	SH	GW
Career	180	110	236	346	64	30	11	21

1993-94: NHL Season No. 15

Date	Opponent	G	A	Pts.	G	A	Pts.
1. Oct. 6	Vancouver	0	0	0	0	0	0
2. Oct. 9	Detroit	2	4	6	2	4	6
3. Oct. 10	San Jose	0	2	2	2	6	8
4. Oct. 12	Islanders	1	2	3	3	8	11
5. Oct. 14	Edmonton	0	2	2	3	10	13
6. Oct. 16	Calgary	1	3	4	4	13	17
7. Oct. 19	Florida	0	0	0	4	13	17
8. Oct. 20	Tampa Bay	1	2	3	5	15	20
9. Oct. 22	Washington	1	1	2	6	16	22
10. Oct. 24	Rangers	1	1	2	7	17	24
11. Oct. 26	Islanders	0	0	0	7	17	24
12. Oct. 27	Detroit	0	2	2	7	19	26
13. Oct. 29	Winnipeg	1	2	3	8	21	29
14. Nov. 3	New Jersey	1	1	2	9	22	31
15. Nov. 6	Pittsburgh	0	4	4	9	26	35
16. Nov. 9	Calgary	0	1	1	9	27	36
17. Nov. 10	Vancouver	0	0	0	9	27	36
18. Nov. 13	St. Louis	0	2	2	9	29	38
19. Nov. 18	Toronto	0	1	1	9	30	39
20. Nov. 20	St.Louis	0	1	1	9	31	40
21. Nov. 21	Dallas	0	1	1	9	32	41
22. Nov. 25	Quebec	1	3	4	10	35	45
23. Nov. 27	Montreal	0	0	0	10	35	45
24. Nov. 30	Winnipeg	2	2	4	12	37	49
25. Dec. 2	Anaheim	0	2	2	12	39	51
26. Dec. 4	Tampa Bay	0	0	0	12	39	51
27. Dec. 8	Florida	0	2	2	12	41	53
28. Dec. 11	St. Louis	0	2	2	12	43	55
29. Dec. 13	Ottawa	1	1	2	13	44	57
30. Dec. 14	Pittsburgh	0	0	0	13	44	57
31. Dec. 17	Buffalo	0	0	0	13	44	57
32. Dec. 18	Toronto	0	0	0	13	44	57
33. Dec. 20	Calgary	2	0	2	15	44	59
34. Dec. 23	Dallas	0	0	0	15	44	59
35. Dec. 26	Anaheim	0	0	0	15	44	59
36. Dec. 28	Vancouver	1	2	3	16	46	62
37. Dec. 31	Detroit	0	1	1	16	47	63
38. Jan. 1	Toronto	1	2	3	17	49	66
39. Jan. 4	Quebec	0	4	4	17	53	70
40. Jan. 8	Detroit	0	0	0	17	53	70
41. Jan. 11	San Jose	0	1	1	17	54	71
42. Jan. 12	Hartford	2	2	4	19	56	75
43. Jan. 15	New Jersey	2	1	3	21	57	78
44. Jan. 16	Philadelphia	1	1	2	22	58	80

Date	Opponent	G	A	Pts.	G	A	Pts.
45. Jan. 18	Dallas	0	2	2	22	60	82
46. Jan. 24	Calgary	1	2	3	23	62	85
47. Jan. 25	Winnipeg	0	2	2	23	64	87
48. Jan. 27	Rangers	1	0	1	24	64	88
49. Jan. 29	Anaheim	0	1	1	24	65	89
50. Jan. 31	Phoenix	0	0	0	24	65	89
51. Feb. 2	Edmonton	1	0	1	25	65	90
52. Feb. 5	Calgary	1	1	2	26	66	92
53. Feb. 9	Chicago	0	1	1	26	67	93
54. Feb. 11	Anaheim	2	3	5	28	70	98
55. Feb. 12	Washington	0	0	0	28	70	98
56. Feb. 14	Boston	0	2	2	28	72	100
57. Feb. 18	Philadelphia	0	1	1	28	73	101
58. Feb. 19	San Jose	0	2	2	28	75	103
59. Feb. 21	Toronto	2	0	2	30	75	105
60. Feb. 23	Dallas	0	0	0	30	75	105
61. Feb. 25	Edmonton	1	0	1	31	75	106
62. Feb. 26	Calgary	1	0	1	32	75	107
63. Feb. 28	Montreal	0	1	1	32	76	108
64. Mar. 2	Hartford	1	1	2	33	77	110
65. Mar. 3	Boston	0	1	1	33	78	111
66. Mar. 6	Chicago	0	0	0	33	78	111
67. Mar. 9	Chicago	0	0	0	33	78	111
68. Mar. 12	Buffalo	0	0	0	33	78	111
69. Mar. 15	Ottawa	1	3	4	34	81	115
70. Mar. 16	Anaheim	0	0	0	34	81	115
71. Mar. 19	San Jose	0	2	2	34	83	117
72. Mar. 20	San Jose	2	0	2	36	83	119
73. Mar. 23	Vancouver	1	0	1	37	83	120
74. Mar. 25	Edmonton	0	1	1	37	84	121
75. Mar. 27	Vancouver	0	2	2	37	86	123
76. Mar. 30	Anaheim	0	0	0	37	86	123
77. Apr. 2	Edmonton	1	1	2	38	87	125
78. Apr. 3	Edmonton	0	3	3	38	90	128
79. Apr. 5	San Jose	0	1	1	38	91	129
80. Apr. 7	St. Louis	0	0	0	38	91	129
81. Apr. 9	Winnipeg	0	1	1	38	92	130
82. Apr. 10	Chicago	Did not play					
83. Apr. 13	Calgary	Did not play					
84. Apr. 14	Edmonton	Did not play					

	GP	G	A	Pts.	+/–	PIM	PP	SH	GW
1993-94	81	38	*92	*130	-25	20	14	4	0
	GP	G	A	Pts.	+/–	PIM	PP	SH	GW
Career	1,125	803	1,655	2,458	+573	467	180	72	78

context

Most scoring titles

Wayne Gretzky		11
Runners Up	5	6

Phil Esposito   Gordie Howe
Mario Lemieux

Lemieux

milestones

1. March 23 Scores 802nd career goal, beating Canucks' Kirk McLean at 14:47 of second period, to pass Gordie Howe as NHL's all-time leading goal-scorer

2. April 14 Leads league with assists (92) and points (130); finishes with career worst minus-25; misses playoffs for the first time

3. Named second all-star, most gentlemanly player

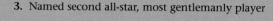

Bruce Bennett/BBS

playoffs

Totals:

	GP	G	A	Pts.	PIM	PP	SH	GW
Career	180	110	236	346	64	30	11	21

1994-95: NHL Season No. 16

Date	Opponent	G	A	Pts.	G	A	Pts.
1. Jan. 20	Toronto	1	1	2	1	1	2
2. Jan. 22	Edmonton	0	2	2	1	3	4
3. Jan. 24	Dallas	0	1	1	1	4	5
4. Jan. 26	St. Louis	1	0	1	2	4	6
5. Jan. 28	Winnipeg	0	0	0	2	4	6
6. Jan. 29	Chicago	0	1	1	2	5	7
7. Feb. 4	Detroit	0	1	1	2	6	8
8. Feb. 5	Anaheim	0	1	1	2	7	9
9. Feb. 7	St. Louis	0	1	1	2	8	10
10. Feb. 11	Toronto	0	1	1	2	9	11
11. Feb. 12	Detroit	0	1	1	2	10	12
12. Feb. 15	Dallas	0	0	0	2	10	12
13. Feb. 17	San Jose	0	0	0	2	10	12
14. Feb. 18	Vancouver	1	1	2	3	11	14
15. Feb. 20	Vancouver	0	1	1	3	12	15
16. Feb. 23	Calgary	1	1	2	4	13	17
17. Feb. 25	Edmonton	0	0	0	4	13	17
18. Feb. 28	Chicago	0	0	0	4	13	17
19. Mar. 4	Vancouver	0	1	1	4	14	18
20. Mar. 6	Dallas	0	1	1	4	15	19
21. Mar. 9	Chicago	0	0	0	4	15	19
22. Mar. 11	Winnipeg	0	0	0	4	15	19
23. Mar. 13	Toronto	1	1	2	5	16	21
24. Mar. 14	Detroit	0	0	0	5	16	21
25. Mar. 16	St. Louis	0	0	0	5	16	21
26. Mar. 18	Toronto	0	2	2	5	18	23

Date	Opponent	G	A	Pts.	G	A	Pts.
27. Mar. 20	St. Louis	2	1	3	7	19	26
28. Mar. 21	Anaheim	0	2	2	7	21	28
29. Mar. 25	San Jose	0	0	0	7	21	28
30. Mar. 26	San Jose	0	2	2	7	23	30
31. Mar. 28	Calgary	0	3	3	7	26	33
32. Mar. 29	Vancouver	0	0	0	7	26	33
33. Apr. 1	Winnipeg	2	0	2	9	26	35
34. Apr. 3	Edmonton	0	2	2	9	28	37
35. Apr. 6	Dallas	1	0	1	10	28	38
36. Apr. 7	Calgary	0	2	2	10	30	40
37. Apr. 9	Anaheim	0	1	1	10	31	41
38. Apr. 12	Calgary	0	0	0	10	31	41
39. Apr. 16	San Jose	0	0	0	10	31	41
40. Apr. 17	Calgary	0	1	1	10	32	42
41. Apr. 19	Edmonton	0	0	0	10	32	42
42. Apr. 21	Edmonton	0	1	1	10	33	43
43. Apr. 23	Anaheim	0	1	1	10	34	44
44. Apr. 25	Detroit	0	1	1	10	35	45
45. Apr. 28	San Jose	0	0	0	10	35	45
46. Apr. 30	Anaheim	1	1	2	11	36	47
47. May 2	Winnipeg	0	0	0	11	36	47
48. May 3	Chicago	0	1	1	11	37	48

	GP	G	A	Pts.	+/−	PIM	PP	SH	GW
1994-95	48	11	37	48	-20	6	3	0	1
	GP	G	A	Pts.	+/−	PIM	PP	SH	GW
Career	1,173	814	1,692	2,506	+553	473	183	72	79

context

Most selections to first and second all-star teams

Wayne Gretzky	15
Ray Bourque and Gordie Howe	17 (Bourque) 21 (Howe)

Bourque

milestones

Fall Gretzky assembles team for goodwill tour against European clubs during NHL lockout

1. April 17 Records 2,500th career point with an assist on Rob Blake's goal at 11:09 of first period

Art Foxall/BBS

Steve Babineau/VA

playoffs

Totals:

	GP	G	A	Pts.	PIM	PP	SH	GW
Career	180	110	236	346	64	30	11	21

1995-96: NHL Season No. 17

Date	Opponent	G	A	Pts.	G	A	Pts.
1. Oct. 7	Colorado	0	2	2	0	2	2
2. Oct. 10	Chicago	0	1	1	0	3	3
3. Oct. 12	Vancouver	1	3	4	1	6	7
4. Oct. 15	Vancouver	0	0	0	1	6	7
5. Oct. 18	Philadelphia	0	0	0	1	6	7
6. Oct. 20	Washington	0	4	4	1	10	11
7. Oct. 21	Pittsburgh	0	1	1	1	11	12
8. Oct. 23	Montreal	0	0	0	1	11	12
9. Oct. 26	Ottawa	0	1	1	1	12	13
10. Oct. 28	Toronto	1	1	2	2	13	15
11. Oct. 31	Calgary	0	0	0	2	13	15
12. Nov. 2	Rangers	1	1	2	3	14	17
13. Nov. 4	New Jersey	0	1	1	3	15	18
14. Nov. 7	St. Louis	0	1	1	3	16	19
15. Nov. 8	Dallas	0	2	2	3	18	21
16. Nov. 11	Pittsburgh	1	1	2	4	19	23
17. Nov. 13	Anaheim	1	2	3	5	21	26
18. Nov. 14	Detroit	1	1	2	6	22	28
19. Nov. 16	Islanders	1	5	6	7	27	34
20. Nov. 18	Florida	0	0	0	7	27	34
21. Nov. 21	Philadelphia	0	0	0	7	27	34
22. Nov. 22	Islanders	0	2	2	7	29	36
23. Nov. 24	Boston	0	0	0	7	29	36
24. Nov. 26	Florida	0	0	0	7	29	36
25. Nov. 27	Tampa Bay	0	0	0	7	29	36
26. Nov. 30	Washington	0	1	1	7	30	37
27. Dec. 2	Dallas	0	0	0	7	30	37
28. Dec. 6	Winnipeg	1	2	3	8	32	40
29. Dec. 9	St. Louis	0	0	0	8	32	40
30. Dec. 11	Calgary	0	1	1	8	33	41
31. Dec. 13	Ottawa	0	2	2	8	35	43
32. Dec. 16	Toronto	0	3	3	8	38	46
33. Dec. 20	Vancouver	1	0	1	9	38	47
34. Dec. 22	San Jose	0	0	0	9	38	47
35. Dec. 23	Colorado	0	0	0	9	38	47
36. Dec. 27	Anaheim	0	2	2	9	40	49
37. Dec. 29	Edmonton	1	0	1	10	40	50
38. Dec. 31	Anaheim	0	0	0	10	40	50
39. Jan. 3	Winnipeg	1	2	3	11	42	53
40. Jan. 5	San Jose	1	3	4	12	45	57
41. Jan. 6	San Jose	1	2	3	13	47	60
42. Jan. 8	Dallas	0	2	2	13	49	62
43. Jan. 10	Toronto	0	1	1	13	50	63
44. Jan. 12	Detroit	0	1	1	13	51	64
45. Jan. 14	Chicago	0	1	1	13	52	65

Date	Opponent	G	A	Pts.	G	A	Pts.
46. Jan. 16	Calgary	0	2	2	13	54	67
47. Jan. 22	Rangers	0	0	0	13	54	67
48. Jan. 23	New Jersey	0	0	0	13	54	67
49. Jan. 25	Hartford	0	1	1	13	55	68
50. Jan. 27	Anaheim	1	3	4	14	58	72
51. Jan. 31	Hartford	0	3	3	14	61	75
52. Feb. 1	San Jose	0	1	1	14	62	76
53. Feb. 3	Calgary	0	0	0	14	62	76
54. Feb. 6	Chicago	0	0	0	14	62	76
55. Feb. 8	Toronto	0	1	1	14	63	77
56. Feb. 10	San Jose	0	0	0	14	63	77
57. Feb. 13	Detroit	0	0	0	14	63	77
58. Feb. 14	Buffalo	Did not play					
59. Feb. 17	Anaheim	Did not play					
60. Feb. 19	Boston	0	1	1	14	64	78
61. Feb. 21	Edmonton	1	0	1	15	64	79
62. Feb. 23	Colorado	0	1	1	15	65	80
63. Feb. 24	St. Louis	0	0	0	15	65	80
64. Feb. 26	Winnipeg	0	1	1	15	66	81
Feb. 27	Traded to St. Louis Blues						
62. Feb. 29	Vancouver	1	0	1	16	66	82
63. Mar. 3	Edmonton	0	1	1	16	67	83
64. Mar. 5	Florida	0	0	0	16	67	83
65. Mar. 7	Calgary	0	2	2	16	69	85
66. Mar. 9	Hartford	2	1	3	18	70	88
67. Mar. 12	Calgary	0	0	0	18	70	88
68. Mar. 15	San Jose	1	2	3	19	72	91
69. Mar. 17	Anaheim	0	1	1	19	73	92
70. Mar. 18	Los Angeles	1	1	2	20	74	94
71. Mar. 20	Dallas	0	1	1	20	75	95
72. Mar. 22	Chicago	0	0	0	20	75	95
73. Mar. 24	Detroit	1	0	1	21	75	96
74. Mar. 26	Pittsburgh	0	1	1	21	76	97
75. Mar. 28	New Jersey	1	2	3	22	78	100
76. Mar. 31	Detroit	0	0	0	22	78	100
77. Apr. 3	Colorado	1	1	2	23	79	102
78. Apr. 4	Toronto	0	0	0	23	79	102
79. Apr. 6	Toronto	Did not play					
80. Apr. 8	Winnipeg	Did not play					
81. Apr. 11	Colorado	Did not play					
82. Apr. 14	Chicago	0	0	0	23	79	102

	GP	G	A	Pts.	+/−	PIM	PP	SH	GW
1995-96	80	23	79	102	-13	34	6	1	3
	GP	G	A	Pts.	+/−	PIM	PP	SH	GW
Career	1,253	837	1,771	2,608	+540	507	189	73	82

context

Most 100-point seasons

Wayne Gretzky			15
Marcel Dionne and Mario Lemieux	8	10	
	Dionne	Lemieux	

Dionne

milestones

1. Feb. 27 After months of speculation, Gretzky is dealt to St. Louis Blues for Craig Johnson, Patrice Tardif, Roman Vopat, the Blues' fifth round draft pick in 1996 (Peter Hogan) and first round draft pick in 1997 (Matt Zultek)

2. Feb. 29 Beats Vancouver's Kirk McLean at 16:24 of first period in first game with Blues

3. March 12 Records three points to reach 100 for NHL-record 15th and final time

playoffs

Date	Opponent	G	A	Pts.	G	A	Pts.
1. Apr. 16	Toronto	0	3	3	0	3	3
2. Apr. 18	Toronto	0	1	1	0	4	4
3. Apr. 21	Toronto	0	1	1	0	5	5
4. Apr. 23	Toronto	0	3	3	0	8	8
5. Apr. 25	Toronto	0	1	1	0	9	9
6. Apr. 27	Toronto	0	0	0	0	9	9
7. May 3	Detroit	0	1	1	0	10	10
8. May 5	Detroit	0	1	1	0	11	11
9. May 8	Detroit	0	1	1	0	12	12

Date	Opponent	G	A	Pts.	G	A	Pts.
10. May 10	Detroit	1	0	1	1	12	13
11. May 12	Detroit	1	1	2	2	13	15
12. May 14	Detroit	0	1	1	2	14	16
13. May 16	Detroit	0	0	0	2	14	16

Totals

	GP	G	A	Pts.	PIM	PP	SH	GW
1996	13	2	14	16	0	1	0	1
	GP	G	A	Pts.	PIM	PP	SH	GW
Career	193	112	250	362	64	31	11	22

1996-97: NHL Season No. 18

Date	Opponent	G	A	Pts.	G	A	Pts.	Date	Opponent	G	A	Pts.	G	A	Pts.
1. Oct. 5	Boston	0	0	0	0	0	0	44. Jan. 6	Colorado	0	0	0	16	43	59
2. Oct. 6	Florida	0	1	1	0	1	1	45. Jan. 8	Tampa Bay	0	1	1	16	44	60
3. Oct. 8	Florida	0	1	1	0	2	2	46. Jan. 9	Washington	0	0	0	16	44	60
4. Oct. 10	Dallas	1	0	1	1	2	3	47. Jan. 12	New Jersey	0	2	2	16	46	62
5. Oct. 12	Montreal	0	1	1	1	3	4	48. Jan. 13	Islanders	0	0	0	16	46	62
6. Oct. 14	Calgary	1	1	2	2	4	6	49. Jan. 21	Edmonton	0	0	0	16	46	62
7. Oct. 16	Pittsburgh	0	2	2	2	6	8	50. Jan. 22	Washington	0	2	2	16	48	64
8. Oct. 18	St. Louis	0	1	1	2	7	9	51. Jan. 25	Pittsburgh	0	3	3	16	51	67
9. Oct. 20	Tampa Bay	1	0	1	3	7	10	52. Jan. 27	Chicago	0	0	0	16	51	67
10. Oct. 23	Washington	0	1	1	3	8	11	53. Feb. 1	Philadelphia	0	1	1	16	52	68
11. Oct. 25	Florida	1	1	2	4	9	13	54. Feb. 2	Boston	0	0	0	16	52	68
12. Oct. 27	Buffalo	1	3	4	5	12	17	55. Feb. 5	Hartford	0	4	4	16	56	72
13. Oct. 29	Florida	1	0	1	6	12	18	56. Feb. 8	Islanders	0	1	1	16	57	73
14. Oct. 30	New Jersey	0	2	2	6	14	20	57. Feb. 9	Florida	0	1	1	16	58	74
15. Nov. 2	Boston	1	0	1	7	14	21	58. Feb. 13	St. Louis	0	1	1	16	59	75
16. Nov. 4	Tampa Bay	0	1	1	7	15	22	59. Feb. 15	Chicago	0	0	0	16	59	75
17. Nov. 6	Islanders	0	0	0	7	15	22	60. Feb. 17	New Jersey	0	2	2	16	61	77
18. Nov. 9	Washington	0	1	1	7	16	23	61. Feb. 19	New Jersey	0	0	0	16	61	77
19. Nov. 11	Vancouver	1	1	2	8	17	25	62. Feb. 21	Hartford	1	0	1	17	61	78
20. Nov. 13	Philadelphia	0	0	0	8	17	25	63. Feb. 23	Philadelphia	0	0	0	17	61	78
21. Nov. 16	Pittsburgh	1	1	2	9	18	27	64. Mar. 1	Detroit	0	0	0	17	61	78
22. Nov. 18	Calgary	0	1	1	9	19	28	65. Mar. 3	San Jose	0	1	1	17	62	79
23. Nov. 21	Edmonton	0	0	0	9	19	28	66. Mar. 6	Los Angeles	1	1	2	18	63	81
24. Nov. 23	Vancouver	0	0	0	9	19	28	67. Mar. 7	Anaheim	0	1	1	18	64	82
25. Nov. 26	Phoenix	0	0	0	9	19	28	68. Mar. 9	San Jose	0	2	2	18	66	84
26. Nov. 27	Colorado	0	1	1	9	20	29	69. Mar. 12	Washington	1	0	1	19	66	85
27. Dec. 1	Montreal	1	1	2	10	21	31	70. Mar. 14	Ottawa	0	0	0	19	66	85
28. Dec. 4	Philadelphia	0	1	1	10	22	32	71. Mar. 17	Ottawa	1	0	1	20	66	86
29. Dec. 6	Toronto	2	2	4	12	24	36	72. Mar. 19	Montreal	1	0	1	21	66	87
30. Dec. 7	Toronto	1	0	1	13	24	37	73. Mar. 21	Detroit	1	0	1	22	66	88
31. Dec. 9	Phoenix	0	3	3	13	27	40	74. Mar. 24	Pittsburgh	1	1	2	23	67	90
32. Dec. 11	Islanders	0	1	1	13	28	41	75. Mar. 27	New Jersey	0	0	0	23	67	90
33. Dec. 13	Buffalo	0	2	2	13	30	43	76. Mar. 29	Hartford	0	1	1	23	68	91
34. Dec. 16	Hartford	1	1	2	14	31	45	77. Apr. 1	Buffalo	0	0	0	23	68	91
35. Dec. 18	Los Angeles	0	3	3	14	34	48	78. Apr. 3	Boston	1	0	1	24	68	92
36. Dec. 21	Montreal	0	3	3	14	37	51	79. Apr. 4	Buffalo	1	0	1	25	68	93
37. Dec. 22	Florida	0	1	1	14	38	52	80. Apr. 7	Philadelphia	0	2	2	25	70	95
38. Dec. 26	Ottawa	0	0	0	14	38	52	81. Apr. 10	Philadelphia	0	2	2	25	72	97
39. Dec. 27	Anaheim	0	0	0	14	38	52	82. Apr. 11	Tampa Bay	0	0	0	25	72	97
40. Dec. 30	Dallas	2	0	2	16	38	54								
41. Dec. 31	Tampa Bay	0	0	0	16	38	54								
42. Jan. 2	Islanders	0	1	1	16	39	55								
43. Jan. 4	Ottawa	0	4	4	16	43	59								

	GP	G	A	Pts.	+/–	PIM	PP	SH	GW
1996-97	82	25	*72	97	+12	28	6	0	2
	GP	G	A	Pts.	+/–	PIM	PP	SH	GW
Career	1,335	862	1,843	2,705	+552	535	195	73	84

context

Most career playoff points

Wayne Gretzky
Playoff Point Leaders   214 | 233   295   382

Glenn Anderson Jari Kurri   Mark Messier

Anderson

milestones

1. July 21 Signs as unrestricted free agent with Rangers

2. Oct. 5 Is held scoreless in first game with Rangers

3. April 11 Shares league lead in assists (72) with Mario Lemieux

4. May 4 Plays in 200th playoff game, becoming one of only five players to reach plateau

5. May 18 Records second hat trick of playoffs to extend NHL record to 10

6. May 25 Records two assists in final playoff game, a 4-2 loss in Philadelphia

Bruce Bennett/BBS

playoffs

Date	Opponent	G	A	Pts.	G	A	Pts.
1. Apr. 17	Florida	0	0	0	0	0	0
2. Apr. 20	Florida	1	1	2	1	1	2
3. Apr. 22	Florida	0	1	1	1	2	3
4. Apr. 23	Florida	3	0	3	4	2	6
5. Apr. 25	Florida	0	0	0	4	2	6
6. May 2	New Jersey	0	0	0	4	2	6
7. May 4	New Jersey	0	1	1	4	3	7
8. May 6	New Jersey	1	1	2	5	4	9
9. May 8	New Jersey	1	0	1	6	4	10
10. May 11	New Jersey	0	1	1	6	5	11

Date	Opponent	G	A	Pts.	G	A	Pts.
11. May 16	Philadelphia	0	1	1	6	6	12
12. May 18	Philadelphia	3	0	3	9	6	15
13. May 20	Philadelphia	1	1	2	10	7	17
14. May 23	Philadelphia	0	1	1	10	8	18
15. May 25	Philadelphia	0	2	2	10	10	20

Totals

	GP	G	A	Pts.	PIM	PP	SH	GW
1997	15	10	10	20	2	3	0	2
	GP	**G**	**A**	**Pts.**	**PIM**	**PP**	**SH**	**GW**
Career	208	122	260	382	66	34	11	24

1997-98: NHL Season No. 19

Date	Opponent	G	A	Pts.	G	A	Pts.
1. Oct. 3	Islanders	0	0	0	0	0	0
2. Oct. 5	Los Angeles	0	1	1	0	1	1
3. Oct. 8	Edmonton	0	1	1	0	2	2
4. Oct. 9	Calgary	0	0	0	0	2	2
5. Oct. 11	Vancouver	3	2	5	3	4	7
6. Oct. 14	Pittsburgh	0	0	0	3	4	7
7. Oct. 15	Ottawa	0	1	1	3	5	8
8. Oct. 18	St. Louis	0	1	1	3	6	9
9. Oct. 20	Carolina	0	0	0	3	6	9
10. Oct. 22	Chicago	0	0	0	3	6	9
11. Oct. 24	Tampa Bay	1	0	1	4	6	10
12. Oct. 26	Anaheim	0	2	2	4	8	12
13. Oct. 28	Dallas	0	1	1	4	9	13
14. Oct. 30	Islanders	0	1	1	4	10	14
15. Nov. 3	Edmonton	0	1	1	4	11	15
16. Nov. 5	Colorado	1	2	3	5	13	18
17. Nov. 7	Dallas	1	0	1	6	13	19
18. Nov. 12	New Jersey	0	1	1	6	14	20
19. Nov. 14	Pittsburgh	0	0	0	6	14	20
20. Nov. 16	Colorado	0	0	0	6	14	20
21. Nov. 18	Florida	0	1	1	6	15	21
22. Nov. 19	Tampa Bay	0	1	1	6	16	22
23. Nov. 21	Carolina	1	2	3	7	18	25
24. Nov. 22	Pittsburgh	0	0	0	7	18	25
25. Nov. 25	Vancouver	0	0	0	7	18	25
26. Nov. 26	Islanders	0	0	0	7	18	25
27. Nov. 28	Buffalo	1	0	1	8	18	26
28. Nov. 30	Florida	0	0	0	8	18	26
29. Dec. 2	Washington	1	0	1	9	18	27
30. Dec. 5	Philadelphia	0	1	1	9	19	28
31. Dec. 6	Montreal	0	1	1	9	20	29
32. Dec. 8	Phoenix	0	1	1	9	21	30
33. Dec. 10	Calgary	0	0	0	9	21	30
34. Dec. 12	Florida	0	0	0	9	21	30
35. Dec. 16	New Jersey	0	0	0	9	21	30
36. Dec. 17	Florida	0	0	0	9	21	30
37. Dec. 20	Tampa Bay	0	1	1	9	22	31
38. Dec. 21	Buffalo	0	0	0	9	22	31
39. Dec. 23	Tampa Bay	0	3	3	9	25	34
40. Dec. 26	Buffalo	0	0	0	9	25	34
41. Dec. 28	Boston	1	1	2	10	26	36
42. Dec. 31	Tampa Bay	0	0	0	10	26	36
43. Jan. 3	Washington	2	0	2	12	26	38
44. Jan. 6	Carolina	0	2	2	12	28	40
45. Jan. 8	Washington	0	2	2	12	30	42
46. Jan. 12	Toronto	0	3	3	12	33	45
47. Jan. 14	New Jersey	0	0	0	12	33	45
48. Jan. 20	St. Louis	0	1	1	12	34	46
49. Jan. 22	Philadelphia	0	1	1	12	35	47
50. Jan. 24	New Jersey	1	2	3	13	37	50
51. Jan. 26	Washington	0	1	1	13	38	51
52. Jan. 29	Ottawa	0	1	1	13	39	52
53. Jan. 31	Boston	0	1	1	13	40	53
54. Feb. 2	San Jose	0	1	1	13	41	54
55. Feb. 4	Anaheim	0	1	1	13	42	55
56. Feb. 5	Los Angeles	0	0	0	13	42	55
57. Feb. 7	Phoenix	0	1	1	13	43	56
58. Feb. 26	Toronto	0	3	3	13	46	59
59. Feb. 28	Philadelphia	0	0	0	13	46	59
60. Mar. 2	Buffalo	0	0	0	13	46	59
61. Mar. 4	Florida	2	1	3	15	47	62
62. Mar. 7	New Jersey	1	0	1	16	47	63
63. Mar. 9	New Jersey	1	0	1	17	47	64
64. Mar. 11	San Jose	1	2	3	18	49	67
65. Mar. 12	Montreal	0	0	0	18	49	67
66. Mar. 14	Boston	0	1	1	18	50	68
67. Mar. 16	Ottawa	0	4	4	18	54	72
68. Mar. 18	Montreal	0	1	1	18	55	73
69. Mar. 21	Detroit	0	2	2	18	57	75
70. Mar. 22	Philadelphia	2	1	3	20	58	78
71. Mar. 25	Ottawa	0	2	2	20	60	80
72. Mar. 26	Carolina	0	0	0	20	60	80
73. Mar. 28	Pittsburgh	0	1	1	20	61	81
74. Mar. 30	Tampa Bay	0	1	1	20	62	82
75. Apr. 1	Boston	1	0	1	21	62	83
76. Apr. 4	Islanders	0	0	0	21	62	83
77. Apr. 5	Chicago	0	1	1	21	63	84
78. Apr. 7	Montreal	1	1	2	22	64	86
79. Apr. 11	Detroit	0	1	1	22	65	87
80. Apr. 14	Washington	0	0	0	22	65	87
81. Apr. 15	Islanders	1	1	2	23	66	89
82. Apr. 18	Philadelphia	0	1	1	23	67	90

	GP	G	A	Pts.	+/–	PIM	PP	SH	GW
1997-98	82	23	*67	90	-11	28	6	0	4
	GP	G	A	Pts.	+/–	PIM	PP	SH	GW
Career	1,417	885	1,910	2,795	+541	563	201	73	88

context

Most career goals*

Wayne Gretzky	894
Marcel Dionne and Gordie Howe	731	801

*Five players in NHL history have scored 700 goals. Mike Gartner (708) and Phil Esposito (717) are the others.

Howe

milestones

1. **Oct. 11** Scores record 50th hat trick against Vancouver's Kirk McLean for final three-goal game of career; adds two assists in last of 66 career five-point games

2. **Oct. 26** Records 1,851st assist on Ulf Samuelsson's goal at 0:32 of third period, to move past Gordie Howe on all-time points list (1,850) on strength of assists alone

3. **April 18** Shares league lead in assists with Jaromir Jagr (67), bringing to 16 number of times leading or sharing lead of assist title

4. Named to second all-star team

Totals:

	GP	G	A	Pts.	PIM	PP	SH	GW
Career	208	122	260	382	66	34	11	24

1998-99: NHL Season No. 20

	Date	Opponent	G	A	Pts.	G	A	Pts.		Date	Opponent	G	A	Pts.	G	A	Pts.
1.	Oct. 9	Philadelphia	0	0	0	0	0	0	44.	Jan. 19	Ottawa	0	1	1	7	36	43
2.	Oct. 10	Montreal	0	1	1	0	1	1	45.	Jan. 21	Florida	0	0	0	7	36	43
3.	Oct. 12	St. Louis	0	1	1	0	2	2	46.	Jan. 26	Washington	0	3	3	7	39	46
4.	Oct. 16	New Jersey	0	1	1	0	3	3	47.	Jan. 28	Carolina	0	0	0	7	39	46
5.	Oct. 17	Pittsburgh	1	1	2	1	4	5	48.	Jan. 30	Detroit	0	1	1	7	40	47
6.	Oct. 20	Edmonton	0	1	1	1	5	6	49.	Feb. 1	Washington	0	0	0	7	40	47
7.	Oct. 22	Islanders	0	0	0	1	5	6	50.	Feb. 4	Vancouver	1	2	3	8	42	50
8.	Oct. 24	Philadelphia	0	1	1	1	6	7	51.	Feb. 7	Boston	0	0	0	8	42	50
9.	Oct. 27	Buffalo	0	0	0	1	6	7	52.	Feb. 12	Carolina	0	0	0	8	42	50
10.	Oct. 30	Carolina	0	1	1	1	7	8	53.	Feb. 14	Detroit	0	0	0	8	42	50
11.	Nov. 3	New Jersey	0	0	0	1	7	8	54.	Feb. 15	Nashville	0	5	5	8	47	55
12.	Nov. 4	Montreal	0	0	0	1	7	8	55.	Feb. 17	Montreal	0	0	0	8	47	55
13.	Nov. 7	Toronto	1	1	2	2	8	10	56.	Feb. 19	Pittsburgh	0	1	1	8	48	56
14.	Nov. 10	Tampa Bay	0	2	2	2	10	12	57.	Feb. 21	Edmonton	0	0	0	8	48	56
15.	Nov. 11	Florida	0	1	1	2	11	13	58.	Feb. 22	Calgary	0	1	1	8	49	57
16.	Nov. 13	Boston	0	2	2	2	13	15	59.	Feb. 26	Phoenix	Did not play					
17.	Nov. 18	Anaheim	0	1	1	2	14	16	60.	Feb. 28	Philadelphia	Did not play					
18.	Nov. 19	Los Angeles	0	1	1	2	15	17	61.	Mar. 2	Dallas	Did not play					
19.	Nov. 21	San Jose	0	0	0	2	15	17	62.	Mar. 4	Washington	Did not play					
20.	Nov. 25	Buffalo	0	0	0	2	15	17	63.	Mar. 7	Boston	Did not play					
21.	Nov. 27	Pittsburgh	0	1	1	2	16	18	64.	Mar. 8	Toronto	Did not play					
22.	Nov. 29	Nashville	1	2	3	3	18	21	65.	Mar. 10	Ottawa	Did not play					
23.	Dec. 1	Florida	1	2	3	4	20	24	66.	Mar. 12	Boston	Did not play					
24.	Dec. 2	Islanders	1	0	1	5	20	25	67.	Mar. 14	Islanders	Did not play					
25.	Dec. 5	Ottawa	0	0	0	5	20	25	68.	Mar. 15	Washington	Did not play					
26.	Dec. 7	Toronto	0	1	1	5	21	26	69.	Mar. 19	Buffalo	Did not play					
27.	Dec. 9	Colorado	0	1	1	5	22	27	70.	Mar. 21	Pittsburgh	Did not play					
28.	Dec. 11	Buffalo	0	0	0	5	22	27	71.	Mar. 22	Tampa Bay	0	0	0	8	49	57
29.	Dec. 14	Calgary	0	3	3	5	25	30	72.	Mar. 24	Florida	0	0	0	8	49	57
30.	Dec. 16	New Jersey	1	2	3	6	27	33	73.	Mar. 27	Philadelphia	0	0	0	8	49	57
31.	Dec. 19	Toronto	0	2	2	6	29	35	74.	Mar. 29	Islanders	1	0	1	9	49	58
32.	Dec. 23	Carolina	0	0	0	6	29	35	75.	Apr. 2	Anaheim	0	0	0	9	49	58
33.	Dec. 26	Carolina	0	0	0	6	29	35	76.	Apr. 4	New Jersey	0	0	0	9	49	58
34.	Dec. 30	Phoenix	0	0	0	6	29	35	77.	Apr. 5	Philadelphia	0	2	2	9	51	60
35.	Dec. 31	Colorado	0	2	2	6	31	37	78.	Apr. 8	Chicago	0	0	0	9	51	60
36.	Jan. 2	St. Louis	0	0	0	6	31	37	79.	Apr. 9	Dallas	0	0	0	9	51	60
37.	Jan. 4	San Jose	0	1	1	6	32	38	80.	Apr. 12	Tampa Bay	0	1	1	9	52	61
38.	Jan. 6	New Jersey	0	0	0	6	32	38	81.	Apr. 15	Ottawa	0	0	0	9	52	61
39.	Jan. 7	Washington	0	0	0	6	32	38	82.	Apr. 18	Pittsburgh	0	1	1	9	53	62
40.	Jan. 10	Tampa Bay	1	1	2	7	33	40									
41.	Jan. 13	Islanders	0	2	2	7	35	42									
42.	Jan. 15	Chicago	0	0	0	7	35	42									
43.	Jan. 16	Montreal	0	0	0	7	35	42									

	GP	G	A	Pts.	+/–	PIM	PP	SH	GW
1998-99	70	9	53	62	-23	14	3	0	3
	GP	**G**	**A**	**Pts.**	**+/–**	**PIM**	**PP**	**SH**	**GW**
Career	1,487	894	1,963	2,857	+518	577	204	73	91

context

Most career NHL awards

Wayne Gretzky	32
Bobby Orr	17

Orr

milestones

1. Dec. 19 Records two assists in last game at Toronto's Maple Leaf Gardens; collects 77 points in 30 games at Gardens

2. Feb. 21 Is held pointless in final game in Edmonton, a 2-1 win

3. March 29 Gretzky scores final goal of career, poking loose puck past Islanders' Wade Flaherty at 17:53 of third period, passing Gordie Howe's record for pro goals with No. 1,072

4. April 15 Is held pointless in final NHL game in Canada, a 2-2 tie with Ottawa

5. April 16 Announces retirement at Madison Square Garden

6. April 18 Plays last game, setting up Brian Leetch's power play goal at 19:30 of second period in 2-1 overtime loss to Pittsburgh

7. Named most gentlemanly player

 # WHA/NHL All-Star Game Record

Date	Opponent	G	A	Pts.	G	A	Pts.
1978-79 WHA All-Star Series							
1. Jan. 2	Soviet Union	2	1	3	2	1	3
2. Jan. 4	Soviet Union	1	1	2	3	2	5
3. Jan. 5	Soviet Union	0	0	0	3	2	5
Member of Campbell Conference All-Stars							
1. 1980	Wales	0	0	0	0	0	0
2. 1981	Wales	0	1	1	0	1	1
3. 1982	Wales	1	0	1	1	1	2
4. 1983	Wales (MVP)	4	0	4	5	1	6
5. 1984	Wales	1	0	1	6	1	7
6. 1985	Wales	1	0	1	7	1	8
7. 1986	Wales	1	0	1	8	1	9
Rendez-Vous 1987: Member of NHL All-Stars							
1. Feb. 11	Soviet Union	0	1	1	0	1	1
2. Feb. 13	Soviet Union	0	3	3	0	4	4
	NHL MVP						
Member of Campbell Conference All-Stars							
8. 1988	Wales	1	0	1	9	1	10

Date	Opponent	G	A	Pts.	G	A	Pts.
9. 1989	Wales (MVP)	1	2	3	10	3	13
10. 1990	Wales	0	0	0	10	3	13
11. 1991	Wales	1	0	1	11	3	14
12. 1992	Wales	1	2	3	12	5	17
13. 1993	Wales	0	0	0	12	5	17
Member of Western Conference All-Stars							
14. 1994	Eastern	0	2	2	12	7	19
15. 1996	Eastern	0	0	0	12	7	19
Member of Eastern Conference All-Stars							
16. 1997	Western	0	1	1	12	8	20
Member of North America All-Stars							
17. 1998	World	0	2	2	12	10	22
18. 1999	World (MVP)	1	2	3	13	12	25
Totals							
NHL All-Star Games		**G**	**A**	**Pts.**			
18 Games		13**	12**	25**			

International Career

Date	Opponent	G	A	Pts.	G	A	Pts.
1977-78 World Junior Championship							
1. Dec. 22	United States	1	1	2	1	1	2
2. Dec. 23	West Germany	3	2	5	4	3	7
3. Dec. 25	Czechoslovakia	3	3	6	7	6	13
4. Dec. 28	Soviet Union	0	0	0	7	6	13
5. Dec. 31	Czechoslovakia	1	0	1	8	6	14
6. Jan. 1	Sweden	0	3	3	8	9	17
Totals		**8**	***9**	***17**			
Canada wins bronze medal							
1981 Canada Cup							
1. Sept. 1	Finland	2	1	3	2	1	3
2. Sept. 3	United States	2	2	4	4	3	7
3. Sept. 5	Czechoslovakia	0	0	0	4	3	7
4. Sept. 7	Sweden	0	1	1	4	4	8
5. Sept. 9	Soviet Union	1	2	3	5	6	11
6. Sept. 11	United States	0	1	1	5	7	12
7. Sept. 13	Soviet Union	0	0	0	5	7	12
Totals		**5**	**7**	***12**			
Canada loses in final							
1982 World Championship							
1. Apr. 15	Finland	0	1	1	0	1	1
2. Apr. 16	Czechoslovakia	0	0	0	0	1	1
3. Apr. 18	Sweden	0	0	0	0	1	1
4. Apr. 19	West Germany	0	2	2	0	3	3
5. Apr. 21	Italy	0	0	0	0	3	3
6. Apr. 22	United States	2	1	3	2	4	6
7. Apr. 24	Soviet Union	0	1	1	2	5	7
8. Apr. 25	Soviet Union	1	0	1	3	5	8
9. Apr. 27	Czechoslovakia	0	1	1	3	6	9
10. Apr. 29	Sweden	3	2	5	6	8	14
Totals		**6**	**8**	***14**			
Canada wins bronze							
1984 Canada Cup							
1. Sept. 1	West Germany	3	1	4	3	1	4
2. Sept. 3	United States	0	0	0	3	1	4
3. Sept. 6	Sweden	0	0	0	3	1	4
4. Sept. 8	Czechoslovakia	0	1	1	3	2	5
5. Sept. 10	Soviet Union	0	2	2	3	4	7
6. Sept. 13	Soviet Union	0	1	1	3	5	8
7. Sept. 16	Sweden	1	2	3	4	7	11
8. Sept. 18	Sweden	1	0	1	5	7	12
Totals		**5**	**7**	***12**			
Canada wins							

Date	Opponent	G	A	Pts.	G	A	Pts.
1987 Canada Cup							
1. Aug. 28	Czechoslovakia	0	2	2	0	2	2
2. Aug. 30	Finland	0	0	0	0	2	2
3. Sept. 2	United States	0	2	2	0	4	4
4. Sept. 4	Sweden	1	3	4	1	7	8
5. Sept. 6	Soviet Union	1	1	2	2	8	10
6. Sept. 9	Czechoslovakia	0	2	2	2	10	12
7. Sept. 11	Soviet Union	1	1	2	3	11	14
8. Sept. 13	Soviet Union	0	5	5	3	16	19
9. Sept. 14	Soviet Union	0	2	2	3	18	21
Totals		**3**	***18**	***21**			
Canada wins							
1991 Canada Cup							
1. Aug. 31	Finland	0	0	0	0	0	0
2. Sept. 2	United States	1	3	4	1	3	4
3. Sept. 5	Sweden	0	3	3	1	6	7
4. Sept. 7	Czechoslovakia	2	1	3	3	7	10
5. Sept. 9	Soviet Union	0	0	0	3	7	10
6. Sept. 12	Sweden	1	0	1	4	7	11
7. Sept. 14	United States	0	1	1	4	8	12
8. Sept. 16	United States	Did not play					
Totals		**4**	***8**	***12**			
Canada wins							
1996 World Cup							
1. Aug. 28	Russia	0	2	2	0	2	2
2. Aug. 31	United States	2	0	2	2	2	4
3. Sept. 1	Slovakia	0	0	0	2	2	4
4. Sept. 5	Germany	1	0	1	3	2	5
5. Sept. 7	Sweden	0	0	0	3	2	5
6. Sept. 10	United States	0	0	0	3	2	5
7. Sept. 12	United States	0	0	0	3	2	5
8. Sept. 14	United States	0	1	1	3	3	6
Totals		**3**	**3**	**6**			
Canada loses in final							
1998 Olympics							
1. Feb. 13	Belarus	0	0	0	0	0	0
2. Feb. 14	Sweden	0	0	0	0	0	0
3. Feb. 16	United States	0	1	1	0	1	1
4. Feb. 18	Kazakhstan	0	2	2	0	3	3
5. Feb. 20	Czech Republic	0	0	0	0	3	3
6. Feb. 21	Finland	0	1	1	0	4	4
Totals		**0**	**4**	**4**			
Canada finishes fourth							

Bruce Bennett/RBS

INDEX

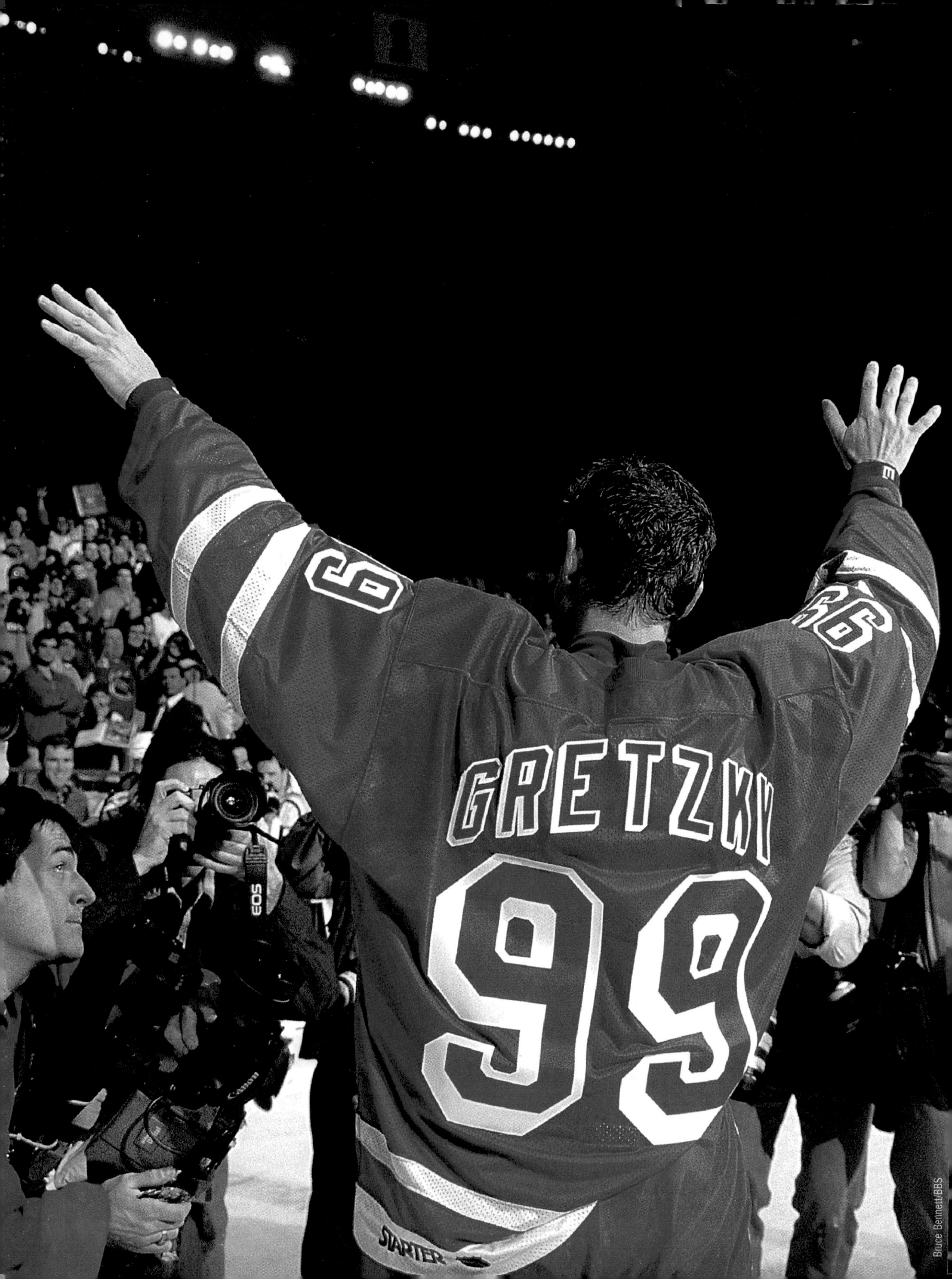

Bruce Bennett/BBS